focus *101*

LaVerne H. Clark

FOCUS 101

An Illustrated Biography of 101 Poets
Of the 60's and 70's

FOCUS 101

Photographs, text and editing
by
LaVerne Harrell Clark

Heidelberg Graphics · Chico, Ca. · 1979

First Edition 1979
Printed in the U.S.A.
ISBN: 0-918606-03-9

Some of the photographs in this book appeared in the following
publications for which grateful acknowledgement is expressed:
The Face of Poetry (by LaVerne Harrell Clark and Mary MacArthur,
Gallimaufry 1977), *Sumac, Poetry Now, Coda: Poets and Writers
Newsletter* and *Blue Moon News.*

Library of Congress Cataloging in Publication Data

Clark, LaVerne Harrell.
  Focus 101.

   1. American poetry—20th century—Bio-biblio-
graphy. 2. Poets, American—20th century—Biography. 3. Poets—Biography. 4. Poetry—Bibliography. I. Title.
PS325.C57   811'.5'409 [B]   78-57156
ISBN 0-918606-03-9

Heidelberg Graphics' publications are available direct from Post
Office Box 3606, Chico, California 95927.

Dedicated to

the 101 poets in this book,

the entire Humanities staff of the University of Arizona
  Library, especially Lois Olsrud,

Larry S. Jackson, for his imagination and helpful concern,

and L.D., again, for standing by.

CONTENTS

The dates in parentheses beneath the poets' captions
indicate when the photographs were taken.

BIRTH: 8/9/'31 in Minneapolis, Minn. was educated in his native state.

EDUCATION: B.A., *magna cum laude,* U. of Minn. ('62); doctoral work in English, Rice Univ. ('62-'65); Ph.D. American Studies, Union Graduate School (Union of Experimenting Colleges & Universities) ('74).

CAREER: After ten years as a professional soldier in the United States, Far East, & Europe, Ackley became a teacher (he had served as an instructor at the Artillery School, U.S. Army immediately prior to leaving the Army), Asst. Instr., U. of Minn. ('61-'62), N.D.E.A. Doctoral Fellow, Rice U. ('62-'65), Instr. U. of Tx.—Austin ('65-'66), Asst. Prof., English, U. of Utah ('66-'67), Asst. Prof., Lit., U. of Americas (Mexico) ('67), Asst. Prof., U. of Tx.—El Paso ('67-'68), St. Mary's College—Notre Dame ('68-'69), Assoc. Prof., McMurray C. ('69-'70), Assoc. Prof., Pembroke St. U. ('70-'72), Seminar Leader, "Alternative Realities," C.I.D.O.C., Cuernavaca, Mexico ('73), Instr.-N.R., Navajo Comm. C., Navajo Nation ('73-'77); Juneau-Douglas Comm. College, U. of Alaska ('77—date). Administrative experiences include: Director, Southwest Poets Conf., '69-'75; Chmm., Div. of

Randall Ackley
(June 1975)

Lang. & Lit., McMurry College, '69-'70; Asst. to Dean for Innovative Programs, Pembroke St. U., '70-'72; Chpsn., Assoc. for Studies in Amr. Indian Literatures, '73-'76; Coord., Henry Berry Lowry Native Amr. Comm. C., '71-'72; Chpsn., Div. of Arts, Comm., Hum.; Navajo Comm. C., '73-'77; Asst. to Academic VP, '77; Asst. to Pres., Navajo Comm. C., '77; present position-Coord., Arts & Scs., Juneau-Douglas C. C.; Member, Exec. Comm., Assoc. of Depts. of English, MLA, '77-date.

EDITORIAL POSTS: In the late "sixties," Ackley founded the literary magazine, *Quetzal,* with the help of Simon Ortiz, Harry Paige, H. Storm, Ricardo Sánchez, as co-editors. With the aid of these poets, and others including Howard McCord, Ron Bayes, Norman Macleod, Harry McCormack, he also began the Quetzal/Vihio Press, which published Simon Ortiz's first book, Storm's first book, as well as a chapbook by Ricardo Sánchez, in the "seventies." Ackley edited *Quetzal* from '70-'73, and has been guest editor for *Out of Sight,* Assoc. Ed. for *Pembroke Magazine,* and has been a contributing editor for *St. Andrews Review* and *Cafe Solo.* He lives with his wife, Mary, and his daughter, Holly, in Juneau, Alaska. He has recently revived *Quetzal* as *Q: Nopacrimmag,* a journal of the North Pacific Rim, working with local faculty, Sheila Nickerson, Ron Bayes, Dick Dauenhauer,

PUBLICATIONS: Troll Songs (Tribal Press '70) & *Lord of All Dreams* (Atlatl Press '74). He is completing another collection of poetry, *Listen to the Wind,* and writing on long term projects, *People of the River, & American Tribual Literatures Today.* His poetry has appeared in numerous journals including *Pembroke, Southern Review, Cafe Solo, Measure,*...and he has also published various reviews and articles on contemporary American Indian literatures. He has worked with the North Carolina Poetry in the schools Project, as a full-time poet-in-residence, and with the Tacoma program.

HONORS: Phi Beta Kappa ('61); Litt. D. (Hon.) Rochdale College ('71), Fellow Int'l Soc. of Poets; & Polish Inst. of Ltrs. & Sciences.

OBSERVATIONS: "My interest is in the lyric and the mythic. My world is impinged upon by the chaos of a disordered society and I seek the beauty of song and the power of myth. Simplicity is more important to me than sophistication, style more important than philosophy. What I have learned has been from books, with teachers like Gerry O'Grady, and from places, with teachers like Simon Ortiz and the places themselves. However, I remain a student and a wanderer, seeking more often than finding. I owe a major debt to the Navajo People whom I worked and lived with for five years, and to my other friends in the Southwest...."

PAULA (FRANCIS) GUNN ALLEN

BIRTH: 10/24/'39, in Albuquerque, N.M. at St. Joseph's Hospital of Am. Indian (Laguna-Sioux), Anglo, and Lebanese descent. She grew up on the Cubero Land Grant just west of the Laguna Indian Pueblo, where she learned much about her native American heritage and her identifications from an Indian grandmother. About her heritage, Ms. Allen writes: "My mother is three-fourths Laguna-Sioux and one-fourth Scotch Irish. My father is Lebanese American....My mother was born in Laguna, and spent her first five years there, and moved to Cubero, where she grew up. My father was born in Seboyeta, N.M., a village on the Seboyeta Land Grant, north of the Laguna Reservation and east of the Cubero Land Grant. My father's father immigrated as a small child from Rhume, Lebanon with his parents. My mother's mother is the daughter of a half-breed Laguna woman whose mother was from Laguna Pueblo and whose father was Scotch-Irish from Ohio. My

Paula Gunn Allen
(June 1975)

mother's father was a Sioux, a musician, who taught at the Albuquerque Indian School." She adds: "Many of my relatives speak Spanish, including my parents, but though I grew up in a Spanish Land Grant Village (as did both my parents), I am

2

but though I grew up in a Spanish Land Grant Village (as did both my parents), I am not Chicana by blood." During her childhood in such interesting and diversified surroundings, she attended schools both on the Cubero Land Grant and in nearby Albuquerque.

EDUCATION: B.A. ('66) & M.F.A. ('68), U. of Oregon; Ph.D. ('75), U. of N.M.

CAREER: She has also taught creative writing in both a university and private workshop setting; also she has taught and widely lectured on Native Americans, Minorities, and Native American women at the College of San Mateo, U. of N.M., and at the Grants, N.M. division of the latter. Additionally she has been in charge of Native Am. Studies at San Francisco St. U., where she was also active in helping to organize programs in Indian literature and culture in the Bay area. Currently she lives in Albuquerque and works for the Cancer Research and Treatment Center. She has three children: Gene (18), Laura (16), and Sulayman (5). Paula Allen has described her life "as a journey in and out of universities, and on and off the streets, in and out of marriage," adding that she "has been writing, looking, living, believing, and disbelieving for a long time."

PUBLICATIONS: The Blind Lion (Thorp Springs Press, '74) & forthcoming *Shadow Country* (Dept. of Ed., Nova Scotia, Canada); included in anthologies, *Voices From Wah'Kon-Tah: Contemporary Poetry of Native Americans* ('74), edited by Robert K. Dodge & Joseph B. McCullough, *Four Indian Poets,* edited by John R. Milton, & *Southwest,* edited by Karl and Jane Kopp & Bart Lanier Stafford III ('77). Her poems appear in various periodicals, including *South Dakota Review* ('73).

HONORS: N.E.A. grant ('78).

OBSERVATIONS: "My own poetry speaks to my experiences," Ms. Allen notes, "my 'history,' perceptions; these in turn are created in concert with where I came from and who I go with. It is seldom happy, it tends to be intense, it is often brief. I try to keep it as close to the springs of my being as I can, toward my own center, because I can only articulate what is a known part of me, my people, my life."

JON (VICTOR) ANDERSON

BIRTH: 7/4/'40, Sommerville, Mass., the son of Henry Victor and Frances (Ladd) Anderson, grew up in Lexington, Mass.

EDUCATION: Northeastern U., B.S. ('64) & M.F.A. ('68), U. of Iowa.

CAREER: Teaching fellowship at U. of Iowa ('67-'68); Instr., Creative Writing, U. of Portland, Ore. ('68-'71); U. of Ohio ('71-'73); U. of Pittsburgh ('74-'75), & U. of Iowa ('76-'77). Twice married and divorced, Anderson lives in '78 in Tucson with his wife Barbara and their son while writing poetry on a Guggenheim grant. Anderson has presented readings at numerous colleges and universities and worked for the Poets-In-The-Schools program in several states.

PUBLICATIONS: Looking for Jonathan (U. of Pittsburgh Press, '68; runner-up for U.S. Poetry Award of the International Poetry Forum, '67); *Death and Friends* (U. of Pittsburgh Press, '70); & *In Sepia* (U. of Pittsburgh Press, '74). Poems of his appear in such periodicals as *Field, Backdoor, Iowa Review, Ohio Review, North American Review, The New Yorker, Beloit Poetry Journal, Hudson Review, Kayak, Poetry, Paris Review, Poetry Northwest, New York Times, Epoch, Humanist, Hornbook, & Choice,* and in such anthologies as *The American Poetry Anthology, Contemporary American* and *Australian Poetry, Young American Poets* ('68), *Intro I* ('68), & *Midland II* ('68).

HONORS: Borestone Mountain Prize ('64), *Kansas City Star* Award ('67),

Writer's Digest Prize ('66), Hallmark Poetry Award ('67, '68), Pushcart Prize ('77), & Guggenheim Fellowship ('77-'78).

OBSERVATIONS: George Starbuck notes that Anderson "has the wit, grace and

Jon Anderson
(March 1971)

flamboyance that wins readers . . . a benign, visionary voice, consoling in presence when the dreams it fills are of despair."

MARVIN (HARTLEY) BELL

BIRTH: 8/3/'37 in New York City, the son of Saul Bell, an immigrant from the Ukraine, and Belle (Spector) Bell, a first-generation American, grew up in Center Moriches, on the south shore of eastern Long Island.

EDUCATION: Alfred U. (B.A., '58); Syracuse U.; U. of Chicago (M.A., '61); U. of Iowa (M.F.A., '63).

CAREER: U.S. Army (Foreign Military Training Officer, '63-'65; discharged 1st.

Marvin Bell
(February 1972)

Lt.) He began his teaching career in '65 at the Writers' Workshop of the U. of Iowa, where he is Professor. He has also taught at Goddard C. ('72) and, during the summers, has been on the faculty of various writing conferences and workshops,

4

including Oregon State U. ('69), U. of Rochester ('74, '77), and Bread Loaf ('73-'77).

EDITORIAL POSTS: Statements, a small magazine he edited and published during his student days ('59-'64); poetry ed., *The North American Review* (64-'69); poetry ed., *The Iowa Review* ('69-'71); since '75, he has written a tri-annual column, "Homage to the Runner," for *The American Poetry Review.* Twice-married, first time to Mary Mammosser in '58. Currently Bell lives in Iowa City with his second wife, Dorothy Murphy, whom he married in '61, and two sons, Nathan Saul and Jason Aaron.

PUBLICATIONS: Poems for Nathan and Saul (chapbook, '66); *Things We Dreamt We Died For* ('66); *A Probable Volume of Dreams* ('69); *The Escape Into You* ('71); *Woo Havoc* (chapbook, '71); *Residue of Song* ('74); *Stars Which See, Stars Which Do Not See* ('77). Anthologies which include his poems are *Where is Vietnam?* ('67); *The Young American Poets* ('68); *The Contemporary American Poets* ('69); *The New Yorker Book of Poems* ('69); *Major Young Poets* ('71); *Preferences* ('74); *The American Poetry Anthology* ('76); and *Fifty Contemporary Poets* ('77). Contributor of poems too numerous for listing here, Bell's publications include *Poetry, The New Yorker, The Nation, New American Review, The Virginia Quarterly Review, Field, Stand, Chicago Review, Choice, Northwest Review,* among others.

HONORS: Lamont Poetry Award ('69); Bess Hokin Prize ('69); Emily Clark Balch Prize ('70); Guggenheim Fellowship ('76); NEA Fellowship ('78).

OBSERVATIONS: "...I believe in writing as a way of understanding what would otherwise remain irrational. But a work of art doesn't need a purpose to come into being," says Bell. "My most cranky answer to the question, 'Why do you write?' is 'Because it feels so good. I write to change my life.' " About *The Escape Into You,* Mark Strand has said: "(It seems) so brave and upright and formal and yet so afflicted and heavy with basic considerations that I really can't figure out how he did it. It is also the only recent poetry I know of in which most of the jokes are sad and in which the wit darkens. This may have something to do with the severity of his consciousness or the way he exaggerates the weight and purpose of morality. I don't know; whichever it is, it works."

LEONARD BIRD

BIRTH: "A Gemini," '36, five miles east of the tuna fleet in San Diego. Recalls his "earliest memories" as "being locked in a closet for breaking a bottle of milk, and listening to a green-eyed Zenith tell the world about Pearl Harbor." Various parts of his youth "in the late 'forties' and early 'fifties' were spent in various reformatories in California."

EDUCATION: San Diego St. (B.A., English), from '61-'65, U. of Utah, M.A., & Ph.D.

CAREER: Marine Corps for four years, as Bird notes, "partly because the Corps promised to turn my 116 lbs. into glinty gray eyes and lean mean, and partly because I swooned watching John Wayne in *Sands of Iowa Jima.*" After discharge from Marines, Bird made his living while in school with assorted jobs: "designed bars and restaurants, joined the Elks and Junior Chamber of Commerce and bought thirteen regimental striped ties." After receiving his Ph.D., he began his teaching career in '65 at Concordia College (Minn.), where he taught until '69 when he assumed his present post as a professor of creative writing and literature at Fort Lewis C., Durango, Colo.

EDITORIAL POSTS: Renaissance Ed. of *Discourse* while at Concordia C., consulting editor of *Quetzal* during its lifetime, and presently editor of *Rocky Mountain Review.* He has given more than a hundred poetry readings at colleges, art galleries and institutions in the western United States, as well as over several P.B.S. affiliates. Called "Red Bird" by his friends and students, he lives in Durango with his wife, the former Barbara Lee Wilderman, and their two children, David (20) and Maria (11).

PUBLICATIONS: River of Lost Souls (Tooth of Time Press, '77). Poems by Bird also appear in such anthologies as *Poets of North America* (So. Ill. U. Press),

Leonard Bird
(June 1975)

Southwest (Red Earth Press, '77), and in many magazines, including *West Coast Poetry Review, Contemporary American Poetry, Quetzal, Creative Arts Quarterly, Albiero Quarterly, Vernal,* & *Rocky Mountain Review.* As a playwright, his three-act drama, "Who Is Gordon Mendez?" was performed at Fort Lewis C. ('74).

OBSERVATIONS: Bird comments: "If I had to choose between publishing and giving readings, I would choose the latter. Most of my poems reek of place (the southwest), and I believe that place is carried in the wind—the wind of place and the wind-breath-spirit-voice of the speaking poet." Bill Tremblay hails Bird's long poem "The Mourning Dove," as "one of the most powerful long-poems to appear in America in several years."

LOUISE BOGAN
BIRTH: 8/11/1897, Livermore Falls, Maine.
DEATH: N.Y.C., 2/4/'70.
EDUCATION: Mount St. Mary's Academy, Manchester, N.H. ('07-'09), the Girls' Latin School, Boston ('10-'15), & Boston U. ('15-'16).
CAREER: From '31 until '69, Bogan served as poetry critic and reviewer for *The New Yorker,* and earned her living in this capacity, as well as with her writings and lecturings on various campuses, including the U. of Wash. ('48), U. of Chicago ('49), U. of Ark. ('52), Salzburg, Austria Seminar in Am. Studies ('58), Brandeis U. ('64-'65), and at Columbia and New York Universities. From '45-'46, she was consultant in poetry for the Library of Congress. Married twice, she had one daughter, Mathilde "Maidie" Alexander (Mrs. Austin J. Scannel) by her first husband Curt Alexander, who died in '20, four years after their marriage. Her second husband was the poet Raymond Holden, whom she married in '25 and

divorced in '37. She spent most of her adult years living in N.Y.C.

PUBLICATIONS: After the publication of her first book, *Body of This Death* ('23), Bogan was recognized as one of America's foremost poets. Other collections of her poetry are *Dark Summer* ('29), *The Sleeping Fury* ('37), *Poems and New Poems* ('41), *Collected Poems: 1923-1953* ('54), & *The Blue Estuaries: Poems 1923-1968.* Her poems appeared in numerous periodicals and with frequency in *The New Yorker, New Republic, Nation,* & *Poetry*; also in a wide range of anthologies: *Yesterday and Today* ('26), *New Poetry* ('32), *New Yorker Book of Verse* ('36), *A Little Treasury of American Poetry* ('48), *Modern Poetry* ('51), *New Poems by American Poets* ('53; '57); *Faber Book of Modern American Verse* ('56), *Modern Verse in English* ('58), *Poetry For Pleasure* ('60), *Poet's Choice* ('62), *Modern Poets* ('63), & *The Voice That Is Great Within Us* ('73). As a translator, she also rendered into English, with Elizabeth Mayer, Goethe's *The Sorrows of Young Werther, Novella,* and *Elective Affinities,* and Ernst Juenger's *The Glass Bees;* with Elizabeth Roget, she likewise edited and translated *The Journals of Jules Renard.* She produced, too, an anthology of poetry for children, *The Golden Journey* ('65), with William Jay Smith. Her reputation as a critic was almost as far-reaching as that she made as a poet. Her three books of criticism include *Achievement in American Poetry: 1900-1950* ('51), *Selected Criticism* ('55), & *A Poet's Alphabet, Reflections on Literary Art and Vocation* ('70), edited in the last year of her life by Robert Phelps and Ruth Limmer, the latter of whom also edited *What the Woman Lived: Selected Letters of Louise Bogan, 1920-70* ('73). Selections from her notebooks and journals are now in the process of appearing. Notebook entries from 1935-36 appear in the Fall '77 issue of *Antaeus,* and a long section of her journal is available in *The New Yorker.* A memoir of Louise Bogan, which contains lengthy quotations from her lectures, written by William Jay Smith, with a bibliography, appeared in '72 and is entitled *Louise Bogan: A Woman's Words.* Additionally Bogan wrote short stories; one of which, "Journey Round My Room" is available in Howard Moss's *The Poet's Story.*

HONORS: John Reed Mem. Prize ('30), Helen Haire Levenson Prize from *Poetry*

Louise Bogan
(February 1967)
deceased

('37), Harriet Monroe Poetry Award ('48), Bollingen Prize ('55), Brandeis U. Creative Arts Award in Poetry ('61), two Guggenheim Fellowships ('33; '37), Fellow in American Letters, Lib. of Congress ('44) and named to the Chair of Poetry—Library of Congress ('45-'46), grant from the National Institute of Arts &

Letters ('51), fellowship of Academy of Amer. poets ('58), member of the Academy of Amer. Arts & Letters, and recipient of two honorary degrees, an Litt.D. from Colby College ('60), & an L.H.D. from Western College for Women, Ohio ('56).

OBSERVATIONS: Bogan once noted: "I think it is a great mistake to throw out form. I do not mean that formless verse cannot be great, but a poet should know form and how to use it." Richard Eberhart has characterized her style in this way: "Louise Bogan's poems adhere to the center of English with a dark lyrical force." In more depth, Marianne Moore explained in '55: "Women are not noted for terseness, but Louise Bogan's art is compactness compacted. Emotions with her, as she has said of certain fiction, is "itself form, the kernel which builds outward from inward intensity. She uses a kind of forged rhetoric that nevertheless seems inevitable....One is struck by her restraint—an unusual courtesy in this day of bombast."

GEORGE BOWERING

BIRTH: 12/1/'35, Keremos, B.C., grew up in various towns in the interior of the same Canadian province, notably in Penctiction, the son of Ewart Harry Bowering, a teacher.

EDUCATION: U. of B.C. (B.A., '60); U. of West Ont. (M.A., '63); post-graduate studies at the latter institution until '67.

CAREER: Did his first writing in high school as a sportswriter for two weekly newspapers published in Oliver and Pentiction, B.C. Served as an aerial photographer in the R.C.A.F. ('54-'57) and helped to develop the U-2 cameras in northern Canada. During his college years, he supported himself by working for the British Columbia Forest Service and for the Federal Dept. of Agriculture. He began his present teaching career in '60 at U. of B.C. as a teaching assistant until '62; Asst. Prof. of English at U. of Calgary ('63-'66), and Writer-in-Residence ('67-'68) at the latter institution; Asst. Prof., Sir George Williams U., Montreal ('68-'72). Since '73 and presently, he is an Assoc. Prof. at Simon Fraser U. In '77-'78, he was on leave and traveling to Italy and Costa Rica.

EDITORIAL POSTS: In '61, Bowering founded TISH, a popular Canadian poetry newsletter, and edited it until '63, in which capacity he was actively associated with such Vancouver poets as Frank Davey, Lionel Kearns, James Reid, Frederic Wah, and David Dawson. Later he founded *Imago,* a magazine for longer poetry, and Imago Press, which publishes chapbooks of poetry, criticism, and interviews, some of which appear as Beaver Kosmos Folios, which he edits irregularly at his present home in Vancouver. On 12/14/'62, he married Angela Luoma. They have one daughter Thea Claire, who was born in Oct. '71.

PUBLICATIONS: Sticks and Stones ('63), *Points on the Grid* ('64), *The Man in the Yellow Boots* ('65), *The Silver Wire* ('66), *Baseball* ('67), *Two Police Poems* ('68), *Rocky Mountain Foot: A Lyric, A Memoir* ('68), *The Gangs of Kosmos* ('69), *Sitting in Mexico* ('70), *George, Vancouver: A Discovery Poem* ('70), *Geneve* ('71), *Touch: Selected Poems 1960-1970* ('71), *The Sensible* ('72), *Layers* ('73), *In the Flesh* ('74), *At War with the U.S.* ('75), *The Catch* ('76), *Poems & Other Baseballs* ('76), *Allophanes* ('77), & *The Concrete Island* ('77), all volumes and chapbooks of poetry. His poems are also included in various anthologies: *Love Where the Nights Are Long* ('65), *Oxford Book of Canadian Verse* ('65), *Penguin Book of Canadian Poetry* ('67), *New Canadian Writing* ('69), & *New American Poetry and Canadian Poetry* ('71). Since '59, his poems have also been published widely in numerous Canadian, U.S.A., and English literary periodicals: *San Francisco Review, The*

Canadian Forum, Canadian Poetry Magazine, Delta, Evidence, Genesis West, Quarry, Talon, Fiddlehead, London Magazine, El Corno Emplumado, & *Tlaloc.* More recently Bowering has confined himself mainly to publishing his poetry in books themselves. A prose writer, too, he has produced two novels, *Mirror on the Floor* ('67) and *A Short Sad Book* ('77), and in '78 is writing *The Dead Sailors.* Additionally he has published a novella *Concentric Circles* ('77), and two collections of short stories, *Flycatcher* ('74) and *Protective Footwear* ('78). As a playwright, he has authored *A Home for Heroes* ('62), and a t.v. play, *What Does Eddie Williams Want?* ('65). His essays appear in these collections: *How I Hear "Howl"* ('68), *Al*

George Bowering
(November 1963)

Purdy ('70), *Autobiology* ('74), & *Curious* ('74), as well as in these periodicals: *Canadian Literature, Canadian Forum, Toronto Globe & Mail, El Corno Emplumado, Walt Whitman Review, Aylesford Review, Kulchur,* & *Minnesota Review.* He has edited *Vibrations: Poems of Youth* ('70), and *The Story So Far* ('71).

HONORS: For his volume of poetry, *Rocky Mountain Foot,* a Gov. General's award ('69), Canada Council pre-doctoral grant ('66-'67), a short-term Canada Council grant in Fiction ('68), and two senior Canada Council Awards ('71 & '77).

OBSERVATIONS: Bowering characterizes his poetry as possessing: "Emphasis on voice, written poem as score for the spoken poem; strong sense of place, locus, in all senses, men as phenomena or objects in confluence of objects, etc. Not to copy nature but to imitate nature, for to copy nature would be a shameful thing, as William Carlos Williams said." Robert Creeley has commented upon Bowering's poems in this way: "The words become a world, sustaining the occasion of thought—which is to think of things, in that complex of all that had been thought, might be, and equally felt....But in the case with words, a world occurs, made possible by that care....Bowering begins to live at this point, finding a world opening to his sense of it."

BOBBY (ROBERT J.) BYRD
BIRTH: 4/15/'42, the son of a pilot who, when Bobby was two-years-old, died in a plane crash in Clarksville, Miss. while instructing young aviators for W.W.II. His mother became a realtor and moved the family back to Memphis, Tennessee, where she raised Bobby, his elder brother, and two sisters with the help of "Tula" (Mrs. Darthula Baldwin), a black woman, who "assumed many of the maternal duties of

our upbringing." These two women, he states, "did real good for and by me, and for themselves."

EDUCATION: U. of Ariz. (B.A.) & U. of Wash. (M.A.). Byrd began writing poetry about the age of 20 or 21, studying first with Barney Childs, composer and poet, at the U. of Ariz. During this time he also met, worked with and learned from Keith Wilson, at that time an Instructor at the U. of Ariz., and Paul Malanga, another creative writing student.

EDITORIAL POSTS: With Paul Malanga, Byrd edited and published *From A Window*, a poetry magazine. The late poet Paul Blackburn, whom Byrd first met in

Bobby Byrd
(May 1975)

'65 at the Aspen Writers' Workshop, also contributed to his poetry. However, his most recent work has been influenced primarily by the practical work and ideas of G. Gurdjieff which Byrd studied under Michael Leffert, a psychologist.

CAREER: Married, the farther of three children, Bobby Byrd lives today with his family in Radium Springs, N.M., where he and his wife Lee help to operate the Radium Springs Hotel and Bath-House. He also works as a technical and free-lance writer.

PUBLICATIONS: Places Is/& Memphis Poems (Grosseteste Press, '71); *Here* (North Atlantic Press, '75); and *the bright sun* (Blackberry Press, '76). Byrd published his first poems in his and Malanga's *From A Window*. Since then, his poems have appeared in *Work, Weed, Desperado, Grosseteste Review, Truck, Sailing the Road Clear, New Mexico Magazine, 10, Coyote's Journal, Stooge, Puerto Del Sol, Tolar Creek Syndicate, Genesis, Monk's Pond, Goat's Head, Fervent Valley, Maps, Desert Review, Poetry Review,* and in such anthologies as *The Indian Rio Grande*, edited by Frumkin & Noyes ('77).

JEFFERSON (MATTHEW) CARTER

BIRTH: 1943, N.Y.C., the third of five children of Allan and Emily Carter, Jeff alternated with his older brother and sister, Jon and Margaret, and his younger sisters, Willow and Gwyneth, between living in Burlington, Vt., where his father got his MD, while working at night to support his family, and in Staten Island, where his father also worked for the Public Health Service. When Jeff was ten years old, he moved to Tucson, where his father set up a private practice as an anesthesiologist, and he tried his best to adjust to the numerous moves his family continued making, while living at the same time in the city where today he still makes his home.

EDUCATION: "Two different grade schools, two different junior highs (Roskruge & Wakefield), and two high schools, Tucson High and Catalina High," diploma from latter ('61); Pomona C. (Claremont, Ca.; B.A. '65; major English to which he switched "after nearly flunking out-of Pre-Med" his Freshman year because he "could not handle chemistry"; U. of Ariz. (Ph.D., '72), where he studied with Dr. Oliver Sigworth, "whose fine mind and wit influenced me into concentrating on the eighteenth century literature."

CAREER: After receiving his Ph.D. in '72, Jeff "flew at once to Europe, trying to rebuild," as he notes, "my mind into some kind of human likeness." Taught

Jefferson Carter
(June 1976)

writing classes for two years at the U. of Maryland night-classes on Army bases in Darmstadt and later Wuerzburg, Germany; later at Columbus International Junior College, an American institution, in Seville, Spain. In '74, Carter returned to the States and to his home in Tucson, where he started devoting as much time as possible to writing and teaching part-time, both at the U. of Ariz. and at the Pima C. He expresses indebtedness to Steve Orlen, whom he says has taught him much. Presently he continues teaching in both Tucson institutions.

PUBLICATIONS: *Taking Chances* (Desert First Works, '76) and *Gentling the Horses* (Maguey Press, '78). Carter recalls he wrote his "first serious (self-conscious) poems," in '70 while studying for his Ph.D. pre-lims. They were published in *Hippocrene*, a little magazine in Houston. He adds that it was "an obscure" publication..."but it was enough to keep me going as I struggled through my 250-page dissertation on the peasant poets of the eighteenth century." Since '74, he has published poems in various small magazines, including: *Ark River Review, Puerto Del Sol, Writer's Forum, Shenandoah, Big Moon, Blue Moon News, Mazagine, Loon, New Times,* and *Ironwood.*

EDITORIAL POSTS: For the past few years, he has been poetry editor of *Mountain Newsreel.*

OBERSVATIONS: "My aim in poetry? Sometimes I feel talking about my aim is bad luck," Carter confides, "but in general, most of the stuff I read today in publications like *American Poetry Review* or *Poetry* leaves me chilled; I'd like to be personal, clear, and use strong but not showy or kinky images in my poems. Somehow, if one gets deeply enough into his own experiences, the experience may become 'universal,' or at least interesting to more than the author; this depends on luck, confidence and hard work. I keep hoping that description can be made to carry emotions and I want to use the desert as an illuminating and illuminated vehicle for this." About Carter's poetry, Bill Johnston has observed: "Most people go through life trying to look good and trying to be secure....Jefferson M. Carter has clearly surpassed both these handicaps to living....*Taking Chances* is a fine book technically, but more importantly because...Jefferson Carter isn't a boring man at all."

JOHN (ANTHONY) CIARDI

BIRTH: 6/24/'16, Boston, Mass., grew up in Medford, Mass.

EDUCATION: Bates C. ('34-'36); Tufts C. ('36-'38; B.A. *magna cum laude*); M.A. ('39, U. of Mich.)

CAREER: Began his career as a teacher in '40 at U. of Kan. City, Mo. for two years. Joined the U.S. Army Air Force in '42; served as gunner during W.W.II, and was discharged with an Air Medal and an Oak Leaf Cluster, '45. Returned to a teaching career at Harvard U. ('46-'53; Asst. Prof. of English.) In '53, Ciardi left Harvard for Rutgers and taught at the latter, as Prof. of English, until '61, when he abandoned his teaching career to devote full-time, except for summer duties with the Breadloaf Writers' Conf. (director from '56-'72, but teacher of poetry-writing since '47), to his writings, lectures, readings, and editorial duties. In '56, he became Poetry Ed. of *Saturday Review,* and began writing his column, "Manner of Speaking," duties he continued until '73 when SR #1 folded, but resumed again in '75 when Norman Cousins regained the editorship of *Saturday Review/World,* with Ciardi having served two years meanwhile as Contrib. Ed. to Cousins' *World.* For a time ('61-'62), he also hosted a weekly C.B.S. TV show, "Accent." Ciardi has traveled widely in Europe, too, especially in Italy, and was, during the year '51, Lect. in Poetry at the Salzburg Seminar in Amer. Studies. With his wife Judith (the former Myra Judith Hosdetter, whom he married in '46), he makes his home in Metuchen, N.J. They have three grown children, a daughter and two sons.

PUBLICATIONS: Homeward to America ('40), *Other Skies* ('47), *Live Another Day* ('49), *From Time to Time* ('51), *As If* ('55), *I Marry You: A Sheaf of Love Poems* ('58), *Thirty-Nine Poems* ('59), *In the Stoneworks* ('61), *In Fact* ('62), *Person to Person* ('64), *This Strangest Everything* ('66), *A Genesis: 15 Poems* ('67), *The Achievement of John Ciardi: A Comprehensive Selection of his Poems,* with a critical introduction, edited by Miller Williams ('69), *An Alphabestiary* ('67), *Lives of X* ('71), and *The Little That Is All* ('74). Ciardi's poems have appeared frequently in *Atlantic Monthly, New Yorker, and Harper's,* as well as in numerous anthologies: *War Poets* ('45), *A Preface to Poetry* ('46), *Mid-Century American Poets* ('50), *Atlantic Book of British and American Poetry* ('58), *Poetry for Pleasure* ('60), *Modern Poets* ('63), *Beastly Boys and Ghastly Girls* ('64), *Poems of Doubt and Belief* ('64), *Today's Poets* ('64), *Modern Ballards and Story Poems* ('65), *Poems on Poetry* ('65), and elsewhere. As a translator, Ciardi has produced three volumes of Dante's *Divine Comedy: The Inferno* ('54), *The Purgatorio* ('61), and *The Paradiso* ('70). As literary critic, he has contributed *Dialogue With An Audience* ('63); *Poetry, A Closer Look,* with James M. Reid & Laurence Perrine ('63), and *Manner of Speaking (Saturday Review* columns, '72). Additionally he has edited various well-known poetry anthologies: *Mid-Century American Poets* ('50) and *How Does a Poem Mean?* ('60). A recording of his reading selections from his *As If* has been produced by Folkway Records. Additionally he has produced nine volumes of children's verse: *The Reason for The Pelican* ('59), *I Met A Man* ('61), *The Man Who Sang the Sillies* ('61), *You Read to Me, I'll Read to You* ('62), *John J.*

Plenty and Fiddler Dan ('63), *The King Who Saved Himself from Being Saved* ('65), *The Monster Den* ('66), *Someone Could Win a Polar Bear* ('70), and *Fast and Slow* ('75). Others of his children's books include *Scrappy the Pup* ('60), *The Wish Tree* ('62), and *You Know Who* ('64).

HONORS: Phi Beta Kappa ('38); Avery Hopwood Award ('39); Blumenthal Prize ('43); Eunice Tietjens Award ('45); Levinson Prize ('47); New England Poetry Club

John Ciardi
(March 1971)

Golden Rose Trophy ('48); Harriet Monroe Memorial Prize ('55); Amer. Acad. in Rome Fellowship ('59); Boys Club of America Junior Book Award ('62); D. Litt. Tufts C. ('60); D. Litt. Ohio Wesleyan ('71); D. Litt. Washington U., St. Louis ('71); Hum.D., Wayne St. ('63); L.L.D., Ursinus C., Pa., ('64); L.H.D., Kalamazoo C. ('64); L.H.D., Bates C. ('70); Fellow of the National Institute of Arts and Letters, and of the Amer. Academy of Arts & Sciences; and former president of the Nat. College English Assoc.

OBSERVATIONS: "Poetry, for me," says Ciardi, "finds voices, but the aim should not be an idiosyncratic single voice immediately recognizable as a given man (style as signature)....The ideal accomplishment of a poem may be put as *homo fecit*. A man did it, and any man may say it of himself as one of the voices of his humanity, of his humanity quickened to itself." David Daiches has called Ciardi "a poet of genuine gifts whose best poetry has wit, perception, and humanity."

NEIL CLAREMON

BIRTH: 1942, N.Y.C., spent the first twenty-eight years of his life, shuffling back and forth between three homes every twelve months: N.Y.C., Hollywood, Fla., and Westchester Co., N.Y.; but at fifteen, began visiting an aunt and uncle in Tucson. He became so attracted to Ariz. he decided to make it his future home.

EDUCATION: After a B.S. degree from Cornell, he moved to Tucson to work upon his M.A. at the U. of Ariz., and began writing poems there, though independently, as he pursued his graduate studies. After completing the latter degree, he spent a year working on a Ph.D. at SUNY, Stony Brook, but found himself concentrating more on the poetry program of the latter institution than on academic subjects.

CAREER: In '69, he moved back to Ariz., settled in Cortaro for a time, and became the director of the newly-formed Southwest Creative Writing Project, which under a grant from the National Endowment for the Arts and the Ariz.

Commission on the Arts was to become the present-day Poetry-in-the-Schools projects of Ariz. and initially of N.M. Until '73, Claremon directed this program, bringing the Arizona Poetry-In-The-Schools project into a separate entity from that of New Mexico, and traveling constantly during these years betweeen Indian, Mexican-American, and schools serving ''low-income'' group students of all nationalities. He abandoned his Ph.D. as a result of this experience, wrote his first

Neil Claremon
(December 1972)

book of poems, *East By Southwest* ('70), which reflected his earlier commuting experience,and in '73, gave up the directorship of the Poetry-In-The-Schools Program of the Arizona Commission on the Arts, to devote himself full-time to his writings, both in poetry and fiction. His work with Mexican-Americans had interested him so deeply that he decided the same year to move from his home in Cortaro to the border city of Nogales, Ariz., where he and his wife Judith and their daughter Amanda live today.

PUBLICATIONS: East By Southwest ('70) and *West of the American Dream* ('73). Most of Claremon's poetry, even initially, has appeared in book form. Additionally he has published one novel, *Borderlands* ('75).

OBSERVATIONS: A.J.M. Smith writes: ''Neil Claremon is a young poet who is working towards the discovery of a possibly unique method of writing the objective and subjective. In poems that are imagistic in their concreteness he juxtaposes disparate and coincidental experiences and produces a metaphysical construct in which thing and idea become one....Working with intersections and junctures,...he has given us poems in which a double or triple vision of separate experiences is brought into sharp and often ironic focus. We read his poems as we would read a map—a chart of the place where events meet, objectively in space and time and abstractly, in the mind.''

LUCILLE CLIFTON
BIRTH: 6/27/'36, Depew, N.Y., grew up and attended public schools there. Descended from a black great-grandmother, Caroline Donald Sale, who at age eight—when a black child slave, walked all the way from New Orleans to Virginia, Ms. Clifton knows a proud heritage, and has written movingly of it and of her ancestor's experiences in her book *Generations: A Memoir* (Random House, '75). This work, an odyssey into the author's own past tells of how this gifted black poet's own roots in ''Dahomey women,'' especially in those of her ''Mammy Ca'line'' (her great-grandmother Sale) who was ''born free in Afrika in 1822'' and ''died free in

America in 1910," as well as of the generations of her family descended from this remarkable woman. Lucille Clifton's own father had grown up in Virginia and taught his New York children strong attachments about his native state.

EDUCATION: Howard U. ('53-'55; Drama major), and N.Y. St. Teacher's C., Fredonia, briefly. No degree.

Career; Married Fred J. Clifton in '58, and lives with him and their six children today in Baltimore, where he is a prominent consultant for various community programs. A dedicated wife and mother, as well as a poet and prose writer, Lucille Clifton had little in print until '69, when she was thirty-two years of age, since "publishing had seemed less important than writing and [she] hadn't thought about it very much." She published her first poem in *Negro Digest*, and then as her children grew older began to concentrate more upon her writing career.

PUBLICATIONS: Good Times ('69), *Good News About the Earth* ('72), and *An Ordinary Woman* ('74). Her poetry also appears in various anthologies: Adoff, *The Poetry of Black America*; Bell, *Afro-American Poetry*, Chametzky & Kaplan, *Black and White in American Culture*, Colley and Moore, *Starting with Poetry*; Hayden, Burrows & Lapides, *Afro-American Literature*; Miller, *Dices and Black Bones*; Randall, *The Black Poets*; Watkins & David, *To Be a Black Woman*; John Malcolm Brinnin's *Twentieth Century Poetry: American and British, 1900-1970*; and Howe & Basso, *No More Masks! An Anthology of Poems by Women.* Among the poetry periodicals carrying her work are these: *Ms., Black World, The Negro Digest, The*

Lucille Clifton
(November 1975)

Massachusetts Review, and *The Iowa Review.* Her experiences as a concerned mother have helped her immensley in producing several well-known children and young adult's books: *Some of the Days of Everett Anderson* ('70), *The Black BC's* ('70), *Everett Anderson's Christmas Coming* ('72), *All Us Come Cross the Water* ('73), *Don't You Remember* ('74), *Everett Anderson's Year* ('74), and *The Times They Used to Be* ('74).

HONORS: In '69, she participated in the YM-YWHA Poetry Center's "Discovery Series," after receiving their "Discovery Award." The same year she also won an N.E.A. grant, and likewise served briefly as a Visiting Writer at Columbia U. School of the Arts. She has also read her poetry at numerous American colleges and universities, and has worked, too, in the Poetry-in-the-Schools program of Maryland, as well as at Coppin St. C., Baltimore, where she has been poet-in-residence.

OBSERVATIONS: Lucille Clifton noted on one occasion: "I am a black woman poet, and I sound like one." On another, she put it this way: "An artist is supposed to tell the truth." Maxine Kumin describes Lucille Clifton as "a lyricist who sings spare and hard songs. *Good Times* is an important contribution to the growing body of black literature."

THOMAS COBB

BIRTH: 7/9/'47, in Chicago, moved to Tucson in Oct. '50 when he was three years old.

EDUCATION: Tucson public schools; Amphitheater High School diploma, U. of Ariz. B.A. ('69) and M.A. ('71), both in English; and M.F.A., Creative Writing ('72).

Thomas Cobb
(June 1976)

CAREER: Began his teaching career at U. of Ariz. as graduate assistant until '72; in '72, became Instr. of English at Eastern Ariz.; from '75-'76, he served as director of the Creative Writing program at the same institution. From '73-'75, Cobb also worked with the Poets'-on-the-Road, Ariz. Commission on the Arts & Humanities. Cobb lives today with his wife Lynn in Tucson, Ariz., where he operates the Sixth Street Bookstore. He is active in prison-poetry workshops, which he also conducts in various Ariz. penal institutions.

PUBLICATIONS: We Shall Curse the Dead (Desert First Works, '75). Anthologies such as these carry his poems: *Poetry of the Desert Southwest*, edited by James Quick (Baleen Press, Phoenix, '73), *Intro V*, edited by Walter Beacham and George Garrett (U. Press of Va., '74), and *New American Verse*, edited by Mark Langhorne (Amer. Poetry Press, Atlanta, '74). Various periodicals, including the following, have published his poetry: *Chameleon, Loon, Mill Mountain Review, Caim, Mazagine, New Mexico Magazine,* and *Arizona Perspective.*

OBSERVATIONS: Jefferson Carter has reviewed Cobb's first collection as "a combination of flat, ironic statement...and vivid, functional description...visually precise...provocative...expression perfectly controlled...."

ROBERT (JACKSON) CONLEY

BIRTH: 12/29/'40, Cushing, Okla., a member of the Cherokee Nation, was educated both in the public schools of Okla. and in north Tex., in the Wichita Falls area, where his family moved while he was growing up.

EDUCATION: B.A. (Drama) and M.A. (English) in '66 and '68 from Midwestern U. (Tex.).

CAREER: Six years in the Infantry of the Marine Corps Reserve. Began teaching career, '66, when he served as a graduate teaching assistant in English and Speech for two years at Midwestern U. In '68, he left Tex. to become an Inst. in English at No. Ill. U., DeKalb, a position he left in '71, to assume duties at Southwest Mo. St. U., Springfield. At the latter institution, in addition to teaching English, he was instrumental in establishing a graduate workshop for area teachers in ethnic literature, and was appointed by the Dean of Humanities to undertake a study of the feasibility of initiating an ethnic studies program on the campus. In '75-'76, he held the position of Coordinator of Indian Culture at Eastern Montana College. He has been a very active member of the National Indian Education Association and a

Robert J. Conley
(June 1976)

consultant to their "Project Media." Today he lives at the Cherokee Tribal Headquarters in Tahlequah, Oklahoma, where he is Assistant Programs Director for the Cherokee Nation.

EDITORIAL POSTS: Co-editor and publisher of *The Blackbird Circle*, a small press poetry magazine with national distribution, Conley has been the recipient of two CCLM publishing grants for his periodicals. As an editor, he has also co-authored four textbooks: *A Return to Vision* (Houghton Mifflin, '71; '74), *The Shadow Within* ('73), *The Essay: Structure and Idea* ('75), all of which he edited with Richard Cherry & Bernard Hirsch, and *Poems for Comparison and Contrast* ('72), which he edited solely with Cherry.

PUBLICATIONS: Conley's first collection, *21 Poems*, was published in '75 by Aux Arcs Press, Springfield, Mo. His poems have been widely published in poetry periodicals, including these: *Quoin, The Blue Cloud Quarterly, Academy, Indian Voice Magazine, Pembroke, The Five Tribes Journal, Quetzal, The Cardinal Poetry Quarterly, Scree 4: Native American Issue, The Blackbird Circle, The Coldspring Journal, Places, Sun Tracks, Phantasm,* & *Wassaja.* His poems have also been anthologized in these collections: *From the Belly of the Shark*, ed. by Walter Lowenfels, *The New Breed: An Anthology of Texas Poets*, ed. by Edward Oliphant, & *Anyone for Tennyson?*, an anthology issued to supplement the PBS-TV show by the same name. Concerning the latter, Conley had the honor of having one of his poems read by Henry Fonda on "The American Dream," a segment of the PBS-TV poetry series, *Anyone for Tennyson?* Additionally a prose writer, Conley has also

17

published four of his short stories in four different issues of *Indian Voice*, and one in *Sun Tracks*. He has conducted poetry readings and workshops at Cazenovia College, N.Y., at So. Missouri St. U., and elsewhere, and has been interviewed on "Native Americans" for an episode in the series, *The Invisible Americans*, produced for TV-3 in Springfield, Mo. in cooperation with the Mayor's Commission on Human Rights.

OBSERVATIONS: Pam Lape has commented: "Conley lets you into his world, he opens up, lets you drift, lets you think, lets you feel, lets you get away from it all. He shows himself."

ROBERT (WHITE) CREELEY

BIRTH: 5/21/'26, Arlington, Mass., received his first schooling at Holderness School in Plymouth, N.H.

EDUCATION: Attended Harvard ('43-'46), but dropped out during W.W.II, and volunteered for the American Field Service, which took him to India and Burma. Afterwards he re-entered Harvard, but left it again for Black Mountain College, N.C., where in '55, he received his B.A.; M.A. (U. of N.M., '60).

CAREER: Creeley's teaching career began at Black Mountain College ('54-'55; Instr. in Writing); also taught for two years in Guatemala on a *finca*; creative writing at U. of N.M. ('61-'62, '63-'66, & '68-'69); '62-'63, Lect. in poetry, U.B.C., Vancouver; '70-'71, Visiting Prof., San Francisco St. C. Since '66, except for leaves of absence and periods of travel, he has been a Prof. of English, SUNY, Buffalo.

EDITORIAL POSTS: For some of the time he was on-campus, and also while abroad, Creeley served as editor of the *Black Mountain Review*, a post he kept during the first seven years of the magazine's existence. During this experience, he was closely associated with such other poets from the school as Charles Olson, Denise Levertov, Robert Duncan, and Edward Dorn, who were in those years just beginning to make their way with their craft. Prior to joining and after leaving the Black Mountain C., both as a student and faculty member, Creeley lived for awhile in Spain and France, where he wrote poetry and operated such small presses as the Divers Press ('53-'55) in Palma de Majorca, which published his work and that of other poets destined to become influential voices of "the sixties and seventies." In the early '50s, he was also associated actively with such small poetry journals as *Wake, Golden Goose, Origin, Fragmente, Vou, Contact, CIV/n,* and *Merlin*, as well as with others, too, subsequently in the late '50s and early '60s. During recent years, he has been commuting regularly between Buffalo, where he and his wife make their home during the academic year, to the Bay Area to teach and work with writing programs in Calif. and to live in Bolinas during the summers. The Creeleys also keep their home, too, in the small town Placitas, outside Albuquerque, where many New Mexican poets, influenced by Robert Creeley, as well as others from throughout the U.S., now live. Divorced twice, Creeley is the father of six children.

PUBLICATIONS: Both collections and chapbooks of poetry of his include these: *Le Fou* ('52), *The Immoral Proposition* ('53), *The Kind Of Act Of* ('53), *A Snarling Garland of Xmas Verses* ('54), *Ferrini and Others*, with others ('55), *All That Is Lovely in Men* ('55), *If You* ('56), *The Whip* ('57), *A Form of Women* ('59), *For Love: Poems 1950-60* ('62, '66), *Distance* ('64), *Two Poems* ('64), *Hi There!* ('65), *About Women* ('66), *Poems: 1950-65* ('66), *For Joel* ('66), *A Sight* ('67), *Words* ('67), *Robert Creeley Reads* (with recording, '67), *The Finger* ('68), *The Charm: Early and Uncollected Poems* ('68, '71), *5 Numbers* ('68), *The Boy* ('68), *Divisions and Other Early Poems* ('68), *Pieces* ('68), *Hero* ('69), *A Wall* ('69), *Mary's Fancy*

('70), *In London* ('70), *For Betsy and Tom* ('70), *For Benny and Sabina* ('70), *As Now It Would Be Snow* ('70), *America* ('70), *Christmas: May 10, 1970* ('70), *St. Martin's* ('71), *Sea* ('71), *1.2.3.4.5.6.7.8.9.0.* ('71), *For the Graduation*('71),

Robert Creeley
(December 1963)

Change ('72), *One Day After Another* ('72), *A Day Book* (with his prose also; '72); *For My Mother* ('73), *Kitchen* ('73), *Sitting Here* ('74), *Thirty Things* ('74), and *Hello* ('78). A great many anthologies carry his poetry, among them: *New American Poets* ('60), *Contemporary American Poetry* ('62), *American Poems* ('64), *Today's Poets* ('64), *American Poetry* ('65), and *A Controversy of Poets* ('65). Numerous periodicals have included his verse; some of them are: *Black Mountain Review, Nation, Evergreen Review, New Directions Annual,* and *Poetry.* As a writer of fiction, Creeley has produced two novels, *The Island* ('63; '64), and *Presences,* with Marisol ('76), and three books of short stories: *The Gold Diggers* ('54), *Mister Blue* ('64), and *The Gold Diggers and Other Stories* ('65). His play, *Listen* ('72), was produced in London the year of its publication. As editor, he produced: *Mayan Letters,* by Charles Olson ('53; '68); *New American Story,* with Donald Allen ('65); *Selected Writings,* by Charles Olson ('66); *The New Writing in the U.S.A.,* with Donald Allen ('67) and *Whitman* ('73). His collections of essays and interviews include *An American Sense* ('65); *Contexts of Poetry* ('68), *A Quick Graph: Collected Notes and Essays* ('70), *A Day Book* ('70), *The Creative* ('73), *A Sense of Measure* (*Essays, '73*), *Contexts of Poetry: Interviews '61-'71* ('73), and *Inside Out: Notes on the Autobiographical Mode* ('74).

HONORS: Creeley's poems have won him various prestigious awards and fellowships: Levinson Prize from *Poetry* ('60), D.H. Lawrence Fellowship for writing from the U. of N.M. ('60), his *For Love: Poems 1950-60* was a leading contender for the '62 National Book Award; two Guggenheim fellowships ('64; '71), Oscar Blumenthal Prize ('64), Rockefeller Fellowship ('65), and Union League Civic & Arts Foundation Prize from *Poetry* ('67).

OBSERVATIONS: Robert Creeley says: "I write to realize the world as one has come to live in it, thus to give testament, I write to move in *words,* a human delight. I write when no other act is possible." William Carlos Williams once noted, especially with regard to Creeley's measure, that it is "the subtlest...that I encounter anywhere except in the verses of Ezra Pound."

VICTOR HERNÁNDEZ CRUZ
BIRTH: 2/6/'49, Aguas Buenas, Puerto Rico, emigrated with his parents to New

York City when he was four years old. He grew up on the Lower East Side of Manhattan.

Victor Hernández Cruz
(November 1971)

PUBLICATIONS: His first collection of poems *Snaps* was published in 1969 by Random House. His *Mainland* came out in 1973 from the same publisher, and *Tropicalization* appeared in 1976 from Reed, Cannon and Johnson.

CAREER: He has read and lectured at colleges and universities throughout the United States. For the last ten years he has been back and forth from the West Coast to the East Coast, getting a flavor of both temperaments which are expressed in his work. His recent work explores the intensities of growing up with two languages; he plays one against the other (Spanish and English). He is currently living in San Francisco and writing a novel.

MICHAEL CUDDIHY
BIRTH: 2/2/'32, N.Y.C., attended elementary school in his birthplace, and then went to Rhode Island where he was enrolled in the Portsmouth Priory school. After

Michael Cuddihy
(May 1976)

graduation, Cuddihy spent two years studying at Notre Dame. Then, in Sept. '51, while working as a counselor at a camp run by the N.Y. *Herald Tribune* Fresh Air Fund, he contracted polio myelitis, spent nine months in an iron lung, and a couple years in a hospital.

EDUCATION: In Sept. '56, unable to cope with New York winters, he moved to Tucson, and transferred to the U. of Ariz., where he completed his B.A. in history (June, '59). For several years, he did reviews, mostly history, for such periodicals as *Thought, America,* and *Jubilee.* Meanwhile he pursued graduate work at the U. of Ariz., with brief stints at Harvard and Berkeley. Around '68 he began writing poems, first working on his own for a year, and then sitting in on a poetry workshop taught by Richard Shelton at the U. of Ariz. Poetry Center for several months. As his interests in poetry grew, Michael also attended workshops elsewhere, including one taught by William Matthews in Ithaca, N.Y., in the summer of '71.

EDITORIAL POSTS: In '72, along with his wife Mary, he started *Ironwood,* a magazine of contemporary poetry. Cuddihy, who continues to live today in Tucson, chose the name *Ironwood* because of regional connotations and because he feels the name is a "strong word," which "suggests the wedding of things vegetable and mineral." The magazine, which has now published more than a dozen issues, has done special numbers on the poetry of George Oppen and James Wright. Cuddihy also publishes a series of chapbooks under his Ironwood Press imprint, which includes such poets as Peter Nelson, Thomas Johnson, Tony Petrosky, Nils Nelson, Steven Orlen, Del Marie Rogers, Lynn Strongin, Frank Stanford, and Michael Buckard, among others.

PUBLICATIONS: Cuddihy's poetry has appeared in numerous periodicals, including *Kayak, Commonweal, Cloud Marauder, Chicago Tribune Magazine, Sumac, Lillabulero, Inscape, Café Solo, Granite,* and more recently, *Iowa Review, Pocket Pal,* & *Rapport.* His work is also included in such anthologies as *Poetry of the Desert Southwest,* edited by James Quick, and *The Indian Rio Grande,* edited by Gene Frumkin and Stanley Noyes. As a translator, Cuddihy rendered into English in '67 a volume by the French philosopher, Jacques Maritain, entitled *The Peasant of the Garonne,* published by Holt, Rinehart, and Winston.

OBSERVATIONS: Cuddihy says of his poetry: "Early I was drawn to what has been called 'the poetry of silence,' the kind of thing W.S. Merwin, Charles Simic, and James Wright were doing. More recently my poems have attempted to deal with childhood experiences, the feelings they evoke."

C(ECIL) DAY LEWIS

BIRTH: 4/27/'04, Ballintubber, So. Ireland.

DEATH: 5/22/'72, Barnet, England. The son of F.C. Day Lewis, an Anglo-Irish clergyman, and Kathleen Blake (Squires) Day Lewis, a collateral descendant of Oliver Goldsmith, he began writing poetry at the age of six.

EDUCATION: Brought up mainly in England, he attended Sherborne School, Dorset, and Wadham C., Oxford. In the "mid-twenties" at Oxford, he met W.H. Auden, whose influence on his work, he discusses in his autobiography, *The Buried Day* ('60).

CAREER: For awhile after leaving Oxford, Day Lewis taught school, serving first as Asst. Master, Summerfields, Oxford ('27-'28), & ('28-'30) as teacher in Larchfield, Helensburgh, Scotland. In '30, he returned to England, to a teaching post at Cheltenham College, which he held until '35. During the same period of time, he was also writing and publishing the first eight volumes of his verse. In 1932, he contributed to, with W.H. Auden, Stephen Spender, and Louis MacNeice, a volume of poetry called *New Signatures,* destined to become a landmark of English poetry for the "thirties." But it was the income he was starting to make from writing the detective fiction he began to publish from '35 forward—work he continued to publish for the rest of his life under the pseudonym of Nicholas Blake, which enabled him to abandon a full-time teaching career. Although Day Lewis devoted much of his future life to his serious writings as poet and literary critic and to the detective works which helped sustain him, he nevertheless held numerous other lecturing posts during his career, as well as others related to publishing and editing. Some critics even felt his detective novels to be equal to his serious work. For instance, *The Times Literary Supplement* has noted that the Nicholas Blake books are "competent and civilized, agreeably relaxed and yet intellectually flattering." Dating from '41, he was an editor with the Ministry of Information, a position he left in '46 at the close of W.W.II. Beginning in 1954 and continuing until his death, he traveled extensively in the U.S.A., and Canada, giving readings of his works and lecturing on various university campuses. His lectures and reading tours were renowned in England long before he crossed the Atlantic. During his career, Day Lewis held appointments as Visiting Lect. & Prof. at such universities as these: Trinity C., Cambridge (Clark Lect., '46), Oxford U. (Prof. of Poetry, '52, '53-'56), Queen's U., Kingston, Ont. (Chancellor Dunning Trust Lect., '54), Harvard (Charles Eliot Norton Prof. of Poetry, '64-'65), and Hull U. (Compton Lect., '68). From '62-67, he was a member of the Arts Council of Great Britain, and from '54, until the end of his life, he was a director of Chatto & Windus Ltd. publishers.

PUBLICATIONS: Day Lewis published the first of his thirty-three volumes of poetry, *Beechen Vigil and Other Poems* in '25. His other contributions were *Country Comets* ('28), *Transitional Poems* ('29), *From Feathers to Iron* ('31), *The Magnetic Mountain* ('33), *Collected Poems, 1929-33* ('35), *A Time to Dance and Other Poems* ('35; '36 Amer.), *Noah and the Waters* ('36), *Overtures to Death and Other Poems* ('38), *Poems in Wartime* ('40), *Selected Poems* ('40), *Word Over All* ('43), *Poems: 1943-47* ('48), *Short is the Time: 1936-43* ('45), *Collected Poems: 1929-36* ('51, '69), *Christmas Eve* ('54), *The Newborn: D.M.B., 29 April, 1957* ('57), *The Gate and Other Poems* ('62), *Requiem for the Living* ('64), *On Not Saying Everything* ('64), *A Marriage Song for Albert and Barbara* ('65), *The Room and Other Poems* ('65), *C. Day Lewis: Selections From His Poetry* ('67), edited by Patric Dickinson, *The Abbey That Refused to Die: A Poem* ('67), *Roots* ('70; Am. ed. entitled *The Whispering Roots and Other Poems* ('70), & *Going My Way* ('70). Among the numerous anthologies carrying Day Lewis's poems are these: *Modern British Poetry* ('36), *Chief Modern Poets* ('43), *Modern Poetry* ('51), *Poetry for Pleasure* ('60), *Faber Book of Modern Verse* ('60), *An Anthology of Modern Verse* ('61), *Poet's Choice* ('62), *Penguin Book of Contemporary Verse* ('62), *Modern Poets* ('63), *Poetry of the Thirties* ('64), *Poems of Doubt and Belief* ('64), & *Earth Is the Lord's* ('65). As a translator, he was the author of four volumes: Virgil's *The Georgics* ('40), Paul Valéry's *Le cimetière marin* (*The Graveyard by the Sea,* '47), Virgil's *The Aenid* ('52), & *The Eclogues* (63). As an editor of poetry and critical anthologies, Day Lewis was widely known for such editions as the following: *Oxford Poetry,* with W.H. Auden ('27); with others, *A Writer in Arms* by Ralph Fox ('37), *The Mind in Chains: Socialism and the Cultural Revolution* ('37), *The Echoing Green* ('37), *A New Anthology of Modern Verse: 1920-1940,* with I.A.G. Strong ('41), *The Golden Treasury* (rev. ed. '54); with others, *Orion, V.I & V.III* ('45, '46), *The Chatto Book of Modern Verse: 1915-55,* with John Lehmann ('56); with Kathleen Nott & Thomas Blackburn, *New Poems 1957* ('57), *A Book of English Lyrics* ('61); *The Collected Poems of Wilfred Owen* ('64; rev. Am. ed. '64), *The Midnight Skaters: Poems For Young Readers* by Edmund Blunden ('68); *The*

C. Day Lewis
(April 1965)
deceased

Poems of Robert Browning ('69 ed.; '71 rev.), *A Choice of Keats's Verse* ('71), & *Crabbe* ('73). Day Lewis's prose writings include various volumes of literary criticism, among them these titles: *A Hope for Poetry* ('34), *The Poetic Image* ('47), *Notable Images of Virtue: Emily Bronte, George Meredith, W.B. Yeats* ('54), *The Lyric Impulse* ('65), *Thomas Hardy,* with R.A. Scott-James ('65), & *A Need For Poetry?* ('68). Among his many shorter prose offerings are his *Introductions* to George Meredith's *Modern Love* ('48), Wilfred Owen's *Collected Poems* ('67), & Robert Frost's *Selected Poems* ('36). He also published his autobiography, *The Buried Day* ('60), and three novels: *The Friendly Tree* ('36), *Starting Point* ('37), & *Child of Misfortune* ('39). Further he wrote children's books, for example, *Dick Willoughby* ('33). The various detective stories, published under the name of Nicholas Blake include *A Question of Proof* ('35), *Thou Shell of Death* ('36), *There's Trouble Brewing* ('37), *The Beast Must Die* ('38), *The Smiler With the Knife* ('39), *Malice in Wonderland* ('40), *The Summer Camp Mystery* ('40), *The Corpse in the Snowman* ('41), *Minute for Murder* ('47), *Head of a Traveler* ('49), *The Dreadful Hollow* ('53), *The Whisper in the Gloom* ('54), *A Tangled Web* ('56), *End of Chapter* ('57), *A Penknife in My Heart* ('58), *The Widow's Cruise* ('59), *The Worm of Death* ('61), *The Deadly Joker* ('63), *The Sad Variety* ('64), *The Morning After Death* ('66), *The Nicholas Blake Omnibus* ('66), & *The Private Wound* ('68).

HONORS: Fellow of the Royal Soc. of Art ('44), Fellow & Vice-Pres. ('58) of the Royal Soc. of Lit. & Companion of Lit. ('64); Commander, Order of the British Empire ('60); D. Litt., Exeter U. ('65), Hon. Member of the Am. Academy of Arts & Letters ('66), Honorary Fellow of Wadham C., Oxford ('66), Litt. D., Trinity C., Dublin ('68), & Litt. D., Hull ('70). He was named Poet Laureate in '68.

OBSERVATIONS: C. Day Lewis once commented upon his writings in this way: "My own basic pattern compelled me to become a person who lives largely by words and for them. In my young days, words were my antennae, my touch stones, my causeway over a quaking bog of mistrust. After some false starts and fruitless detours, they began to lead me towards the human condition as I knew it within myself; I gradually understood the paradox that a poet must make sense of 'real' things through the process of creating works of a quite different order of reality. For me, poetry comes and goes. I write verse quite prolifically for a year or two; then the impulse is exhausted, and for the next year or two I have none to write, unless I try my hand at translation. These fallow times used to disquiet me, making me think I had run dry for ever, so that I questioned whether my way of life was the right one for me as a poet, and would have changed it radically if I had known what way would be more productive. Now I have grown habituated to this ebb and flow; I can wait more patiently for the season when the world around me and within me shall bloom again with poetic significance." R.M. Elman has described Day Lewis's poetry as "thoroughly Georgian in tone, cultivated, very English, highly eclectic, but also quite original." Twice married, Day Lewis was the father of four children, and is survived by them and by his widow, Jill Angela Henriette Day Lewis (Jill Balcon, the actress), with whom he made his last home in the Greenwich section of London.

ABELARDO B. DELGADO

BIRTH: 11/27/'31, in a rural community, Boquilla de Conchos, in the state of Chihuahua, Mexico, spent his earliest years in the Mexican cities of Parrall and Chihuahua, and as a child also moved to El Paso, Tex., where he grew up in an impoverished Chicano *barrio.*

EDUCATION: El Paso, Tex. public schools; B.S. in secondary education with a major in Spanish and Speech, and some post-graduate work.

CAREER: Delgado worked as the executive director to a Migrant Council in Denver for almost two years; also in a similar capacity in Los Angeles for another. For the past ten years he has been an outstanding leader in the Chicano movement. In '71, he observed that as a young man he had learned much about such leadership

Abelardo Delgado
(June 1975)

"from two persons, a Jesuit priest I worked with for ten years in South El Paso; and from Salvador Ramierez, who successfully assembled a good set of talented Chicanos to start a chain reaction of institutional change in El Paso—which only God knows where it will end." He has traveled widely over the U.S., especially in the West and Southwest, working for the Chicano cause and giving readings of his poetry and lectures. For several years now, he has been teaching Chicano Studies on the faculty of the U. of Utah, where he operates the Barrio Publications, which publish his works, as well as those of some other important Chicano voices of today. He makes his home in Salt Lake City with his wife "Lola" of twenty-five years and their eight children when he is not participating in many of the out-of-town conferences related to writing or Minority Studies at which he is a popular participant. He delights in his first grandchildren.

PUBLICATIONS: A major voice of Chicano poetry, Abelardo, or "Lalo," as he is affectionately known to his many friends, has published the following books and chapbooks of poetry: *Chicano, 25 Pieces of a Chicano Mind* ('70), *Los Cuatro,* with poetry also by Sánchez, Pérez, & Avila, ('71), *Reflexiones* ('72), *Mortal Sin Kit* ('72), *Bajo el Sol de Aztlán* ('73), & *It's Cold* (also contains prose, '74). Additionally he is the author of a prose book-length manifesto, *The Chicano Movement* ('71), and of such posters as "Stupid America," "La Raza Habla," and "It's Buy-cent-anal time, Carnales..." His poetry is included in such important anthologies of Chicano literature of the Southwest as these: *La Raza,* ed. by Stan Steiner ('69), *South El Paso, El Segundo Barrio,* ed. by Los Atrevidos ('71), *Aztlán,* ed. by Luis Valdez & Stan Steiner, *From the Belly of the Shark,* ed. by Walter Lowenfels ('73), *Passing Through: An Anthology of Contemporary Southwest Literature,* ed. by W. Burns Taylor, Richard Santelli & Kathleen McGary ('74), *Voices of Aztlán: Chicano Literature of Today,* ed. by Dorothy E. Harth & Lewis M. Baldwin ('74), & *Chicano Voices,* edited by Carlota Cárdenas de Dwyer ('75). Poems by Abelardo Delgado have also appeared with increasing frequency since '71 in numerous magazines and newspapers, especially in connection with protest literature: *Legal Newsletter* (Boulder, Colo.), *La Guardia* (Milwaukee), *El Barrio* (U. of Tex. at El Paso magazine), *The American College Poetry Society Anthology* ('61), *El Alacrán* (El Paso), *El Sol* (Moorehead, Minn. magazine), *Ahora* (farmwork magazine, Alamosa, Colo.), *Menuda* (El Paso magazine), *El Gallo* (Denver newspaper), *Caracol* (San Antonio magazine), *Xalman* (Santa Barbara magazine) and elsewhere. His protest articles have also appeared in a number of magazines and newspapers since '67, including: *Wilson Library Bulletin, La Luz Magazine, El Paso Herald Post,* and in the *Conference Book* of the Southwest Educational Council, San Antonio. His works are always written in English, Spanish, and *Pocho* dialect. (The latter is a term used by Mexican nationals to characterize a person of Mexican ancestry born in the United States, and is a dialect formed of a mixture of Spanish and English, which is characterized by Spanish pronunciation of English words.)

OBSERVATIONS: Delgado writes that currently "there is an effort on my part to include a couple of pieces of prose to balance out the verses" in his publications. This is because "I want to be known as a *cuentista* (story-teller) also. My present mood is excitement and tranquility at the same time." He adds: "All I can ever say about my writings, is that they come out of me with their own force and gather life and shape of their own and at times I do not recognize them as my own." About his poetry, two prominent Chicano literary critics have spoken. Philip D. Ortego has noted: "Delgado writes of the impatient *raza*, but tempers that impatience with an appeal to Anglo-Americans for brotherhood...." Arnulfo D. Trejo has written: "The poet's [Abelardo's] main concern is to narrate the experiences of the people of the *barrios.* Because of his intense desire to tell rather than make the reader feel, the thoughts are direct and the elements of poetry such as melody, rhythm, and imagery play only a minor role."

R.(OBERT) P.(RESTON) DICKEY

BIRTH: 9/23/'36, the son of Delno Miren Dickey, a lead miner, and Naomi (Jackson) Dickey, Flat River, Mo., grew up in nearby Elvins, Mo. In '54, at seventeen, he joined the U.S.A.F., and was discharged in '56.

EDUCATION: B.A. ('68); M.A. ('69), both in English from the U. of Mo.; Ph.D. ('75), Walden U. (Fla.).

CAREER: Career as a teacher of courses in poetry, fiction, literature, and creative writing began at the U. of Mo. ('67-'69); Asst. Prof., U. of So. Colo., Pueblo ('69-'73); director of his own school of creative writing Sept. '74—May, '75, Tucson. Presently Dickey adds: "To celebrate getting my Ph.D. and also being informed that I would be listed in the 39th edition of *Who's Who in America,* both increasingly dubvious distinctions, I took a six nights-a-week job clerking at a convenience market in Tucson, was held up by armed bandits four weeks later, and so resigned. I am now a member of the Assoc. Faculty at Pima C., teaching fiction writing and Freshman Composition." He devotes as much time as possible to writing his poetry, a fifth novel, and a biography of Alan Swallow. He has one son, Shannon Ezra, born 11/9/'69 to him by his marriage to poet Victoria McCabe.

PUBLICATIONS: Dickey began writing poetry at the age of seventeen shortly after he entered the Air Force "and met this guy about 39, named Tony Yanello, four bunks down who had an extra footlocker" full of poems. "Since that day," he continues: "Poetry has been...a central and continuous truth of my life." His first book of poetry *Four Poets* (with Donald Justice, Thomas McAfee, & Donald Drummond) appeared in '67 from C.U.I. Press, Pella, Iowa. It has been followed by such collections as *Running Lucky* ('69), *Acting Immortal* ('70), *Concise Dictionary of Lead River, Missouri* ('72), and 5 chapbooks: *Life-Cycle of Seven Songs* ('72), *McCabe Wants Chimes* ('73), *The McCabes: A Family Sketch* ('73), *Drunk on a Greyhound* ('73), & *One Man in Pueblo* ('74). Additionally his poems have appeared in some three dozen trade and textbook anthologies, including: *Tambourine* (St. Louis, '67), *Contemporary American Poets* (Paris, Fr., '69), *New Generations of Poets* (N.Y., '69), *A Place To Be* (Addison-Wesley, '70), *Poems One Line and Longer* (N.Y. '73), & *Traveling American With Today's Poets* (N.Y., '76). His poems have also appeared in over five hundred periodicals in nine countries, including *Saturday Review, Grosseteste Review, The New Yorker, Atlantic, Choice, Prairie Schooner, Poetry Northwest, Perspective, Southern Review, Paris Review, Poetry, & Poetry Australia.* He has also recorded an hour tape of his work for the Library of Congress (Feb. '74). Additionally he has published a college-level textbook entitled *The Basic Stuff of Poetry* ('72), as well as many reviews and articles. Especially of note among the latter is his essay, "The New Genteel Tradition in American Poetry," appearing in the Fall, '74 *Sewanee Review.* As a playwright, he has had three plays produced in seven productions. His *This is Our Living Room* was staged at the Changing Scene Theater, Denver, Feb., '71. Gerhard Track's opera *Minnequa,* with libretto by Dickey had its premiere with three performances, 1/29-31, '76, at the Bicentennial-Centennial celebration in Pueblo, Colo. A third libretto, *The Witch of Tucson* is currently being set to music. Dickey has given nearly 400 readings at universities, colleges, high schools, galleries, and other institutions throughout America. He has also held workshops and brief residencies in the Poetry-In-The-Schools programs in Ill., Mo., Kan., Wyo., and in May, '75, did a month-long tour of readings at Georgia colleges and universities.

HONORS: Mahan Award for Poetry ('65 & '66), two prizes of $100 each in Kansas City Poetry Contests, and the Swallow Press New Poetry Series Award ('69), the year his *Running Lucky* was a contender for the Lamont Award.

EDITORIAL POSTS: From '66-'77, Dickey was founder and editor of an important little quarterly magazine, *The Poetry Bag,* which published the works of over eighty previously unpublished poets, as well as such names as Aiken, Neihart, Stafford, Mailer, Bly, Neruda, Van Dyn, X.J. Kennedy, Rolfe Humphries, Nancy

Sullivan, Winfield Townley Scott. As a small press publisher, Dickey's *Poetry Bag Press* published during this time a half a dozen books of other writers' works.

OBSERVATIONS: Dickey wrote in Feb., '76: "Concerning the problem of trying to perfect one's work. Continually through my mind, almost daily, runs the first two lines of Yeats' "The Choice":

> The intellect of man is forced to choose
> Perfection of the life, or of the work.

Like everyone else, I'd *like* to and keep sort of wistfully hoping that I might be able to accomplish both—but it just can't be done....The fence straddling

R.P. Dickey
(February 1976)

wish-and-attempt to work hard at both is what makes of most writers fifth-rate versions of what they might have become had they really concentrated more on perfecting their work. It's a terrible choice, but it is one we all one way or several ways have to make....Further, I am appalled at the larger contours peculiar to my time, so I study it closely, and study my craft, hoping to be able to redeem some tiny sliver of my time by writing well. I do not at all feel "of" my time, just "in" it, alas, and, of course, almost certainly would have felt the same way had I lived in any other time! All this perhaps sounds high and maybe moralistically condemnatory—and I try to balance that streak in my temperament by working into a lot of my poems, expressions and explorations of another streak, that of humor. On one level everything is funny, and I find myself working on that level more than a little...." Dale Doepke has characterized Dickey's poetry in this way: "He uses effectively natural speech rhythms, breath phrasing, short lines, expressive word positioning, and compressed syntax in the experimental tradition of Cummings, Williams, and more recently, the Projectivist poets."

NORMAN DUBIE
BIRTH: 4/10/'45, in Barre, Vermont, during a snowstorm. Norman's father, ever and still a radical New England Protestant clergyman took him and his family to various parts of New England to live. His mother was a nurse; he has a brother and sister. As a child, Norman lived first in the mountains of New Hampshire, then on a peninsula off the Maine coast, next in Bangor, again in New Hampshire—in Manchester, and later in Andover, Mass. Today Dubie takes some pride in the fact that his daughter Hannah was born (7/18/'69) on a hill within a thirty mile radius of the birthplaces of all members of his family on both sides, "all the way back to

pre-colonial times." After Hannah's birth, Norman and her mother were divorced (7/4/'73). He and his second wife, poet Pamela Stewart, and Hannah, live in Tempe, Ariz. currently, where Dubie, beginning the academic year of '75, serves as Poet-in-Residence at Ariz. St. U.

EDITORIAL POSTS: From '71-'72, Dubie was Poetry Ed. of *The Iowa Review*, and in the Summer, '72, he directed the Graduate Poetry Workshop of the Iowa Writer's Workshop. He has also worked with various prisoners' groups, and from

Norman Dubie
(January 1976)

'73-'74, was Director of Poetry for the Prisoners' Writers' and Artists' Workshop. In '73-'74, he served as poetry editor of *Now* magazine, a journal for prison writers and artists.

EDUCATION: B.A. in English, Goddard ('64-'69); M.A. in Creative Writing, U. of Iowa, '69-'71.

CAREER: Dubie has earned his living since his undergraduate days as a teacher; Teaching Asst., Goddard C., '68-'69; Teaching Asst., Rhetoric, U. of Iowa ('69-'70); Writing Fellow, U. of Iowa ('70-'71); Lecturer, Grad. C., U. of Iowa ('71-'74); and Asst. Prof., Ohio U. ('74-'75). During the years, '75-'78, in addition to being Writer-in-Residence, Ariz. St. U., Tempe, he has likewise served as Consultant in Poetry to the Ariz. Commission on the Arts & Humanities.

PUBLICATIONS: The Horsehair Sofa ('69), *Alehouse Sonnets* ('71), *The Prayers of the North American Martyrs* ('75), *In the Dead of the Night* ('75), *Popham of the New Song* ('75), *The Illustrations* ('76), *The City of the Olesha Fruit* ('78), *Comes Winter, the Sea Hunting* ('78), and *Dialesque in White* ('78). Since '74, his poems have appeared in such publications as these: *North American Review, The New Yorker, Quarterly Review of Literature, The Antioch Review, American Review, Antaeus, The Iowa Review, Salmagundi, Field, The American Poetry Review, Poetry Now,* and *Poetry.*

HONORS: Bess Hokin Award from *Poetry*, and Guggenheim Fellowship ('77-'78).

OBSERVATIONS: Paul Zimmer has described Dubie's poetry as "a dazzling collection of special facts and realizations from history and the present, woven together in a highly individual style. At time his poems are frightening, yet entertaining, like being swept along by events over which you have no control. For instance, Dubie heightens the small 'historical' incidents he writes about to a point where the reader somehow enters into them and comes away with the experience of them."

ALAN DUGAN

BIRTH: 2/12/'23, in Brooklyn, New York, grew up there and in Jamaica, Queens, attending elementary and high school in both boroughs of N.Y.C.

EDUCATION: Dugan started college at Queens C., Flushing, N.Y. in '41, but was drafted into the army in '43 before he could complete his degree. He returned to college on the G.I. Bill in '46, this time attending Olivet College, Olivet, Mich. for a time, and then transferring to Mexico City College, Mexico, D.F., where he received his B.A., still on the G.I. Bill, in '49. He also did a year of graduate study at the latter institution which is now called la Universidad de las Americas.

CAREER: Dugan spent most of the next ten years in New York City, writing poetry while he worked at numerous jobs, none with literary or academic connections; for instance, he worked as a caster in a medical supply house, failed with a commercial press venture, and even put in a stint working in advertising.

HONORS & CAREER (cont'd): In '61, his first book *Poems* won the Yale Younger Poets' Prize. The next year, in '62, he was propelled from relative obscurity when the same book, *Poems*, won him, all in one year, the National Book Award, the Pulitzer Prize, and the Prix de Rome from the National Institute of Arts and Letters. The latter prize took him to Rome for the year '62-'63 as a Fellow of the American Academy in Rome. Thus, he began a varied career of living, traveling, and writing on grants, reading tours, and residencies at various universities, teaching poetry writing. He spent '63-'64 living in Paris on a Guggenheim Foundation Fellowship, and '64-'65 on poetry reading tours throughout the U.S., reading at numerous colleges and Universities, discussing student work with students. In '65-'66, he was Visiting Lecturer in Poetry at Connecticut College replacing William Meredith, the regular Poet-in-Residence, during his sabbatical year. In '66-'67, he was the

Alan Dugan
(December 1966)

recipient of a Rockefeller Foundation grant, and spent the year in Mexico and travelling in Central and South America. From '67-'69, he was appointed Poet-in-Residence and taught poetry at Sarah Lawrence C. in Bronxville, N.Y. Since '69, he has been living for the most part in Truro, Mass. and has been associated with the Fine Arts Work Center in Provincetown as a Staff Member for Poetry—a position he holds presently, one in which he participates in poetry workshops and conferences with mature young writers. However he often travels away for periods as Visiting Lecturer ('76-'77 at the U. of Colorado, Boulder) or else to participate in several short term teaching, reading, and lecturing assignments ranging in length from a week to several months. Among these are: Western Washington State College, Bellingham, Wash. (Spring, '67); The State University of New York's Writers' Conference at Star Lake, N.Y. (Spring, '68); The U. of Colo., Boulder, Writers' Workshop (Summer, '69); The U. of Ark., Fayetteville (Fall, '69); The U. of N.C., Greensboro (Spring, '70); and Poet-in-Residence to the Public and High Schools of Falmouth, Mass., a program of the Mass. Council on Arts & Humanities (Fall, '71). Additionally in '72-'73 when he held a second Guggenheim Fellowship, he spent part of '73 in Mexico completing his *Poems 4.* In addition to the honors previously noted, Dugan has also received *Poetry's* Levinson Prize ('67).

PUBLICATIONS: His *Poems* ('61), *Poems 2* ('63), *Poems 3* ('67), and *Collected Poems* ('69) have all been published by Yale University Press, and *Collected Poems* was also issued by Faber & Faber in London in '70. His *Poems 4* appeared from Atlantic-Little, Brown, in '74, and Dolphin Editions, Cambridge, Mass., published his *Sequence* in '76. Additionally his poems have appeared frequently in *Poetry* and in various other periodicals. Some of the anthologies featuring it are *New Modern Poetry* ('67), *Twentieth Century Poetry: American and British, 1900-1970* ('70), *The Norton Anthology of Modern Poetry* ('73), and *Modern Poets: An Introduction to Poetry* ('76).

OBSERVATIONS: Dugan declares: "Poetry is not and should not be separated from one's life....only the bravest can continue the 'free' life. Most often economic necessity forces the 'often spirited' ones back into the mainstream of middle class society." Robert Boyers discusses Dugan's poems, saying that they "have variety, but they might all be drawn together as a single long poem. The same alert but static sensibility is operant in all of them, and the speaker rarely indulges the sort of emotional extremism which might distinguish his more inspired from his more characteristically quotidian utterances. Particulars in the work are easily reducible to an elementary abstraction in which polarities are anxiously opposed until, under the wry focus of Dugan's imagination, they somehow coalesce. Alternatives become merely matter of perspective, and the wise man gradually learns that as between one choice and another, we had best avoid choices altogether."

STEPHEN DUNN

BIRTH: 6/24/'39, N.Y.C., the son of Charles F. and Ellen (Fleishman) Dunn, grew up and attended schools in the metropolitan area where his father was a salesman.

EDUCATION: B.A. ('62), Hofstra U.; M.A. ('64-'70, creative writing), New School for Social Research, N.Y.C., & Syracuse ('70).

CAREER: U.S. Army ('62). After his discharge, Dunn had a varied career: professional basketball player ('63-'66) for Williamsport, Pa. Billies; for three years ('63-'66), he was a copywriter for the Ziff-Davis Pub. Co., N.Y.C.; promoted to post of asst. ed. at latter for a year ('67-'68); traveled to Europe several times and spent one year living in Spain. His teaching career began ('70) at Southwest Minn. St. C., where for several years he was Asst. Prof. of English and Creative Writing. Since '74, he has been Poet-in-Residence at Stockton St. C. in Pomona, N.J. Beginning in '70, he has also been active in the Poet-in-the Classroom Programs in Minn., N.Y., & N.J. Presently he lives with his wife Lois (Kelly), a yoga teacher whom he married 9/26/'65, and their daughter Andrea Ellen in Absecon, N.J. Currently he spends as much time as possible writing poetry.

Stephen Dunn
(December 1975)

PUBLICATIONS: 5 Impersonations ('71), *Looking for Holes in the Ceiling* ('74), and *Full of Lust & Good Usage* ('76). Various anthologies carry Dunn's poems: *Intro #2, New Voices in American Poetry, Syracuse Poets, Heartland II, Minnesota Poets' Anthology,* and *The American Poetry Anthology.* His poems are also scattered through a wide variety of periodicals: *New York Quarterly, New York Times, Poetry, The New Republic, Poetry Northwest, Kayak, The Atlantic, The New American Poetry Review, The Antioch Review, Beloit Poetry Journal,* and *Antaeus.* As editor, he has produced *A Cat of Wind, An Alibi of Gifts* (New Jersey State Arts Council, '77).

HONORS: Dunn has been awarded an N.E.A. grant ('73); won the Florida Poetry Contest ('72), the "Discovery Award" from the YM-YWHA Poetry Center ('71), and the Syracuse U. Award for poetry from the Academy of Amer. Poets ('70).

OBSERVATIONS: Philip Booth in writing of Dunn's poetry has noted: "So casually as to seem beyond strain, these poems drive, and play, their way through a landscape which is clearly American-Surreal. But Stephen Dunn is a realist: even from its most trying perspectives, he affirms the crazy country "through which one must search out his real self. Here is a poet who has earned his own way. All the way. He has found right words for the life/time these poems embrace. His work is a joy."

RICHARD (GHORMLEY) EBERHART
BIRTH: 4/5/'04, Austin, Minn., the second son of A.L. Eberhart, who held important positions with the Hormel Packing Company during Richard's childhood, among them a vice-presidency, and the brother of Dryden, the oldest child, and Elizabeth, the youngest, in his eighteenth year ('22) took care of his mother whom he nursed while she died from cancer—the same year his father's fortune collapsed.

EDUCATION: Despite financial strain, the young poet managed to receive his education at Dartmouth (B.A., '25); St. John's C., Cambridge, England (B.A., '29 & M.A., '33), and also spent the year '32-'33 studying at Harvard.

CAREER: During his years as a student, he worked in a department store, at a slaughter house, and also served for a year as a tutor to a prince from Siam, who was the son of King Projadhipok. He continued his teaching career, by becoming

Master of English at St. Mark's School, Southborough, Mass., in '33, and held the position until '41; at this school Robert Lowell was one of his students. He joined the U.S. Naval Reserve during W.W. II in '41, and was discharged in '46 as Lt. Col. On 5/21/'41, he married Helen ("Betty") Butcher, whose father and brother had been partners in the Butcher Polish Company of Boston. After the war, from '46-'52, Eberhart worked with the firm, and still serves today as honorary Vice-Pres. and a member of the Board of Directors. In '50, he founded and became first director of the Poets' Theatre, Inc., Cambridge, Mass.; since '55, he has also been a member and starting in '64, a director of Yaddo Corp. It was in '52 that he turned again to the teaching career interrupted by W.W.II. At Dartmouth C., from '56-'68, he was Prof. of English, and Poet-in-Residence, and since '70, Prof. Emeritus. However during this period, and afterwards, he has also taught on numerous other campuses, and earlier at the following: U. of Wash. ('52-'53; '67); U. of Conn. ('53-'54), and Wheaton C. ('54-'55), Princeton U. (Gauss Lectr., '55-'56). He was Phi Beta Kappa poet at Tufts U. ('57), Swarthmore C. ('63), Trinity C. (Hartford, Conn., '63), C. of William and Mary ('63), U. of N.H. ('64), and Harvard ('67), and has also been Elliston Lecturer, U. of Conn. ('61). Since his semi-retirement from Dartmouth, where at Hanover, he and his wife Betty make their home during part of every year, Eberhart continues as visiting professor or poet-in-residence at various universities: U. of Wash. ('72), U. of Fla. ('73, '76, & '78), U. of Calif., Davis ('75), and Columbia U. ('75). During the summers, Dick and Betty Eberhart

Richard Eberhart
(March 1971)

live at their cottage by the sea in Maine. Their two children, a son Rick, and a daughter Gretchen are both married now, and living in their own homes.

PUBLICATIONS: Richard Eberhart is the author of over twenty volumes of poetry: *A Bravery of Earth* ('30), *Reading the Spirit* ('36), *Song and Idea* ('40), *Poems: New and Selected* ('44), *Burr Oaks* ('47), *Brotherhood of Men* ('49), *An Herb Basket* ('50), *Selected Poems* ('51), *Undercliff: Poems 1946-1953* ('53), *Great Praises* ('57), *The Oak: A Poem* ('57), *Collected Poems: 1930-1960* ('60), *The Quarry* ('64), *The Vastness and Indifference of the World* ('65), *Fishing for Snakes* ('65), *Selected Poems 1930-1965* ('65), *Thirty-One Sonnets* ('67), *Shifts of Being* ('68), *The Achievement of Richard Eberhart: A Comprehensive Selection of his Poetry*, ed. by Bernard F. Engle ('68), *Three Poems* ('68), *Fields of Grace* ('72), and *Collected Poems: 1930-1976* ('76). His poems have appeared in poetry periodicals and anthologies too numerous for mention here. However, some of the latter volumes include such titles as these: *Twentieth Century American Poetry* ('44), *Anthology of Famous English and American Poetry* ('45), *War Poets* ('45), *A Little Treasury of Great Poetry* ('47), *One Hundred American Poets* ('48), *One Hundred Modern Poems* ('49), *Mid-Century American Poets* ('50), *Modern Poetry* ('51), *Penguin Book of Modern American Verse* ('54), *Modern American Poetry and Modern British Poetry* ('55), *New Pocket Anthology of American Verse* ('55), *Seven Centuries of Poetry* ('55), *Fifteen Modern American Poets* ('56), *Modern Verse in English* ('58), *How Does a Poem Mean?* ('59), *Poem* ('59), *American Poetry* ('60), *Poetry for Pleasure* ('60), *Poet's Choice* ('62), *Erotic Poetry* ('63), *Modern Poets* ('63), *Modern Religious Poems* ('64), *Of Poetry and Power* ('64), *Poems of Doubt and Belief* ('64), *Faber Book of Modern Verse* ('65), *Poems on Poetry* ('65), *The Norton Anthology of Modern Poetry* ('73), & *Modern Poems: An Introduction to Poetry* ('73, '76). Eberhart has also written successful verse plays, which appear in *Collected Verse Plays* ('62), an adaptation of a play by Lope de Vega, "The Bride From Mantua," which was produced in Hanover, N.H. in '64; (the de Vega work is *Justice Without Revenge*). As an editor of poetry, Eberhart has produced, with Seldon Rodman, *War and the Poet: An Anthology of Poetry Expressing Man's Attitudes to War From Ancient Times to the Present* ('45), and *Dartmouth Poems*, 12 vols. ('58-'59; '62-'71). His *Selected Prose* was published in '78. Additionally in the realm of prose, he has also contributed the "Introductions" to John Milton's *Paradise Lost, Paradise Regained,* and *Samson Agonistes* for the '69 Doubleday-Literary Guild edition of these works. An essay of his entitled "Pure Poetry and the Idea of Value" also appears in *Quality in the Arts* ('69).

HONORS: For his poems, he has received most of the distinguished poetry prizes available in the U.S.A. These include the following: Guarantor's Prize ('46), Harriet Monroe Memorial Prize ('50), New England Poetry Club Golden Rose ('50), Harriet Monroe Memorial Award ('55), Nat. Inst. of Arts & Letters grant ('55), Bollingen Prize ('62), Pulitzer Prize ('66), Fellowship of the Academy of Am. Poets ('69), Cons. in Poetry at the Lib. of Congress ('59-'61), and Hon. Conslt. in Am. Letters ('63-'69), Hon. Member, Phi Beta Kappa ('67, Harvard), Mem. of the Nat. Inst. of Arts & Letters ('60), and the Nat. Academy of Arts & Sciences ('67), and the National Book Award ('77). Since '73, he has been Hon. Pres. of the Poetry Soc. of Am. He holds honorary degrees from the following institutions; all of them D. Litt.: Dartmouth ('54), Skidmore C. ('66), Worcester C. ('69), & Colgate ('74).

OBSERVATIONS: Richard Eberhart declares: "Poetry is a confrontation of the whole being with reality. It is a basic struggle of the soul, the mind, and the body to comprehend life, to bring order to chaos or phenomena, and by will and insight to create communicable verbal forms for the pleasure of mankind." About Eberhart's poetry, Robert Lowell once noted: "...he writes with a resolute absent-mindedness, a wondering of sophistication, and a wonderful openness and energy." *The Norton Anthology* ('73) observes: "Eberhart retains a fierceness of perception; but his later poems, though remaining rough-hewn, are more carefully organized. The effect of unpremeditativeness combined with deliberativeness is a preserve Eberhart has to himself."

GENE FRUMKIN

BIRTH: 1/29/'28, N.Y.C., the son of Samuel and Sarah Blackman Frumkin, spent his first ten years in the Bronx where his father was a tailor. He started his poetry career at the age of four by writing poems in Yiddish, but by the age of seven had lost his interest in that language, abandoning it as well as his poetry writing. He moved to Los Angeles at the age of ten, arriving on July 14, Bastille Day.

EDUCATION: He studied at U.C.L.A. ('46-'51; B.A.—English). It was soon after graduation, in a workshop taught at Los Angeles State College one evening a week by Thomas McGrath, that Frumkin started to write poems again, this time "approximately in English," he notes.

CAREER: From '52, until he began his teaching career, Frumkin worked in Los Angeles, as managing editor of *California Apparel News*, a weekly trade newspaper. Frumkin's teaching career began in the spring of '64, when as an Instr. at the U.C.L.A. Extension Division, he conducted a Poetry Workshop—one he also

Gene Frumkin
(June 1975)

offered the following spring. In '66, he was offered a position at the U. of N.M. as Lect. in English and a teacher of creative writing, at which time he moved to Albuquerque. He served as Director of Creative Writing through the spring of '76, and is now an Associate Professor of English at the U. of N.M. From '66-'70, he was Chairman of the Poetry Reading Series Committee and is presently faculty advisor to that committee. During the summer of '75, he also conducted two courses at SUNY, Buffalo, in the Summer Modern Literature program there. As a member of the D.H. Lawrence Fellowship Committee in '69, '72, and as chairman of that committee at the U. of N.M. from '75 to the present, Frumkin has also helped select the creative writers and artists who have had grants to live at Lawrence's Kiowa Ranch, twenty-two miles north of Taos in the Sangre de Cristo Mountains. By his marriage to Lydia (Samuels), a painter, he is the father of two children: Celena and Paul. He is presently divorced.

EDITORIAL POSTS: During his Los Angeles years, he was co-editor of *Coastlines Literary Magazine* in '55, serving as its editor from '58-'62. From '55-'56, he was also a member of the editorial board of *California Quarterly;* later he served as special editor of the Winter-Spring ('69) issue of *New Mexico Quarterly.* Presently he is co-editor of *San Marcos Review.*

PUBLICATIONS: The Hawk & the Lizard ('63), *The Orange-Tree* ('65, chapbook), *The Rainbow Walker* ('69), *Dostoevsky & Other Nature Poems* ('72), *Locust Cry: Poems 1958-65* ('73), and *The Mystic Writing Pad* ('77). With Stanley Noyes, he is co-editor of the poetry anthology *The Indian Rio Grande: Recent Poems From 3 Cultures* (San Marcos Press, '77). In addition, his poems have appeared in numerous anthologies: *The Golden Quill Anthology for '58,* ed. by Abbe, Davidson, & Williams ('58); *Poets of Today,* ed. by Walter Lowenfels ('64), *3 Poets (Road Apple Review),* ed. by Douglas Flaherty ('70); *Forty Poems, Touching on Recent American History*, ed. by Robert Bly ('71); *Their Place in the Heat, Contemporary Poetic Statements*, ed. by Douglas Flaherty ('71); *Contemporary Poetry in America*, ed. by Miller Williams ('73), *The Poetry of the Desert Southwest*, ed by James Quick ('73), *Voices From the Rio Grande*, ed. by James A. Fisher, Jr. ('76), and *Southwest*, ed. by Kopp, Kopp, & Stafford ('77). Poems of his have appeared in a wide variety of periodicals, including: *Poetry, Saturday Review, The Nation, The Paris Review, Minnesota Review, Chicago Review, Evergreen Review, New Mexico Quarterly, New Mexico Magazine, Choice, Kayak, Prairie Schooner, Beloit Poetry Journal, Coastlines, California Quarterly, South Dakota Review, Invisible City, Paunch, Three Rivers Poetry Journal,* and *Trace.*

RITA GARITANO

BIRTH: 5/22/'39, Coffeyville, Kansas, attended public schools in her native state.

EDUCATION: B.A., U. of Kansas ('61); M.F.A., U. of Ariz. ('72); post-graduate study in Creative Writing, prose and poetry ('75-'76), U. of Ariz.

CAREER: In '65 until presently, except for sabbaticals and leaves-of-absence, she has served as a teacher of English in both the junior and senior Tucson High Schools. During the years, '72-'73, '74-'75, & '75-'76, she has also been employed by the "Poets on the Road" program of the Ariz. Arts & Humanities Commission. During the fall of '75 she also served as a substitute writing teacher at Pima C. Today she makes her home in Tucson, with her husband Robert and their son Lyle, and works as a classroom teacher at Sahuaro High School. Her husband is an administrator in the Tucson public schools system.

PUBLICATIONS: Rita Garitano's first collection of poems, *We Do What We Can,* appeared in '75 by Desert First Works. Such anthologies as these also carry her

Rita Garitano
(May 1976)

work: *Southwest: A Contemporary Anthology,* edited by Kopp, Kopp, & Stafford (Red Earth Press, '77), *Poetry of the Desert Southwest,* edited by James Quick (Baleen Press, Phoenix, '73), and *Intro V,* edited by Walter Beacham and George Garrett (Univ. Press of Va., '74). These magazines have also carried her poetry: *Inscape, Obsidian, Arizona English Teacher, Mazagine, Dragonfly, Mill Mountain Review, Huerfano, Women: A Journal of Liberation, Isthmus,* & *New Mexico Magazine.* A prose writer as well as a poet, Rita wrote her first novel, *Power Plays,* which is currently seeking a publisher, during her sabbatical leave from teaching during the '75-'76 school year.

HONORS: During her graduate years at the U. of Ariz., she served as a student member ('71-'72) on the Board of Directors of the Poetry Center. In '76, she was nominated as one of fifty poets from ten western states to be considered for selection and participation in the Western Arts Commission's "Artists on Tour."

OBSERVATIONS: Rita Garitano says: "Writing is a process of self discovery for me. A unification of the inner and outer worlds occurs during that process. I am compelled to communicate and poetry is the vehicle." After reading her poetry, Donald Hall made this statement: "Her rhythms dance. She handles language with a natural grace."

DAN GERBER

BIRTH: 8/12/'40, in Grand Rapids, Mich., the son of Daniel F. and Dorothy (Scott) Gerber, grew up in his home state where his father was a business executive.

EDUCATION: Mich. State U. (B.A., '62).

CAREER: Began his career as a racing car driver for five years. After a bad accident which broke many bones in his body, he decided to give up the sport and turn to teaching as a profession. He has since taught in High School, Fremont, Mich., for two years; at Thomas Jefferson C. (Allendale, Mich.) as poet-in-residence, '69-'70; and at Mich. St. U. ('70-'71), likewise in the latter capacity. He has also worked widely in the Poetry-In-The-Schools programs in such states as Minn., Ind., Mich., & Ariz., and has given numerous readings at colleges and institutions throughout the country. Today he lives in Fremont, Mich. with his wife, the former Virginia Hartjen, whom he married 8/12/'61, and their three children: Wendy, Frank, and Tamara. He devotes his time to poetry, fiction, and journalism.

Dan Gerber
(December 1971)

EDITORIAL POSTS: In '68, Gerber founded, with poet Jim Harrison, the Sumac Press, and for a time the two poets served as co-editors of the quarterly named SUMAC, but in '72, they disbanded a regular issuing of the journal to devote more time to book publishing instead.

PUBLICATIONS: The Waiting ('66), *The Revenant* ('71), and *Departure* ('73). Gerber's poems are found in various anthologies, including: *Inside Outer Space* ('70), *Five Blind Men* ('69), *Michigan Signatures* ('69), *Heartland* (No. Ill. U. Press), *Contemporary American Poetry* (Japan), & *The Third Coast* (Wayne St. U.

Press). They are also available in many poetry periodicals, including *Abraxas, December, Equal Time, Epos, Greenfield Review, Hearse, Inscape, Mikrokosmos, The Nation, The New Yorker, The Partisan Review, Pebble, Stony Brook Poetry Journal, Sumac, Voyages, Playboy, Poetry Now, Los, Periodical Lunch, Fireweed, New York Magazine, Pembroke, New Letters, The Red Cedar Review, Sports Illustrated, Grey's Sporting Journal, X, A Magazine of the Arts,* and *Hoto.* A novelist, he has also published *American Atlas* ('73), *Out of Control* ('75), and is currently working on a third novel, *Last Days in the Field.* Gerber's first book of non-fiction, *Indy—The World's Fastest Carnival Ride* is scheduled by Prentice-Hall. He has also published numerous photographs, especially in issues of *Sumac* magazine.

OBSERVATIONS: Dan Gerber feels that "the poet is the translator of the conditions of the imagination, into language, song, whatever singing goes on in his head and must come out. I think the poet is seer, in that he is overwhelmed by what most men take for granted. In this sense he is a pair of glasses, a focus through which others may see themselves." Writing about Gerber's poetry, J.D. Reed has noticed that "one of its strengths..." is "Mr. Gerber's refusal to make circular action too easy. It comes with difficulty and only by taking the most difficult leaps of language and imagination."

MIGUEL GONZÁLEZ-GERTH

BIRTH: 8/15/'26, in Mexico City, the son of an army officer of Spanish descent named González and a mother named Gerth, who was a music student of German descent. Between '34 and '35, while still a child, he lived in Spain with his parents, an "experience," which as he notes, "led to a life-long interest in Hispanic culture." In '40, he came from Mexico to the U.S.A. to make his home.

EDUCATION: After completing high school in Texas, he started studying engineering, chemistry, and international law, but abandoned his "fleeting" interest in each of these fields in order to concentrate finally on Spanish, French, and English literatures while he studied for his B.A., M.A., and Ph.D. degrees from the U. of Tex., Austin, and at Princeton.

CAREER: González-Gerth has spent the major part of his teaching career in Austin, where today he is a Prof. of Spanish at the U. of Tex. In addition to writing poetry, he also engages in multilingual translation, in working as a free-lance writer, and calls himself "a self-employed week-end farmer" at the hideaway he and his wife own outside Gatesville, Tex. "This rural commitment, which I happily share with my wife, is particularly rewarding to me," he notes "because it brings us closer to the earth and the animals we love." Since his period of study at Princeton, and six years of teaching at Bryn Mawr and Swarthmore, the González-Gerths have made their home mostly in Austin, the city where they still live today.

EDITORIAL POSTS: For several years now, González-Gerth has served as co-editor of *The Texas Quarterly,* and general editor of The University of Texas Iberian Series.

PUBLICATIONS: The Infinite Absence: La Ausencia Infinita ('55, '64, & '71, bilingual edition); *Desert Sequence and Other Poems* ('56), *En Vísperas de Olvido* ('67), and *The Musician and Other Poems* ('77). Presently he continues work on a long trilingual poem entitled "Flussferd," which has engaged his attention for some time, and also on a new collection of "lyrical aphorisms inspired by Japanese Haiku" and tentatively entitled "Dandelion Green." His poems have been

Miguel Gonzáles-Gerth
(August 1976)

published in various anthologies both here and abroad, as well as in a variety of magazines, particularly in *The New York Times Book Review* and *Texas Quarterly*. The latter magazine produced his "The Brandywine in Winter" (Winter, '71 issue), in which he integrated his verse and photography, a medium which also interests him, and one in which he intends to experiment further. As a translator, González-Gerth is perhaps best known for his translations from such poets as Lorca, Jorge Guillén, Luis Cernuda, Vicente Aleixandre, Vallejo, and Pablo Neruda, all of whom have, as he notes, "influenced me, as have (platitudinously) the various members of my family, including my cats."

HONORS: The '64 edition of his *The Infinite Absence*, produced in a limited edition by the Stone Wall Press in Iowa City, won a place among the fifty books of the year selected by the American Institute of Graphic Arts.

OBSERVATIONS: "For me, poetry is putting words together in a way that makes both sense and music," González-Gerth notes. "But the finished poem must be more than that; it must be a revelation that points to yet another mystery. After all, art is so close to religion that traditionally it has been allied to it, sometimes to its disadvantage. One might ask whether intellectual power and verbal skill are not enough to produce poetry. The first is only desirable while the second is utterly necessary, and yet the notions of vision and design apply to both technique and intuition. Seldom found in equally high degree, together they characterize the truly great. Though of meagre talent, I am thoroughly dedicated to literature; I try to learn and teach, to enjoy and suffer literature..., to feel and to try to understand whatever literature is and does." James Boyer May has reflected upon his contribution in this way: "González-Gerth...quietly has been developing and fashioning his own idiom. His [*The Infinite Absence*] later longer works contain expanded treatments seen presaged in close reading....Among other qualities, his poetry must be defined as philosophical. He conveys impressions of intense personal and unique thought and experience not so much through images as through *manner*."

LARRY GOODELL

BIRTH: 6/20/'35, the only child of Dorothy and Lawrence Goodell, Sr., in Roswell, N.M., grew up in his birthplace in southeastern N.M.

EDUCATION: U. of So. Calif. ('53-'57; B.A.; graduate work at U. of N.M. ('58-'59, '61-'62, & '68-'69).

CAREER: After receiving his B.A. from U.N.M., Goodell taught one year at the New Mexico Military Institute, and was then drafted into the U.S. Army and assigned to Camp Irwin in the Mojave Desert, where he was a chaplain's assistant in a tank battalion. In '61, he was discharged only to be recalled during the Cuban Missile Crisis. After his final discharge, this time from Fort Polk, Louisiana, he returned to U.N.M. to graduate school and studied under Robert Creeley. Creeley's invitation was instrumental in Goodell's attending the important Vancouver Poetry Conference the following summer of '63. There he was influenced deeply by Olson, Duncan, Ginsberg, Whalen, Levertov, and Creeley, who were all there. He brought many impressions back with him to N.M., the strongest of them, the importance of *place* in writing and a need to start his own publishing venture.

Goodell had just moved to Placitas, N.M. at this time and meanwhile, for two years—'63-and '64, he taught at a nearby prep school, now the Albuquerque Academy. In the summer of '65, he attended poetry readings at a Berkeley Conference and became better acquainted with some of the same poets he had first met in Vancouver in addition to numerous others, to wit, Jack Spicer, Ed Dorn, and Ann Quinn, a young British novelist.

For a number of years now, Goodell has worked at an important Southwestern avant-guard bookstore, "The Living Batch," which faces the gates to U.N.M. in Albuquerque. However, he continues to make his home in the nearby Sandia mountain village of Placitas, where he and his wife, Lenore and their son Joel, are enjoying a new adobe home on the edge of a village orchard. His wife is a painter and toy and costume-maker. One costume—a "Muscle Shirt"—has been exhibited

Larry Goodell
(June 1975)

at the Museum of International Folk Art in Santa Fe. Goodell frequently wears this shirt, or dresses in other costumes and masks when he gives readings. He has developed his readings into full events encompassing his own local and inner mythology and given song. He reads in bars, over FM radio, and in local university areas.

EDITORIAL POSTS: Goodell founded Duende Magazine and Press in '64. It has published an important series of books by such poets as Ronald Bayes, Ken Irby, Margaret Randall, Larry Eigner, Robert Kelly, David Franks, Bill Pearlman, and Gino Clays, among others. Since '72, he has edited and published several issues of *Fervent Valley,* which has carried his own work as well as that of many other new names among Southwestern poets and also the works of such well-known poets today as Charles Bukowski and Keith Wilson. Duende Press has also spurred a new series called the Pick Pocket Series—with such titles as *Villon*, a new translation by Jean Calais (Stephen Rodefer) and *One or Two Love Poems from the White World*, also by Stephen Rodefer.

PUBLICATIONS: In '78, Duende Press published Goodell's *Dried Apricots* (a book of religious prose), and Truck Press produced his collection of poetry entitled *The Staff & Bowl of Ometeotl*, a book of ceremonial event poems. Among the anthologies presenting his poems is *The Indian Rio Grande*, ed. by Frumkin and Noyes ('77).

THOM(SON WILLIAM) GUNN

BIRTH: 8/29/'29, Gravesend, Kent, England, moved frequently during the first ten years of his life, both because of the War, and because his father, the son of a merchant seaman, and himself a journalist, worked for various newspapers. Thom's mother was the daughter of a tenant farmer. He has one brother, Alexander, or "Ander," who is a professional photographer with whom he has collaborated on one book of photographs and poems. As a youth, he went to a variety of schools before his family settled in Hampstead, and he attended Univ.C. School there.

EDUCATION: Trinity C., Cambridge, A.B., '53,; Post-graduate study, creative writing, Stanford '58.

CAREER: Gunn spent two years doing National Service in the British Army. After this, he went to Paris and worked in the offices of the *Metro* (subway) while he tried to write a novel. He then went to Cambridge, where he wrote the poems that were to make up his first book. He first came to the U.S.A. in '54 after having spent six months in Rome. He came to the States to attend Stanford on a fellowship and to study in the creative writing program there with Yvor Winters. After leaving Stanford without a degree, he taught English at the U. of Calif., Berkeley ('58-'66). Since '66, when he gave up his teaching post at the Berkeley campus, he has earned his living both as a free-lance writer, and as, he notes, "by various jobs." Sometimes he teaches "for a term," or "sometimes" does "other things, none regular," and only as needed, so as to permit him as much free time as possible to write. He has traveled widely, taught for a year in San Antonio, Tex., in '55, and today lives in San Francisco, where he has made his home regularly since '60, though he makes brief visits back to England.

EDITORIAL POSTS: During the years '58-'64, Thom Gunn served as poetry reviewer for the *Yale Review.*

PUBLICATIONS: Poems ('53, chapbook), *Fighting Terms* ('54), *The Sense of Movement* ('57, '59), *My Sad Captains* ('61), *Selected Poems*, with Ted Hughes ('62), *A Geography* ('66, chapbook), *Positives*, a book of poems with photos by his brother Ander Gunn ('66), *Touch* ('67; '68), *The Garden of the Gods* ('68, chapbook), *The Explorer: Poems* (chapbook, '69), *The Fair In the Woods* ('69, chapbook), *Poems 1950-1966: A Selection* ('69), *Sunlight* (chapbook, '69), *Last Days at Teddington* (chapbook, '71), *Moly* ('71), *Mandrakes* ('74), *Song Book* (chapbook, '74), *To the Air* (chapbook, '74), and *Jack Straw's Castle and Other Poems* ('76). He has also made several recordings and has contributed poems to various American magazines, including *Poetry*, and to such English periodicals as *Listener, Encounter,* and *New Statesman.* Widely anthologized, Gunn's poems appear in the following, as well as in other collections: *New Lines and New Lines II* ('56, '63), *Poetry Now* ('56), *New Poets of England and America* ('57, '62), *New Poetry* ('62),

Penguin Book of Contemporary Verse ('62), *Poet's Choice* ('62), *An Anthology of Commonwealth Verse* ('63), *Anthology of Modern Poetry* ('63), *Erotic Poetry* ('63), *Modern Poets* ('63), *Poetry in English* ('63), *Golden Treasury* ('64), *Today's Poets* ('64), *Case For Poetry* ('65), *Earth Is the Lord's* ('65), *Faber Book of Modern Verse* ('65), *Faber Book of Twentieth Century Verse* ('65), *Corgi Modern Poets in Focus 5* ('71), *The Norton Anthology of Modern Poetry* ('73), and *Modern Poems: An Introduction to Poetry* ('73; '76). As an editor, himself of poetry, he has

Thom Gunn
(October 1972)

compiled these anthologies: *Poetry From Cambridge, 1951-'52* ('53), *Five American Poets* ('63), with Ted Hughes, *Selected Poems of Fulke Greville* ('68), and *Ben Jonson* ('74).

HONORS: Levinson Prize ('55), Somerset Maugham Award ('59), Arts Council Award of Great Britain ('59), National Institute of Arts and Letters Grant ('64), a Rockefeller Award ('66), and a Guggenheim fellowship ('71).

OBSERVATIONS: Thom Gunn writes: "Most of my poetry has been metrical, but I have experimented with syllabics for some years and lately with free verse.... One's writing is intended for other people ultimately, but the process of doing it is *private* and lonely, and most poets benefit from being able to slip around anonymously. This I expect to continue doing." Of his poetry, Edwin Muir once wrote: "He states afresh and with great force questions which have troubled poets and thinkers in all ages. But he is aware of them as existing now, in his life, and he contributes something new to the old debate."

DRUMMOND B. HADLEY
BIRTH: 5/27/'38, spent his early years in Missouri. He later moved to the Southwest to attend college.

EDUCATION: B.A., '64 (U. of Ariz.); M.A., '66 (U. of Ariz.). He wrote his M.A. thesis on Charles Olson under whom he studied at a summer workshop. He began writing poetry at the U. of Ariz. Poetry Center, where he studied with Barney Childs. For several years, he served as a student member of the Board of Directors of the then newly established Poetry Center, and was very active in the student readings and programs sponsored by the latter.

CAREER: For several years in the "sixties," Drum Hadley attended numerous poetry conferences and workshops, both on the West Coast, and the Vancouver Poetry Conference of '63, where he was inspired by the readings of Robert Creeley, Charles Olson, Robert Duncan, Allen Ginsberg, and Philip Whalen. His long standing friendship with Keith Wilson has also been a great source of satisfaction and inspiration. For several years in the late '60s, Hadley worked as a cowboy on various ranches in southern Ariz. and in northern Mexico. He composed some of his poetry on a tape recorder while riding horseback, working cattle. Later as he continued to work at his writing, he lived for a number of years in Santa Fe,

Drummond Hadley
(February 1971)

presenting numerous readings in the Southwest and also working for the New Mexico Poetry-In-The-Schools program for a time. For several years now, with his family, he has been ranching in southern Arizona near the Mexican border. His wife Diana has illustrated several of his books of poetry with her photographs of cowboys and ranching life.

PUBLICATIONS: The Webbing ('67), *The Spirit of the Deep Well Tank* ('72), & *Strands of Rawhide* ('72). He is currently working on a long poem about horse breaking. His poems have also appeared in various periodicals, including *El Corno Emplumado, From A Window, Sum, Wild Dog, New Mexico Magazine, Puerto Del Sol,* and elsewhere, and in such anthologies as *Southwest,* edited by Kopp, Kopp & Stafford ('77), & *The Indian Rio Grande,* edited by Frumkin & Noyes ('77).

OBSERVATIONS: About Hadley's poetry, Keith Wilson has written: "Drummond Hadley speaks with more than just authenticity about this Southwest....His voice is the spirit behind and around the rocks, the men, this land. His poems are what many men dream, out here."

DONALD (ANDREW) HALL

BIRTH: 9/20/'28, New Haven, Conn., grew up in Hamden, Conn., where his father, for whom he was named (Jr.) helped to run the family business, a dairy. Summers he spent on Eagle Pond Farm in New Hampshire with his mother's parents who were farmers. He remembers reading and writing in the mornings, and pitching hay in the afternoons. He always preferred N.H. to Conn., but attended grammar school through two years of high school in Hamden, Conn. He started writing at age twelve, became serious about it by fourteen, and by sixteen had published some poems.

EDUCATION: He studied the last two years of high school at the Phillips Exeter Academy, the preparatory school where he received his diploma. After a year of illness when he was seventeen, he took his B.A. ('51) from Harvard, his B. Litt. from Oxford ('53), attended Stanford in '53-'54, when he studied with Yvor Winters on a creative writing fellowship in poetry. From '54-'57, he was a Junior Fellow in the Soc. of Fellows at Harvard, and did nothing for three years but read and write. At the latter institution, he had studied as an undergraduate student with Richard Wilbur, Archibald MacLeish, John Ciardi, and Theodore Morison.

CAREER: From '57-'75, he taught at the U. of Mich., where he was Prof. of English.

EDITORIAL POSTS: As a student at Harvard, he was on *The Advocate* with Robert Bly, John Asbury & Kenneth Koch. From '53 to '62, he served as poetry ed. of *Paris Review*, and as a member of the editorial board for poetry for the Wesleyan U. Press ('58-'64). At present, he is literary consultant to Harper & Row Pub. Co. He has made frequent trips to England, a country in which he has lived upon two occasions. In '59-'60, as well as in '63-'64, he lived in the village of Thaxted, Essex. He now makes his home at Eagle Pond Farm in Danbury, N.H., the same home that belonged to his grandparents during his youth, with his second wife, Jane Kenyon, a poet whom he married in '72. Since '78, he has been associated with the Goddard College MFA Writing Program in Vermont; however in recent years, Hall has been spending less of his time teaching and devoting more and more of it to his writings. He is the father of a son Andrew (born in '54) and a daughter Phillipa ('59) born to him by his first marriage to Kirby Thompson in '52.

PUBLICATIONS: Poems ('52), *Exile* (privately printed, '52), *To the Loud Wind and Other Poems* ('55), *Exiles and Marriages* ('55), *The Dark Houses* ('58), *A Roof of Tiger Lilies: Poems* ('64), *The Alligator Bride* (chapbook, '68), *The Alligator Bride: Poems New and Selected* ('69), *The Yellow Room Love Poems* ('71), *A Blue Wing Tilts at the Edge of the Sea* ('75), and *Kicking the Leaves* ('78). He has recorded his poetry on *Today's Poets I*, with others, by Folkways, '67. His poems have appeared in various periodicals, including *Nation, New Yorker, Saturday Review, Poetry, Listener, New Statesman,* and *Times Literary Supplement.* They have also been included in many anthologies: *New Pocket Anthology of American Verse* ('55), *New Poets of England and America* ('57; '62), *Understanding Poetry* ('60), *New Modern Poetry* ('67), and *100 Postwar Poems* ('68). Widely-known himself as an anthologizer, he has edited fourteen anthologies of poetry: *The Harvard Advocate Anthology* ('50); with Robert Pack and Louis Simpson, *New Poets of England and America* ('57), *Whittier* ('61); *New Poets of England and America; Second Selection* ('62), with Pack; *Contemporary American Poetry* ('62; rev. ed., '71); *A Poetry Sampler* ('62); with Warren Taylor, *Poetry in English* ('63;

Donald Hall
(October 1972)

rev. ed., '70); *The Faber Book of Modern Verse* (rev. ed., '65); *The Modern Stylists: Writers on the Art of Writing* ('68); *Man and Boy: An Anthology* ('68); *American Poetry: An Introductory Anthology* ('69), and *The Pleasures of Poetry* ('71). A prose writer, as well as a poet, he has had fiction published in various periodicals, including *Trans-Atlantic Review, Iowa Review,* and elsewhere, and has produced two books of juvenile fiction: *Andrew the Lion Farmer* ('59) and *Riddle Rat* ('77). Other prose works of a critical, biographical, and autobiographical nature include these: *String Too Short To Be Saved* ('61; '62), *Henry Moore: The Life and Work of a Great Sculptor* ('66), *Marianne Moore: The Cage and The Animal* ('70), *As The Eye Moves: A Sculpture by Henry Moore* ('70), *The Gentleman's Alphabet Book* ('72), *Writing Well* ('73), *Playing Around* ('74), *Dock Ellis in the Country of Baseball* ('76), and *Remembering Poets* ('78). The latter concerns reminiscences and opinions about Robert Frost, Dylan Thomas, T.S. Eliot, and Ezra Pound.

HONORS: Henry Fellowship for study at Oxford ('51-'53); Newdigate Prize from Oxford for poetry ('52), Lamont Poetry Selection Prize ('55), Edna St. Vincent Millay Mem. Prize ('56), Longview Foundation Award ('60); and two Guggenheim Fellowships ('63; '72).

OBSERVATIONS: Donald Hall writes that he identifies with "the school of fantasy or neo-surrealism, or whatever you want to call it, as exemplified in the works of Wright, Bly, Merwin, Kinnell, etc." Concerning Hall's poetry, Richard Eberhart has praised Hall as "one of the best poets of his generation. He puts a mental stamp on each poem, each remarkable for economy, depth of thought, sureness of feeling. He is always entering into others, strongly emphatic. He is original...can be philosophical or witty in turn...has controlled intriguing changes of rhythm."

JOY HARJO

BIRTH: 5/9/'51, in Tulsa, Okla., she belongs to the Creek Indian peoples via her father. Her mother is from Arkansas. She grew up in Okla., as did her father. However her ancestors came from Ala. originally and lived there until the Creek Indian removal in the 1830's.

EDUCATION: In Santa Fe, she attended high school at the famous Inst. of Am. Indian Arts ('68 diploma); B.A., U.N.M. ('76).

CAREER: After her graduation from the Inst. of Am. Indian Arts, she moved to Albuquerque in order to attend the U. of N.M. She began work at the U. of N.M. as a student of painting, but more and more she pursued the study and writing of poetry until she turned mainly to it, and received her degree in creative writing on a Bureau of Indian Affairs student scholarship. Twice divorced, she is the mother of a son named Phil by her first marriage, and of a little daughter Rainy Dawn, age five, whose father is the Am. Indian (Acoma Pueblo) poet, Simon Ortiz. Ms. Harjo has presented readings at the U. of N.M., and elsewhere, and participated during June '76 in an Indian Women Writers' Conf., hosted by the Navajo Community College, Tsaile, Ariz. Additionally she has worked with poetry projects in the New Mexico schools. Presently she is studying for her M.F.A. degree on an assistantship at the Iowa Writers' Workshop and living in Iowa City. She is also a photographer.

PUBLICATIONS: Her first collection, *The Last Song,* which she also illustrated, appeared in '75 from the Puerto Del Sol Press at N.M. St. U., Las Cruces. Currently she is at work on a new poetry manuscript tentatively entitled *She Had Some Horses.* Her poems have also appeared in anthologies entitled *Southwest: A Contemporary Anthology,* ed. by Kopp, Kopp, & Stafford ('77), *The Indian Rio Grande,* edited by Frumkin & Noyes ('77), *The Ethnic American Woman,* ed. by

Edith Blicksilver ('78), *Settling America: The Ethnic Experience of 14 Contemporary Poets,* edited by David Kheridan (Macmillan, '74), *Passing Through: An Anthology of Contemporary Southwest Literature,* ed. by W. Burns Taylor, Richard Santelli & Kathleen McGary ('71), & *Traveling America With Today's Poets.* Other poems of hers appear in these magazines, and elsewhere: *Dakotah Territory, Puerto Del Sol, Best Friends, Thunderbird Magazine, New Mexico Magazine, Phantasm, Southwest Women's Poetry Exchange, Literary Quarterly of U. of Colorado,* & *Yardbird Reader.*

Joy Harjo
(June 1975)

HONORS: In '76, she shared with Carol S. Merrill, the Prize for Poetry at U.N.M. offered by the Academy of American Poets, and was awarded an NEA creative writing grant in '78.

OBSERVATIONS: Joy Harjo has written about her poetry in this way: "There is that rhythm of wind that shapes the woman-body of land and mountains that surrounds the inside and outside of me. That seems to be most inherent in how I see and why I write. I have to be able to feel that rhythm and listen to it from a long way off, and to be gentle enough to feel it and know what it means when it is silent and strong within me." Keith Wilson comments upon her writing in this way: "Ms. Harjo's poems are images, moving. A strong sense of desert, mountain, person, growth. I'm glad these poems [have been] published—they establish a new voice in the Southwest."

MICHAEL (STEVEN) HARPER
BIRTH: 3/18/'38, in Brooklyn, spent much of his youth in Los Angeles.

EDUCATION: City College of L.A., A.A. ('59); Calif. St. U., Los Angeles, M.A. ('61); M.F.A., U. of Iowa Writers' Workshop ('63); post-doctoral fellow, U. of Ill. ('70-'71).

CAREER: Contra Costa College ('64-'68); Reed C. ('68-'69, Visiting Prof. in Lit.); Lewis & Clark ('68-'69; Poet-in-Residence), Calif. St. U., Hayward ('69-'70). Since '71, and currently, he is director of the writing program and Prof. of English at Brown U. He and his wife, the former Shirley Ann Buffington, whom he married in '65, their two sons, and a daughter divide their time living between their homes in Taunton, Mass. in the school year and in New London, Minn. in the summer.

PUBLICATIONS: Dear John, Dear Coltrane ('70); *History Is Your Own Heartbeat* ('71); *Song: I want a Witness* ('72); *Photographs: Negatives: History as Apple Tree*

('72), *Debridement* ('73), *Nightmare Begins Responsibility* ('75), & *Images of Kin* ('77). He is likewise the author of poems anthologized in Adoff, *The Poetry of Black America;* Brown, Lee & Ward, *To Gwen With Love;* Colley and Moore, *Black Poetry,* Randall, *The Black Poets;* & Wilentz and Weatherly, *Natural Process.* Periodicals, including the following, have carried his verse: *Black Scholar, Black World, Chicago Review, Negro American Literature Forum, Negro Digest, Poetry, Poetry Northwest, Quarterly Review of Literature, Massachusetts Review,* & *New Yorker.* Harper, himself, has also produced an anthology: *Heartblow: Black Veils,* a collection of black poetry of the '70s, published by the U. of Ill. Press, '78.

HONORS: Fellow at the Center for Advanced Study, U. of Ill. ('70-'71); in '72, his *History Is Your Own Heartbeat* received a special award from the Black Academy of Arts and Letters, and the year before ('71), he was one of the final nominees for the Nat. Inst. Book Award in poetry; in '72, the Nat. Inst. of Arts and Letters presented to him an award for literature, which read: "(his) grave, blunt poems deal with human and black experience simultaneously, welcoming white Americans into their music as far as our imagination and our hearts permit and our history entitles us to go." Additionally he received a Guggenheim fellowship ('76), & an N.E.A. grant ('78).

OBSERVATIONS: Michael Harper notes: "My poems are rhythmic rather than metric; the pulse is jazz, the tradition generally oral; my major influences musical;

Michael Harper
(April 1973)

my debts, mostly to the musicians (John Coltrane, Miles Davis, Billie Holliday, Bud Powell, etc.) who taught me to see about experience, pain and love, and who made it artful and archetypal." About Harper's writing, Gwendolyn Brooks has written: "Michael Harper's poetry is vigorous as well as brilliant. It has an unafraid strength. Altogether technically dexterous, it differs magnificently from the customary methodical product of today, which is so often without fire, without tense pulse, without rich guts. Here is obvious blood-stuffed life. Here is illumination, black-based and other."

JIM (JAMES THOMAS) HARRISON

BIRTH: 12/11/'37, Grayling, Mich., the son of an agriculturalist, Winfield Sprague Harrison and Norma (Walgren) Harrison, he spent his childhood enjoying life in Osceola County where his father was a federal government agricultural agent.

EDUCATION: B.A. ('60) & M.A. ('62) from Mich. St. U., where for the latter degree, he specialized in Comp. Lit. and studied with Prof. Herbert Weisinger, whom he says influenced his work.

CAREER: Early in his career, particularly while a student, Harrison was a sometimes clerk, farm, and construction worker. He traveled for awhile, living in Boston, San Francisco, and N.Y.C., and for a brief time, taught at S.U.N.Y., Stony Brook, where he was an Asst. Prof. of English, but gave up teaching to devote his full-time in the early "seventies" to writing and editing, although he has traveled and read extensively in the U.S., and worked for the Poetry-In-The-Schools program in Ariz., Mich., and elsewhere. Married to the former Linda King (Oct., '60), he lives today with his wife and their two children on a farm in his native state at Lake Leelanau, Mich.

EDITORIAL POSTS: With Dan Gerber, in '70, Harrison founded *Sumac,* a literary quarterly, which disbanded from a regular printing in '72; he was likewise affiliated with Sumac Press, which focused upon publishing books until '75 when it disbanded too, but not before leaving a distinguished, quality listing of influential "seventies" books of poetry.

PUBLICATIONS: Plain Song ('65), *Locations* ('68), *Walking* ('69), *Outlyer and Ghazals* ('71), & *Letters to Yesenen* ('74). Various anthologies carry his poems: *Out of the War Shadow* ('67), *Lyric Poems* ('68), *31 New American Poets* ('69, *Contemporary American Poetry* ('70), *The Norton Anthology of Modern Poetry* ('73), &

Jim Harrison
(November 1970)

Modern Poems: An Introduction to Poetry ('73; '76). His poems have appeared in *Poetry, Tri-Quarterly Review, Stony Brook Journal, The Nation, New York Times Book Review, Sumac,* and elsewhere. A novelist as well as a poet, Harrison has also authored *Wolf—A False Memoir* ('71), *A Good Day to Die* ('73), & *Farmer* ('76).

HONORS: Two prizes from the Nat. Lit. Anthology; grants in '67, '68, & '69, from the N.E.A., and a Guggenheim Fellowship ('69-'70). Harrison, an avid sports enthusiast, also contributes to *Sports Illustrated.* Fishing is one of his main avocations.

OBSERVATIONS: Jim Harrison comments: "I have learned a great deal...from fellow poets Denise Levertov, Robert Duncan & Louis Simpson, among others." He adds: "I write 'free verse,' which is absurdly indefinite as a name for what any poet writes. I consider myself an 'internationalist' and my main influences to be Neruda, Rilke, Yeats, Bunting, Lorca, and in my own country, Whitman, Hart Crane, Robert Duncan, and Ezra Pound. Not that this helps much other than to name those I esteem and, perhaps vacantly wish to emulate. Most of my poems seem rural, vaguely surrealistic though after the Spanish rather than the French. My sympathies run hotly to the impure, the inclusive, as the realm of poetry. A poet, at best, speaks in the outloud speech of his tribe, deals in essences whether political, social, or personal. All of world literature is his province though he sees it as a 'guild' only to be learned from, as he must speak in his own voice." About Harrison's poetry, Richard Ellman and Robert O'Clair have observed: "Most of Jim Harrison's early poems are concerned with rural subjects—a parody of a job application form by a comic yokel, a dilapidated landscape....Harrison treats his subjects with a surrealist energy and invention."

GEORGE HITCHCOCK

BIRTH: 6/2/'14, Hood River, Ore., grew up in his native state.

EDUCATION: B.A., U. of Ore., Eugene ('35).

CAREER: Early in his career, Hitchcock worked at many odd jobs. He was a laborer, shipfitter, smelterman, mason, carpenter, and gardener. For a time he was with the theater too, serving as author, actor, and director. Later he was a journalist. His teaching career began at San Francisco State C. where he was a Lect. in English. For several years now, he has been a Lecturer at the U. of Calif., Santa Cruz, where he teaches poetry writing and makes his home.

EDITORIAL POSTS: From '61-'62, Hitchcock held the post of editor of the *San Francisco Review*. In '64, he founded his magazine, *Kayak,* and since that time has also began his distinguished series, *Kayak Books*. A master of design and typesetting, Hitchcock directs his own press publications. As Geof Hewitt has written, "Through his Kayak Press, Hitchcock has become an important force in

George Hitchcock
(December 1969)

the new American poetry: his magazine, *Kayak,* sometimes the most exciting of all the little magazines, has made available a variety of new forms, many of which Hitchcock has explored in his own work. These include found poetry, 'cut-ups,' and collaborations."

PUBLICATIONS: Poems and Prints, with Mel Fowler ('62), *Tactics of Survival* ('64), *The Dolphin With a Revolver in Its Teeth* ('67), *A Ship of Bells* ('68, '72), *Twelve Stanzas in Praise of the Holy Chariot* ('69), *The Rococo Eye* ('70), *Lessons in Alchemy* ('76), *& The Piano Beneath the Skin* ('77). His poems have appeared in such periodicals as *The Sixties* and *Choice,* as well as elsewhere, and in such anthologies as these: *Poets of Today* ('64), *Where Is Vietnam?* ('67), & *The Voice That Is Great Within Us* ('73), among others. An editor of poetry anthologies, himself, Hitchcock has also produced these collections: *Pioneers of Modern Poetry* ('67, with Robert Peters), & *Losers Weepers: Poems Found Practically Anywhere* ('69). As a fiction writer, he has published a novel, *Another Shore* ('72), and a collection of stories, *Notes of the Siege of the Year* ('74); and as a playwright, has authored seven plays, one of which, *The Busy Martyr*, was published in *First Stage* (Lafayette, Ind., '63). The latter play was also produced in Medford, Mass. in the '62-'63 Winter season.

HONORS: For his magazine *Kayak* and his Kayak Press, Hitchcock has received two awards in '68 & '69 from the N.E.A. for graphics.

OBSERVATIONS: George Hitchcock confides: "My verse is largely subconscious in its origins and rational tampering with these well-springs, in my case at least, is likely to pollute the water." About Hitchcock's poetry, Kenneth Irby writes that in it "so much relish of the world is felt, and at heart, a peace not often to come to in poems these days."

ANN MARIE (HARALAMBIE) HUCK

BIRTH: 11/15/'51, Brooklyn, N.Y., grew up in Larchmont in the same state.

EDUCATION: B.A., Creative Writing, U. of Ariz. ('72); M.A., English, U. of Ariz. ('74); J.D., U. of Ariz. ('76). Divorced and now living in Tucson with her daughter, Kathy, Ann Huck works as a civil liberties and general practice lawyer, continues writing seriously as a poet in any free time she can manage, and conducts

Ann Marie (Haralambie) Huck
(May 1975)

poetry workshops and readings. Her major interests otherwise are music. astronomy and backpacking.

PUBLICATIONS: Becoming (Desert First Works, '75).

EDITORIAL POSTS: With three other editors, she helps plan and edit the chapbook series of Desert First Works, Tucson.

OBSERVATIONS: About her goals for her poetry, Ann M. Huck writes: "What I'm trying to do in my poetry...I suppose I come out of the 'confessional/cathartic' school of poetry-trying to deal with my own feelings of relationship. Currently I am trying to write some good, contemporary Christian poetry—Tennyson, Hopkins, and others did not sacrifice poetry to sentimentality, but today most so-called religious poetry is no more than greeting card triviality. God deserves better than that, so this is the task at hand for me at the moment." About Ms. Huck's poetry,

Jeff Carter has noted: "[She] has a knack for clean, brittle imagery...I get a sense of something important being said here and being said well...an idea alive with emotion...an emotion strengthened by idea...." Mark Halperin has written of *Becoming:* "The typical motif in these poems is the voyage of discovery, their world is a lonely place where things, concrete objects, rarely support us, but tend, rather, when pressed, to convey messages."

James Humphrey
(March 1972)

JAMES HUMPHREY

BIRTH: 2/20/'39, Sioux City, Iowa.

EDUCATION: B.A. & M.A., Brown U. ('77).

CAREER: Humphrey has worked as a truck driver, construction worker, card dealer, cotton picker, lumberjack, painter of murals in bars, florist, and bartender. He has also, more recently, worked for the Poetry-in-the-Schools program in many states: Iowa, Maine, Massachusetts, Connecticut, Rhode Island, Arizona, California, and has conducted poetry writing workshops for art councils in several states, as well as given readings on various college campuses and at other institutions, especially those located in New England. He has also been a member of the board of directors of the Attleboro, Mass. Drug Rehabilitation Program. With his second wife Norma, a librarian whom he married on 2/28/'66, and their son Saroyan (named for William Saroyan), he lives in Attleboro, Mass. in "a renovated railroad station in the country." Of his home, Humphrey writes: "Freight trains still go by 3 and 4 times a day...it is something, and for me that is better than concrete." Presently he is an auto racing writer for the weekly magazine *New England Speedway Scene*, and devotes all the time he can possibly manage to his poetry and play writing. Since '75, Humphrey's poetry writing curriculum has been used in the Attleboro Public School System.

EDITORIAL POSTS: For a brief time, Humphrey edited a little magazine he called *Captain May I.*

PUBLICATIONS: Argument for Love ('70); *The Visitor* (chapbook, '72), *An Homage: The End of Some More Land* (chapbook, '72), & *The Re-Learning* ('76), the latter of which was published by Hellcoal Press, Brown University, Providence, R.I., and nominated for the Pulitzer Prize and the National Book Award the same year. Humphrey is a contributor to such an anthology as *Poets in the Schools: Connecticut Commission on the Arts,* edited by Kathleen Meagher ('73) and to such poetry periodicals as these: *Madrona, West End, Sumac, Penumbra, Suction,*

Cronopious, The Iowa Defender, Bones, Tentacle, Iowa Arts Council Newsletter, Abraxas, Crucible, Ploughshares, Softball, The Stone Times, & In These Hard Times.

HONORS: In addition to the nominations mentioned above which his last collection, *The Re-Learning,* received from Hellcoal Press, Humphrey has received grants from the International P.E.N. American Center in '72, '73 & '75, and from the Authors' League, '72.

OBSERVATIONS: About Humphrey's first book, *Argument for Love,* Darrell Gray wrote: "What I like most about [his] poems is their unflinching honesty. They are 'arguments' for preserving in life that which makes us most human. A disarming simplicity of diction, plain and hard meaning without descriptive qualification, reverberates in the highly charged condensation of these poems. His is the language in which men dream of what their lives ought to be." Concerning his latest book, *The Re-Learning,* James Schevill has commented: "The poetry of James Humphrey is direct and personal in tone and subject. Here is a poetry that does not evade and at its best suggests important confrontations."

DAVID IGNATOW

BIRTH: 2/17/'14, in Brooklyn, the son of Max and Yetta (Reinbach) Ignatow, grew up there and has lived most of his life in the area of metropolitan New York.

EDUCATION: He graduated from high school in '29, and therein completed his formal education. But from boyhood, he was encouraged by two friends—Prof. Milton Hindus and Raun Weber, and later with his poetry by a third professor, Lawrence Chauncey Woodman. The poets William Carlos Williams and Kenneth Fearing also influenced his career and gave him their interest in it.

CAREER: In his early years, Ignatow managed his father's business. In '64-'65, he began his teaching career as an Instr. at the New School for Social Research. Since that time, he has held posts as Visiting Lect. (U. of Kentucky, '65-'66); Lectr., U. of Kansas ('66-'67); Lectr., Vassar C. ('67-'69), and since '69, has served both as Poet-in-Residence at York C., City U. of N.Y., and as Adj. Prof. of the faculty at Columbia U. School of Fine Arts.

EDITORIAL POSTS: Since 1969, he has served as consulting editor of *Chelsea,* a literary magazine, and also beginning the same year and presently as Assoc. Ed. of *American Poetry Review.* Previously he served as poetry ed. for *The Nation* ('62-'63) and as co-editor of *Beloit Poetry Journal* ('50-'59). Today he lives in Jamaica, Long Island, N.Y., with his wife artist and prose-writer Rose Graubert Ignatow, whom he married in July, '39, and who is additionally a co-editor of *Chelsea,* and their daughter Yaedi. Their son David is now grown.

PUBLICATIONS: Poems ('48), *The Gentle Weight Lifter* ('55), *Say Pardon* ('61), *Figures Out of the Human* ('64), *Rescue the Dead* ('68), *Earth Hard: Selected Poems* ('68), *Poems: 1934-69* ('70), *Facing the Tree* ('73; '75), *The Notebooks of David Ignatow,* ed. by Ralph J. Mills, Jr. ('73), *Selected Poems,* ed. by Robert Bly ('75), & *Tread the Dark* ('78). Ignatow has also recorded his poetry, with others, on *Today's Poets 3* (Folkways). Some of the anthologies carrying his poetry are *Antioch Anthology* ('55), *A Treasury of Jewish Poetry* ('57), *Erotic Poetry* ('63), *A Treasury of Contemporary American-Jewish Literature* ('64), *Of Poetry and Power* ('64), *Civil Liberties and the Arts* ('64), *Poems on Poetry* ('65), *Where is Vietnam?* ('67), *America Forever New* ('68), *Possibilities of Poetry* ('69), *The City* ('69), *Decade* ('69), & *Contemporary American Poetry* ('70). Widely published in periodicals, Ignatow has poems appearing in *The Nation, Chelsea, The New York*

David Ignatow
(February 1971)

Times, Poetry, Kayak, Quarterly Review of Literature, & *The Sixties,* among others. As an editor of poetry, he has also published one anthology, *Political Poetry* ('60) and two pamphlets: *Walt Whitman: A Centennial Celebration* ('63), & *William Carlos Williams: A Memorial Chapbook* ('63).

HONORS: Nat. Inst. of Arts & Letters Award ('64), two Guggenheim fellowships ('65; '73), Shelley Memorial Prize ('66), a Rockefeller grant ('68-'69), an N.E.A. grant ('69), & Bollingen Prize ('77).

OBSERVATIONS: Ignatow states: "My form is usually very free, content and/or ideas determining it. While I use every conceivable devise, traditional and new for the proper realization of the poem....I search for *now,* using the method of introspection and dream in tandem with objective events or things." About his work, Ralph J. Mills observes: "Running through all of his work is what might be called a spiritual, even religious quest, a search for qualities which will redeem the violence, suffering and guilt in life....Never a participant in the momentary fads and fancies of the literary life, David Ignatow has quietly and persistently developed his art over the past two decades and now emerges as one of the very best poets of his generation."

LAWSON FUSAO INADA

BIRTH: 5/26/'38, Fresno, Calif., the son of Fusaji and Masako (Saito) Inada, is a Sansei (third-generation Japanese American). During W.W.II, he was "interned" with his family in concentration camps in Fresno, Calif., Ark., & Colo.; after the War they returned once again to the multi-ethnic West Side of Fresno.

EDUCATION: Fresno State C. ('55-'56, '57-'59; B.A., '59), U. of Calif., Berkeley ('56'-57); graduate work at the U. of Iowa ('60-'62); U. of Ore. ('65-'66; M.F.A., '66).

CAREER: Inada began his teaching career at the U. of New Hampshire as an Instr. ('62-'65); since '66 he has been on the faculty of So. Ore. St. C., where he is now a Prof. of English. The father of two sons, Miles Fusao and Lowell Masao, he lives today in Ashland, Ore., with his wife the former Janet Francis, whom he married 2/19/'62. Additionally Inada has been a Visit. Prof. at Lewis and Clark in '69-'70, Eastern Ore. St. C., the summer of '76, and the U. of Hawaii, the summer of '78. He is also the founder of a special services program for minority and disadvantaged students called S.O.S.C.: Students of Other Cultures. Additionally he is a director of C.A.R.P. (Combined Asian American Resources Project), which published the late John Okada's novel, *No-No Boy* ('76).

PUBLICATIONS: Three Northwest Poets: Drake, Inada, Lawder ('70), *Before the War: Poems as They Happened* ('71), & *The Buddha Bandits Down 99: Hongo, Inada, Lau* ('78). He is the co-editor, with J. Chan and F. Chin, of *Aiiieeeee! An Anthology of Asian American Writers* ('75). His poems have been anthologized in numerous anthologies, among them: *New Directions # 23* ('71) & *An Asian American Reader* ('71), as well as in such periodicals as *Aion, The Carleton Miscellany, Chicago Review, Evergreen Review, Kayak, Quixote, Northwest Review, San Francisco Review,* & *United Church Herald,* among others. As a short story writer, he has also published in *Yardbird III* & *Roots II.* A film based on Inada's life, *I Told You So: Lawson Fusao Inada* ('75) was produced by Visual Communications, with a grant from *HEW* and the Los Angeles Public Schools.

HONORS: From '76-'77, he served as a panelist who judged the work of prose writers for *The Directory of American Fiction Writers* (Poets & Writers, Inc., N.Y.C.).

Lawson Fusao Inada
(January 1972)

OBSERVATIONS: Inada notes: "Fresno is my Father, and Camps is a Mother to me. You don't fool with that. Thus, I work in the tradition of Andres Huesca, Lester Young, & Toshio Mori. And all the others of us. We just happened to get it out and set it down." Denise Levertov describes Inada's work in this way: "[His] poems about the Japanese American experience would have documentary value even if he were not such a good poet; but, in fact, his work goes far beyond that level of interest."

JEREMY INGALLS
BIRTH: 4/2/1911, Gloucester, Mass., the daughter of Charles Augustine and May-Estelle (Dodge) Ingalls.

EDUCATION: Tufts U. (B.A., '32); (M.A., '33); (Litt.D., '65); from '45-'47, Fellow and Research Associate, Chinese Studies, U. of Chicago; Hon. L.H.D. degree, Rockford C. ('60).

CAREER: Asst. Prof. of Am. Lit., Western C., Oxford, Ohio ('41-'43). For a number of years, she wrote poetry and traveled widely on grants and fellowships from various foundations. (See below). In '46, she was appointed Poet-in-Residence at Rockford C., Ill., where from '48-'60, she was also Prof. of English and Asian Studies. Until her early retirement due to health problems in '60, she was also from '53, chairman of the literature department at Rockford. She now continues her writing career full-time at her home in Tucson, and is currently at work on her two long poems, *Seacross* and *Patmos,* as well as on various translations. Since '48, Jeremy Ingalls has also served as a sponsor and hostess for several students from foreign countries, as well as for American Indian children.

PUBLICATIONS: The Metaphysical Sword ('41; winner the same year of the Yale Series of Younger Poets' Award; *Tahl* ('45), *The Woman From the Island* ('58), & *These Islands Also* ('59). Her poems have been translated into Italian, French, Korean, & Japanese, and have appeared in various anthologies, including Bartlett's *Familiar Quotations.* They have likewise been published in numerous magazines, some of which follow: *Accent, Atlantic Monthly, Beloit Poetry Journal, Chicago Review, New Republic, Poetry, Saturday Review,* & *Western Review.* Additionally, Ms. Ingalls is also a translator: Li Hsien-Nung's *A Political History of China, 1842-1928,* with S.Y. Teng ('56); *The Malice of Empire,* by Yao Hsin-Nung ('70); and *Tenno Yūgao* by Yoichi Nakagawa (a Japanese novel, '75). One of her poems, "Ballad of the Times of Men," from *The Metaphysical Sword,* was set for symphony orchestra and women's chorus by the composer, Everett Helm, and performed by the Cincinnati Symphony Orchestra. Additionally as a prose writer, she has published *A Book of Legends* ('41), a work which contains fifteen re-tellings of famous tales from past civilizations, & *The Galilean Way* ('53), an analyses, from the perspective of world history of the Galilean Christian world view. Articles of hers have also appeared in *Classical Journal, Journal of Modern History, Religion in Life,* and elsewhere.

Jeremy Ingalls
(October 1964)

HONORS: In addition to the Yale Younger Series Award ('41), she has been awarded a Guggenheim Fellowship in Poetry ('43-'44); an Am. Academy of Arts & Letters grant for poetry ('44-'45); a fellowship from the Republic of China for classical Chinese research ('45-'47); Ford Foundation Fellowship, Asian Studies ('52-'53); Fulbright Prof. in Am. Lit. & a Rockefeller Foundation Lecturer in Japan ('57-'58). For her poetry, she has also received the Shelley Memorial Award ('50), Lola Ridge Mem. Award for poetry ('51, '52), & Steinman Foundation lectureship in poetry ('60).

OBSERVATIONS: About Jeremy Ingalls' poetry, particularly about her work *Tahl,* William Rose Benét wrote in *Book-of-the-Month Club News:* "This poem, as well as being a swift-moving and absorbing tale, is a tremendous analogy and allegory. *Tahl* is surrounded by other lives, by a fascinating association of human beings in their private and public relationships....The orchestration of the verse, the architecture of the poem, the sheer poetry of the many-sided discussion, of the many-countried descriptions, the central musical figure, the variations in the progress of the music, the rich and full-bodied story, make a magnificent work of art. This book is a work for the ages."

WILL INMAN

BIRTH: 5/4/'23, in Wilmington, North Carolina, the son of William Archibald McGirt and Delia Ellen Inman McGirt was named after his father, who sold real

Will Inman
(May 1976)

estate and insurance. In '53, Inman took the pen name which in '73 in Maryland he changed into his legal name—Will for William and Inman from his mother's maiden name, or as he explains, "Will Inman, or will in man, not my will, but the universal Will." He grew up just outside the east city limits of Wilmington and spent much time hiking; he has loved nature all his life.

EDUCATION: Public schools (Forest Hills and New Hanover High) of New Hanover County, diploma ('39); Duke U. (B.A., '43).

CAREER: From an early age, Inman had strong spiritual stirrings and, even as a boy in the South, was troubled by race hatred. In '47, feeling that no other group seriously opposed color discrimination, he joined the Communist Party, remained a member during the McCarthy period, but left the party in '56 when he discovered he had become a Communist first, a human being second, "a situation," he recalls "that was an anathema to me." During his years as a Communist, he worked for the Food & Tobacco Workers trade union in Winston-Salem ('49) and served as a pall-bearer when a black woman trade union leader named Moranda Smith died. Ms. Smith's leadership in the South had been acknowledged by Paul Robeson's presence at her funeral. Later, Inman worked in meat and fish markets, and upon moving to N.Y.C. in '56, quit the Communist party, and "began to rediscover the vertical dimensions" of his life, "the spiritual." In N.Y.C., in the late "fifties" and early "sixties," he worked in libraries, mostly at N.Y.U., and began writing heavily. In '67, he began his teaching career when he served as poet-in-residence at the American U., Washington, D.C. for the spring semester. He was also active for several years in the Free U. of N.Y. during the "mid-sixties," and served as Vice-President under Allen Krebs. In June, '69, he married Barbara Ann Inman (a poet known as Bai) and began teaching full-time in the English Department of Montgomery C., Rockville, Maryland. In '73, when he had just earned tenure, his wife's ill health forced the Inmans to seek a better climate in Tucson, where Inman lives alone today after a '75 divorce. Currently he devotes his full time to writing poetry, while directing a poetry seminar at the Unitarian-Universalist Church in Tucson and to writing a weekly column, *Conchsound,* for a small paper in Pa. He also does counselling for "gay" men, is in a prison reform group, and has one grown son, Will Stanley.

EDITORIAL POSTS: In '64, Inman began publishing *Kauri,* a small mimeo magazine, which he continued producing until '71, and which in its thirty-three issues, published hundreds of new poets, many of whom are well-known today. Upon its ceasing publication, William Packard, editor of *New York Quarterly,* noted: "*Kauri* touched my life and made a difference. At a time when other literary publications were catering to coteries and promoting their own self-interest, it was obvious that you were doing *Kauri* out of love and concern for things that were far larger than the latest fashion....Your basic editorial plea—for us to change in ourselves, that man can create the good and beautiful out of his own will—is as American as the Declaration of Independence....Our thanks for reminding us."

PUBLICATIONS: I Am The Snakehandler (privately published, '60), *Lament and Psalm* (privately published, '60), *A River of Laughter* (privately published, '61), *Honey in Hot Blood* (privately published, '62), *108 Verges unto Now* ('64), *108 Prayers for J. Edgar* ('65), *A Generation of Heights* ('69; & originally published in the *Quark* series of *Camels Coming Press*), *Whose Heaven, Whose Earth?* ('69, with Bai Inman & Tom & Marjorie Melville), *The Voice of The Beech Oracle* ('77), & *The Wakers in the Tongue* ('77). Numerous anthologies carry Will Inman's poetry: *Poets of North Carolina,* ed. R. Walser, Garrett & Massie ('63); *New Orlando Poetry Anthology, V. II* ('63); *Of Poetry and Power: JFK Memorial* ('64); *Where Is Vietnam?,* ed. by Walter Lowenfels ('67); *Southern Poetry Review: A Decade of Poems* ('69); *In a Time of Revolution,* ed. by W. Lowenfels ('69; later Vintage Books V-553); *Only Humans With Songs to Sing,* ed. by Dan Georgakas ('67); *North Carolina Poetry: 1970,* ed. by Guy Owen ('70); *Campfires of Resistance: Poetry From the Movement,* ed. by Todd Gitlin ('71); *Mad Windows,* ed. by Phil Perry ('69); *The East Side Scene: American Poetry, 1960-65,* ed. by Allen De Loach ('72); *Poems From the Capitol.,* ed. by Ron Arck ('72), *For Neruda, For Chile,* ed. by W. Lowenfels ('75), *Fired Up With You,* ed. by Will Inman ('77); *Southwest,* ed. by Kopp, Kopp, & Stafford ('77), & *A Geography of Poets,* ed. by Edward Field ('78). Poems by Inman have also appeared in numerous periodicals, notably these: *Pembroke, Southwest Review, Blue Cloud Quarterly, Kaldron, The News & Observer, Mutiny, Epos, New York Herald Tribune, The New York Quarterly, Phoebe, Motive, Minotaur, Poet* (India), *Fiddlehead, The Georgia Review, Flame, Prairie Poet, The Carolina Times,* & *Mainstream.* In addition, he has edited in '64, an American issue of *Poet* (Madras, India) for Krishna Srinivas, chief editor, and a record, ed. by Walter Lowenfels and produced by Broadside Records, *New Jazz Poets* (N.Y.C., '67), also includes him reading his poetry. As a fiction writer, his short stories have been published in various late "fifties" and early "sixties" issues of *Breakthru* magazine.

HONORS: In '78, *Kaldron* magazine devoted a whole issue to Inman's work.

OBSERVATIONS: Will Inman says of his writing: "The paradox of being works in us like a cross between a cosmic pulse and a cankerous snail, generating our life even as it saps our strength. So must we learn that sacred balance wherein we can live aware and serene, sometimes even rejoicing, at the verge of our passing, at the point-end of risk and grief...and, surviving to ask why, then to experience harmony in the teeth of the hurricane, and now and then, to find a kin eye in the opening flower or an inward caress along a quiet dawn or dusk." About his writing, Ann Beattie has observed: "Inman is one of the aware people, a reformer in his own right, a man who knows there's a lot happening, and wants to make things happen...himself."

JUNE (MEYER) JORDAN

BIRTH: 7/9/'36, in Harlem, grew up in Brooklyn, in Bedford-Stuyvesant.

EDUCATION: Barnard College & the U. of Chicago.

CAREER: Early in her career, she worked writing film scripts and assisted in producing a film entitled *The Cool World.* For a time she also worked as a research associate and writer for the Technical Housing Department of Mobilization for Youth. Later she taught courses in writing and English at the City C. of N.Y., Conn. C., Sarah Lawrence C., & Yale Univ. For a time, she was co-director with Terri Bush, of the Creative Writing Workshop for children in Brooklyn, mostly of Black and Puerto Rican descent, which was called "The Voice of the Children, Inc." Presently she teaches at S.U.N.Y., at Stony Brook, and divides her time, living sometimes in N.Y.C., and sometimes on Long Island in East Hampton. Under the sponsorship of the Academy of Am. Poets, she has read her poetry in many of the public schools of New York City and at the Guggenheim Museum, and under the sponsorship of Black Poets' Reading, Inc., at many of the colleges, universities and institutions throughout the country. In '71, she was also one of a number of poets asked to read at the Las Vegas, Nev. meeting of the National Council of English Teachers.

PUBLICATIONS: Some Changes ('71), *New Days: Poems of Exile and Return* ('73), & *Selected Poems: Things That I Do in the Dark* ('77). Widely anthologized, June Jordan's poems appear in these collections: Adoff, *The Poetry of Black*

June Jordan
(November 1971)

America; Harper, *Heartbow: Black Veils;* Howe & Basso, *No More Masks;* King, *Blackspirits;* Lowenfels, *In the Time of Revolution;* Major, *The New Black Poetry;* Patterson, *A Rock Against the Wind;* Randall, *The Black Poets;* & Welburn, *Dices.* Ms. Jordan's poems have also appeared in many periodicals, including these: *Negro Digest, Liberator, American Dialog, Black Creation, Black World, Essence, Freedom Ways, Second Quarter, Harper's Bazaar, Library Journal, New York Times, Encore, Newsday, America Report, The Nation, Village Voice, Partisan Review, Blackstage, Esquire,* & *Chelsea.* Additionally, an editor of poetry anthologies, in '70, she edited two: *Soulscript,* a collection of Afro-American poetry, and *The Voices of the Children,* a collection of the writings of Black and Puerto Rican children, which she prepared, with Terri Bush, as a part of the workshop for which she served as co-editor in Brooklyn. Articles and essays of June Jordan's have also been published by *Esquire, Mademoiselle, The Nation, Village Voice, Evergreen Review, Partisan Review, The Urban Review,* and *The New York Times. Okay Now,* her first adult novel, is in-press with Simon and Schuster; however, she is already well-known for her children and young adult books, especially her poems for children and biographies, which include *Who Look at Me* ('69), *His Own Where* ('71), *Fannie Lou Homer* (biography, '72), & *New Room: New Life* ('74). Her non-fiction articles concerning writing and teaching and young people have appeared in *Partisan Review* and *Wilson Library Bulletin.*

HONORS: Ms. Jordan's poetry has brought her various honors, which include a Rockefeller Foundation fellowship in creative writing ('69-'70); the Prix de Rome of the Am. Acad. in Rome ('70-'71); and a nomination for the National Book Award for *His Own Where* in '72.

OBSERVATIONS: June Jordan comments: "Language, our words of experience, controls what we know and what we believe. Black poetry controls language in the spirit of Creative Revolution. We must all be poets at this and every time. We must create the revolution of our experiences. I am trying to develop my own language of love and pride, to share." Hayden Carruth, reviewing her work as a poet and particularly in her latest collection *Selected Poems: Things That I Do in the Dark,* in *N.Y. Times Book Review* (10/9/'77) wrote: "Whatever becomes of poetry in English hereafter, Jordan's poems will likely be a conspicuous part of it." Julius Lester has further observed of June Jordan's writing: "For some, her poetry may not qualify as 'black poetry' because she doesn't rage or scream. No, she's quiet, but the intensity is frightening. Her poetry is highly disciplined, highly controlled....There is nothing wasted, and it is impossible to separate what she says from how she says it. Indeed, how she writes is as much what is being said as what is being said intellectually. She isn't concerned with converting the listener (and her poetry must be listened to, not merely read) to a particular point of view. Her concern is the concern of the poet who is also a musician, of the poet for whom words are merely the beginning and not the end of the experience. She wants the listener to feel what she feels, she what she sees, and then do with it what he may. Hopefully, he will become more human, more caring, more intensely alive to the suffering, and the joy. Her poems only begin to live in the space around the words, that space representing the spaces inside the listener."

DONALD (RODNEY) JUSTICE

BIRTH: 8/12/'25, grew up in his birthplace, Miami, Fla., where his earliest recollections are of "the Depression" and of Miami, when it was a half-deserted resort town.

EDUCATION: As a young man, he studied music, first under Carl Ruggles on a scholarship at the U. of Miami, where he received his B.A. ('45). He took an M.A. ('47) at the U. of No. Carolina, and married his wife, the former Jean Ross, the same year. From '47-'48, he studied on a Stanford U. fellowship in writing with Yvor Winters; but later with a Rockefeller grant, he received his Ph.D. at Iowa ('54), where he studied with John Berryman, Paul Engle, Robert Lowell and Karl Shapiro.

CAREER: His teaching career began at the U. of Mo. ('55-'56), Hamline U., St.

Paul, Minn. ('56-'57), at the U. of Iowa ('57-'66), at the U. of New York, Syracuse ('66-'70), and currently, and since '71, he has been a Prof. of English at the Writers' Workshop, U. of Iowa. Additionally he has been a Visiting Prof., U. of Calif., Irvine ('70-'71), Poet-in-Residence, Reed C. ('62), Poet-in-Residence at Princeton ('75-'76), and on the faculty of the Breadloaf Writers' Conference (summer, '75-'76). The father of a son, Nathaniel, he lives today in Iowa City with his wife.

PUBLICATIONS: The Summer Anniversaries ('59), *A Local Storm* ('63), *Night Light* ('67), *Sixteen Poems* ('70), *From a Notebook* ('72), and *Departures* ('73). Justice's poems have been published in such magazines as *Poetry, The New Yorker,* and *Poetry Now*, as well as in scores of others. They have been included in such anthologies as these, among others: *New Poets of England and America, First Selection* ('57); *Second Selection* ('62); *Penguin's Contemporary American Poetry* ('62); *Modern Library's Twentieth-Century American Poetry* ('63); *Four Poets,* with others ('67); *The Contemporary American Poets* ('69); *Twentieth Century American Poetry: American and British: 1900-'70* ('70); & *Contemporary Poetry in America* ('73). An editor of poetry, additionally, Justice has also produced these volumes: *The Collected Poems of Weldon Kees* ('60), *Contemporary French Poetry*, with Alexander Aspel ('65), *Midland*, with Paul Engle and Henri Coulette ('61), & *Syracuse Poems* ('68). He has also translated Mexican poetry and has written plays, uncollected presently, and has also won O. Henry awards for his short stories.

Donald Justice
(April 1970)

HONORS: Other than the latter honors, he has received various honors solely for his poetry: Lamont Award ('59), Inez Boulton Prize ('60), Ford Fellowship in the Theatre ('64), Harriet Monroe Memorial Prize ('65), N.E.A. grant in poetry ('67), Iowa-Rockefeller grant in poetry ('64), Nat. Inst. of Arts & Letters Award ('74), and Guggenheim fellowship ('76).

OBSERVATIONS: Justice writes: "Major themes: none. Characteristic subjects: childhood, death, madness, love. Usual verse forms: I began with standard meters, including some accentuals, and the usual forms associated with these, moved on toward syllabics, and a general relaxation of meters and 'form,' and now write mostly free, or relatively free. Sources and influences: memory and language itself chief sources; influences many, both in English and other languages. Stylistic devices; none I know of." Concerning Donald Justice's poetry, Mark Strand has commented: "If absence and loss are inescapable conditions of life, the poem for

Justice is an act of recovery. It synthesizes, for all its meagreness, what is with what is no longer; it conjures up a life that persists by denial, gathering strength from its own hopelessness, and exists, finally, and positively, as an emblem of survival."

ROLLY KENT

BIRTH: 1946, in New Jersey.

EDUCATION: Middlebury (B.A.) & U. of Ariz. (M.F.A.)

CAREER: Kent works through the Arizona Commission for the Arts, the Nevada State Council on the Arts, and the Western States Art Foundation (Denver) doing poetry-in-the-schools and community writing workshops in small western towns.

EDITORIAL POSTS: He edits the literature projects of The Maguey Press, Tucson.

PUBLICATIONS: The Wreck in Post Office Canyon ('76). His poems have also appeared in numerous magazines, including *American Poetry Review, American Review, The Atlantic, Nation,* and *Poetry.* Additionally they are anthologized in *The Ardis Anthology.*

OBSERVATIONS: Concerning his poetry, Rolly Kent writes: "What I do when I write is probably something only I can understand, and, if I truly understand it

Rolly Kent
(May 1976)

myself, that happens just during the actual writing....I have lived in three places: New Jersey, where I grew up; Vermont, and Arizona. The places I have gotten to know and in which I have gotten to know a little about myself, are within the regions of these three places.... Writing is a way I take toward myself, toward my life as a thing that moves. Much of my work results from a sudden recognition, perhaps after years of inattention to a particular memory or quality of place and feeling, that certain events and perceptions were overlooked by ignorance. The writing of a poem is a way to realign myself, a way to take away from Time certain experiences and put them through one centralizing activity, writing. Actually, it's pretty simple: using certain techniques, I just pay attention.... Another life seems to exist alongside the ordinary one, and the more I write, the more developed this parallel life becomes. When I write, this additional life is rather like a guide, an adviser.... The poems themselves are the end of what amounts to a small articulation of one move I have noticed myself making. You could say the poems become reminders. Taken together, they are a set of directions."

KARL C. KOPP

BIRTH: 2/12/'34, Havre de Grace, Maryland, grew up in the western mountains of that state.

EDUCATION: Yale, B.A. ('55); M.A. ('60), and Ph.D. ('63), both in English at the U. of Calif., Berkeley.

CAREER: Kopp began his academic career during his Berkeley years ('59-'62) when he was employed as a Teaching Asst. in the Department of Speech; U. of Maine, Instr. & Asst. Prof. of English ('62-'66); American U. of Beirut, Asst. Prof. of English ('66-'69); Asst. Prof. of English, Pierce College, Athens, Greece ('69-'70); Kenyon C., Asst. Prof. of English ('70-'72). In '72, Kopp's career took a new direction through a decision he made at Kenyon to abandon the succession of teaching jobs that his Ph.D. would warrant and to combine writing and farming in the Ark. Ozarks with his second wife Jane C. Kopp, a poet herself, and their infant son Zachary, born 4/22/'72. Since that time he has devoted as much time as possible to writing poetry and to editing various anthologies of poetry and prose, and teaching when the need arises. He has also taught creative writing in '74-'75 as Poet-in-Residence at Arkansas Polytechnic College, Russellville, and from '75-'77, part-time, creative writing, at the U. of Albuquerque. In '77-'78, he also presented many readings throughout the western U.S.A. as one of the poets chosen for the Western States Arts Foundation Tour. Today, he lives with his wife Jane, who helps him with his editing and also teaches at the U. of New Mexico, and their son Zachary in Albuquerque; however, they still know an attachment for their former home in Batson, Arkansas, and visit in whenever possible. As Kopp notes of the Ozarks: "It's land very dear to me and almost identical in essence as well as in many superficial aspects, to my childhood stamping grounds in the mountains of Western Maryland," adding that living there was an experience of "tremendous value" to him and to his poetry, so much of which concerns his time there.

PUBLICATIONS: Tarot Poems ('74), *Yell County Machine Shop* ('76), *Yarbrough Mountain* ('77), and additionally, one chapbook, *beyond sleep beyond* ('72). His poems have been published extensively in magazines, including: *Poetry Now, Amotfa, Kaldron, Kuksu, Fiddlehead, Weid, Inscape, Dragonfly, Haiku Highlights, The Rufus, Yankee, The Smith, New, Nimrod, Descant, The Little Magazine, Ball St. U. Forum, Nitty-Gritty, The Gar, Quartet, New America, Bitterroot, New Mexico Magazine, Big Moon, Slough, South Dakota Review, Painted Bride Quarterly, Hyperion, San Marcos Review, Road-Apple Review,* Chariton Review, and *Wind.* Among the anthologies carrying his work are *Pushcart Press Anthology: Best of Small Presses: 1975* ('76), *Voices From the Rio Grande* ('76), and *The Indian Rio Grande* ('77).

EDITORIAL POSTS: As an editor, both of poetry and prose, Karl Kopp directs the publications of Red Earth Press. He has likewise been a co-ordinating editor of John Gill's *Anthology of the Regional Poetry of the U.S. and Canada* (Crossing Press, '77), and in '77 produced with his wife Jane and Bart Lanier Stafford III, a popular anthology of regional poetry and prose entitled *Southwest: A Contemporary Anthology.* The latter was published by his Red Earth Press, Albuquerque, and is now in its second printing; it has been praised by *Choice* and elsewhere, and is in use as a text at numerous universities, particularly those located in the Southwest. With Jane Kopp, a poet in her own right, Karl has additionally published various articles concerning Arkansas vineyards and wine-making. As an essayist, he has contributed a piece to *The Writer's Sense of Place,* edited by John R. Milton, as a special issue of *South Dakota Review* ('75), and to *The Smith,* among other periodicals. A short story of his has also appeared in *Maine Review* (June, '75).

OBSERVATIONS: About his own writing goals, Kopp has written elsewhere (*South Dakota Review,* Autumn, '75): "Know, most of all, the language. Listen to

Karl Kopp
(June 1975)

what they don't say, too. And catch, if you can, the hidden non-human language of the place itself. This is the real task. (Isn't this the aim of the artist anywhere? The point of our being on this planet at all?)" About Kopp's *Tarot Poems,* the poet Al Young has observed: "In my favorite particular selections, I find you in your highest form, full of soft intensity in a region where humor and wit (which normally don't go together) blend in such a natural, off-handed fashion as to make me want to laugh and, at the same time, hold back tears. Your voice, sophisticated and carefully well-tempered, is one of a kind." Bill Katz has praised Kopp's *Yarbrough Mountain* for *Library Journal* (12/15/'77) as: "Regional poetry at its moving best....Kopp's salute to Arkansas and its peoples."

MAXINE KUMIN

BIRTH: 6/6/'25, in Philadelphia, Pa., the daughter of Peter and Doll (Simon) Winokur.

EDUCATION: B.A. ('46) & M.A. ('48), both from Radcliffe College.

CAREER: She has been a lecturer and instructor in English at Tufts ('58-'61; '65-'68); a scholar at the Radcliffe Inst. for Independent Study ('61-'63), and a member of the faculty of the Bread Loaf Writers' Conference. Additionally Kumin has served as Lect. in English, Newton C. of the Sacred Heart, Mass.; Vist. Lect. in English at the U. of Mass., & Fannie Hurst Professor of Literature at Brandeis. During the spring of '75, she taught creative writing courses in the M.F.A. program of Columbia U., and in '76, she also served as Chairperson for the Lit. Program Adv. Panel for grants for the N.E.A. In the spring of '77, she was Visiting Professor at Princeton, and in the fall of that year traveled to Washington U., St. Louis, as Hurst Prof. of Literature. She married Victor M. Kumin in '46, and they have three children: Jane, Judith, and Daniel. The Kumins live on a farm in Warner, New Hampshire.

PUBLICATIONS: Halfway ('61), *The Privilege* ('65), *The Nightmare Factory* ('70), *Up Country* ('72), and *House, Bride, Fountain, Gate* ('75). As a novelist, Ms. Kumin has written *Through Dooms of Love* ('65), *The Passions of Uxport* ('68), *The*

Abduction ('71), and *The Designated Heir* ('74). She has also written many children's books, all published by Putnam except for the title noted. With the late Anne Sexton, she co-authored these four: *The Wizard's Tears* ('74). *Joey and the Birthday Present* ('71), *More Eggs of Things* (McGraw-Hill, '64), and *Eggs of Thing* ('63). Individual Kumin titles include *Sebastian and the Dragon* ('60), *Spring Things* ('61), *Summer Story* ('61), *Follow the Fall* ('61), *A Winter Friend* ('61), *Mittens in May* ('62), *No One Writes a Letter to a Snail* ('62), *Archibald the Traveling Poodle* ('63), *Speedy Digs Downside Up* ('64), *The Beach Before Breakfast* ('64), *Paul Bunyan* ('66), *Faraway Farm* (Norton, '67), *The Wonderful*

Maxine Kumin
(January 1975)

Babies of 1809 and Other Great Years ('68), *When Grandmother Was Young* ('69), *When Mother Was Young* ('70), and *When Great-grandmother Was Young* ('71).

HONORS: Lowell Mason Palmer Award from the Poetry Soc. of Am. ('60), a grant from the Nat. Council on the Arts & Humanities ('66), William Reedy Award ('68),Eunice Tietjins Memorial Prize ('72); Pulitzer Prize ('73) & member of the Arts Endowment Literature Advisory Panel ('74-'77).

OBSERVATIONS: Maxine Kumin has said of her poetry that "Marianne Moore's statement, 'We must be clear as our natural reticence allows us to be' marked her for life. I have tried always to do this, both in diction and in intent to the point of pain." John Ciardi has commented about her work in this way: "...She teaches me, by example, to use my own eyes. When she looks at something I have seen, she makes me see it better. When she looks at something I do not know, I therefore trust her."

PHILIP LEVINE
BIRTH: 1/10/'28, in Detroit, the son of Harry A. Levine, a businessman, grew up in that city.

EDUCATION: B.A. ('50) and M.A. ('54) from Wayne St. U., where he studied with John Berryman. In '57, he was awarded his M.F.A. degree from the U. of Iowa Workshop. He also attended Stanford U. on a fellowship in poetry in '57.

CAREER: While attending college, Levine worked at various factories in Detroit and learned much from rural southern industrial workers, both black and white, to whom he often expresses gratitude in his writings. His teaching career began in '55 at the U. of Iowa, where he taught until '57, joining the English faculty at Fresno St. C. two years later—an institution where he still teaches poetry writing.

He makes his home today in Fresno with his wife, a former film star Frances Artley, and their three sons: Mark, John, and Theodore Henri. The Levines have traveled in Europe and lived for two years in Spain. In '76, Philip spent the year writing poetry on a Creative Writing Fellowship from the N.E.A. Likewise in the summer of '76 he was one of six poets to travel over England giving poetry readings, and also

Philip Levine
(April 1972)

to conduct poetry workshops at the Fort Worden Writers' Conf., in Port Townsend, Wa., with Kenneth Rexroth for whose work Levine has always acknowledged deep admiration.

PUBLICATIONS: On the Edge ('63), *Silent in America* (chapbook, '65), *Not This Pig: Poems* ('68), *Five Detroits* ('70), *Thistles: A Poem Sequence* ('70), *Pili's Wall* ('71), *Red Dust* ('71), *They Feed They Lion* ('72), *1933: Poems* ('74), and *The Names of the Lost* ('76). Levine's poems have appeared in *Poetry, Hudson Review, New Yorker, New York Review of Books, Kayak, North American Review, Northwest Review, Encounter, Paris Review, Contact,* and *Harper's,* among other periodicals. Some of the anthologies including his work are *Midland, New Poets of England and America, Poet's Choice, American Poems, Contemporary American Poets, Naked Poetry, The Norton Anthology of Modern Poetry* ('73), and *Modern Poems: An Introduction to Poetry* ('73; '76). Besides writing poetry, Philip Levine has also edited, with Henri Coulette, *Character and Crisis* (McGraw Hill, '66).

HONORS: In addition to the fellowship awarded to him for the study of poetry from Stanford ('57), Levine has received many major prizes: Joseph Henry Jackson award from San Francisco Foundation ('61), a Chapelbook Award for poetry ('68), N.E.A. grant ('69, '70-refused, '76-'77), Frank O'Hara Prize from *Poetry* ('72), Nat. Inst. of Arts & Letters grant ('73), and Lenore Marshall Poetry Prize ('77).

OBSERVATIONS: Concerning the major themes in his work, Levine has characterized them as follows: "Major obsessions: Detroit, the dying of America, search for communion, admiration for cactus, pigs, thistles, thorny people who refuse to die." Lucien Stryk writes about Philip Levine's poetry in this way: "In recent years, Philip Levine has travelled, particularly in Spain, and what is most striking about the poems that have come of that experience is that they display the same toughness with self, and, when called for, an equal degree of compassion for others. Whether in Fresno or Barcelona, the poet is never much less than fully human and one finds oneself admiring the man as much as the poet. On the evidence of work done in the last few years he is a poet who is not likely to stop growing."

JOHN (BURTON) LOGAN

BIRTH: 1/23/'23, in Red Oak, Iowa, where he attended public schools and grew up.

EDUCATION: B.A. in Zoology, Coe College, Cedar Rapids ('43); M.A. in English, U. of Iowa ('49); post-graduate study at Georgetown U., Washington, D.C. Logan now recalls that such teachers as Austin Warren impressed him in English Literature classes and Catesby Taliaferro in his study of philosophy. The discovery of Ranier Maria Rilke's work led him into an active study of poetry.

CAREER: He began his career as a teacher in '47, when he served as Tutor until '51 at St. John's C., Annapolis, Maryland. He continued it as Prof. of General Program, Notre Dame U. ('51-'63); Visiting Prof. of English, U. of Wash. ('65), Visiting Prof. of English, San Francisco State U. ('65-'66), and since '66, except for the year '76, at the U. of Hawaii, when he again served as Visiting Prof. of English, he has been on the Fac. of English at SUNY, Buffalo.

EDITORIAL POSTS: Founder and for years editor of *Choice*, a magazine of poetry and photography, he has also served as poetry editor for two other magazines—*The Nation* and *Critic*. Married and the father of nine children, he lives today in Buffalo, New York. With his son John Logan, Jr., who teaches guitar at the U. of Wyo., he occasionally gives readings of his poetry while his son either presents musical accompaniment or else his own songs; however Logan as a reader of his own poetry is much in demand for solo appearances, too, and frequently presents readings throughout the United States.

PUBLICATIONS: Cycle for Mother Cabrini ('55), *Ghosts of the Heart* ('60), *Spring of the Thief* ('63), *The Zig-Zag Walk* ('69), *The Anonymous Lover* ('73), and *Poems in Progress* ('76). His poems have also appeared in a variety of publications too numerous to list, but include such periodicals as *Poetry, Sewanee Review*, and *Minnesota Review*. Represented in more than forty anthologies, he has contributed

John Logan
(May 1976)

poems to such titles as the following: *New Poets of England and America* ('62), *Contemporary American Poetry* ('62), *Erotic Poetry* ('63), *American Poetry* ('64), *A Book of Love Poems* ('65), *New Modern Poetry* ('67), *Contemporary American Poets* ('69), & *Contemporary Poetry in America* ('73). Logan's novella, *The House That Jack Built*, actually a book of his childhood reminiscences, was published in

'74, and he has had fiction published in such magazines as *The New Yorker, Kenyon Review, The Critic, Sewanee Review,* and *Epoch.* As a critic, Logan has also contributed numerous discerning essays on various contemporary and nineteenth-century poets and novelists, including these: "Dylan Thomas and The Ark of Art," *Renascence* (Milwaukee, '60), "The Organ Grinders and the Cockatoo: Poetry of e.e. cummings," *Critic* (Chicago, '61), and "Psychological Motifs in Melville's *Pierre*," *Minnesota Review* (St. Paul, '67).

HONORS: Rockefeller Foundation grant ('68), Miles Modern Poetry Award ('67), two Indiana School of Letters Fellowships ('68; '69), and Morton Dauen Zabel Award of the National Inst. of Arts and Letters ('73).

OBSERVATIONS: John Logan has commented upon his philosophy behind his own work in this way: "I think of poetry as a reaching, an anonymous loving, which occasionally becomes personal where there are those present who care to listen. I began using stresses, in my first book, moved to syllabic writing in my second and third books, invented the thirteen syllable line for my "Monologues of the Son of Saul" in my third book and then moved toward a form which adapts slant rhyme to free verse couplets and triplets, which I used for my fourth book....Stories of the lives of poets (Southwell, Heine, Rimbaud, Keats, Cummings, Crane) are important sources. So are stories from the Old Testament." James Dickey has observed about John Logan's poetry these thoughts: "One closes Logan's books...thinking: 'Yes, this is what poetry can sometimes do; this is what it can sometimes be.' "

ARCHIBALD MacLEISH

BIRTH: 5/7/1892, in the village of Glencoe, Ill., son of Andrew and Martha Hillard MacLeish. Andrew MacLeish, born in Scotland in 1838, was a Chicago business man, an active (Baptist) churchman and one of the founders of the second (present) University of Chicago of which he was a trustee for many years. Martha Hillard was the daughter of a Connecticut Congregational minister and the descendant of generations of seamen and sea-captains out of New England ports. She graduated from Vassar in one of the early classes, taught there for several years and became the President of what is now Rockford College in her middle twenties.

EDUCATION: MacLeish attended public school in the village of Glencoe, New Trier High School, Hotchkiss School, and graduated with an A.B. from Yale in 1915. He entered Harvard Law School that fall, enlisted, after the American declaration of War, in the spring of 1917, served in the field artillery in France as lieutenant and captain and returned to the Law School early in 1919, graduating with his LL.B. *cum laude* in the fall of that year in a special class for service men.

CAREER & PUBLICATIONS: He then taught Constitutional Law at Harvard College and practiced law in a Boston office while finishing his second book of verse (the first having been published in 1917 while he was overseas). In '23, he left the law and went to Paris with his wife, the former Ada Hitchcock, who was a singer, and two small children, Kenneth and Mary Hillard, to devote himself entirely to writing. The family remained in Paris, where *Streets in the Moon, The Hamlet of A. MacLeish, Einstein* and *New Found Land* were written and where *Conquistador* was begun, for five years. In '28, they settled in Conway Mass., where they had bought a farm and where their second son, William, was born, but with the onset of the Great Depression, MacLeish was forced to look for a job which would support his family and found one with Henry Luce who was starting a new magazine to be called *Fortune* and who made terms which would enable MacLeish to work long enough in a day one year to pay his bills and then to go back to his own writing. This unusual arrangement was continued for nine years during which period *Conquistador* was finished and published to win the Pulitzer prize for the year '32. Also the *Frescoes for Mr. Rockefeller's City*; the verse play *Panic* which ran for three nights on Broadway in '35; a new book of poems called *Public Speech*; a collection of poems from '24 to '33; *The Land of the Free*; a book of photographs of the Depression "illustrated by a poem"; and two verse plays for radio, *The Fall of the City* and *Air Raid*, broadcast by C.B.S. in '37 and '38. (These were the first of a number of verse plays for radio: *The Trojan Horse* ('52), *This Music Crept By Me Upon the Waters*, '53, were others.) In '38 MacLeish resigned from *Fortune* and returned to Harvard to start the Nieman Foundation in journalism. The following year he was asked by President Roosevelt to become Librarian of Congress, a position which he first refused and later accepted, serving from '39 to '44 and, for part of that time, from '41 to '42, serving also as Director of the Office of Facts and Figures, the first war-time information agency. In '44 President Roosevelt appointed him Assistant Secretary of State, as post he resigned on Mr. Roosevelt's death in '45. Thereafter President Truman appointed MacLeish Chairman of the U.S. Delegation to the London U.N. Conference to establish an educational and cultural organizaton (UNESCO). He served as the first American member of the UNESCO board and as Chairman of the American delegation to UNESCO's first general conference in Paris. During the years of the War, MacLeish wrote only a few poems—*The Young Dead Soldiers* and *America Was Promises*. Once back in

Archibald MacLeish
(November 1965)

civilian life he began a poem (*Act Five*) which attempted to draw together his experiences of that period in an image (image-in-action) of the human situation in the century of two world wars and the Great Depression. The poem was published in '48 but was not reviewed. A second collection of poems, published in '52, received the Pulitzer Prize, MacLeish's second. Meantime he had been offered the Boylston Chair of "Rhetoric and Oratory" (in practise, Poetry) at Harvard which he accepted and held for thirteen years. During his incumbency he wrote two new books of verse, *Songs for Eve*, ('54) and *The Wild Old Wicked Man* as well as the verse play, JB, which won the Pulitzer Prize in Drama and ran on Broadway for close to a year and, outside New York, (including outside the U.S.) for many years thereafter.

MacLeish retired from Harvard at age 70 in '62, since which time he has lived on the farm at Conway which has been the family home over the past fifty years. Since his term at Harvard he has written a verse play for the stage, *Herakles*, which was produced at Ann Arbor, Michigan; a prose play (*Scratch*) which played for a number of weeks in Boston but lasted only a few days in New York, and a verse play for radio (*The Great American Fourth of July Parade*) which was presented in '76 as a stage play in Pittsburgh, and, country-wide as a radio play, by Earplay. His one serious motion picture experiment was *The Eleanor Roosevelt Story*, released in '65 which won the Academy Award that year in the documentary classification. He made also, one trial of ballet, *Union Pacific* ('34), with music by Nicholas Nabakov which was performed by the Monte Carlo Ballet Russe first in Philadelphia and thereafter in the principal American cities and abroad—with no remuneration to the composer or the poet. A prolific prose writer as well as a poet and playwright, MacLeish has also produced numerous long books, pamphlets, and shorter prose works. These offerings include two works of literary criticism—*Poetry and Opinion: The Pisan Cantos of Ezra Pound* ('50), *Poetry and Experience* ('65), *Libraries in Contemporary Crisis* ('39), *Deposit of the Magna Carta in the Library of Congress on November 28, 1939* ('39), *The American Experience* ('39), *The Irresponsibles* ('40), *The Next Harvard* ('41), *A Time to Speak* ('41), *The Free Company Presents....*('41), *The Duty of Freedom* ('41), *The American Cause* ('41), *Report to the Nation* ('42), *In Honor of a Man and an Ideal: Three Talks on Freedom by Archibald MacLeish, William S. Paley, and Edward R. Murrow* ('42), *American Opinion and the War* ('42), *A Time to Act* ('43), *The American Story: Ten Broadcasts* ('44, '60), *Freedom is the Right to Choose* ('51), *Poetry and Journalism* ('58), *The Dialogues of Archibald MacLeish and Mark Van Doren* (ed. by Warren V. Bush, '64), and *A Continuing Journey* ('68). In addition to these works, he has contributed forewords and introductions to the following books: Felix Frankfurther's *Law and Politics: Occasional Papers, 1913-38*, ed. by MacLeish and E.F. Prichard; William Meredith's *Love Letters from an Impossible Land;* Gerald Fitzgerald's *The Worldless Flesh*. Finally, he has also edited and introduced in a limited, privately published edition, the story of his mother, *Martha Hillard MacLeish: 1856-1947*. His poems have appeared in periodicals too numerous for mention here. Likewise they have been widely anthologized, a partial list of the collections being these: *Poetry of Flight* ('41), *Chief Modern Poets of England and America* ('43), *New Poetry* ('47), *Modern American Poetry* ('50), *Oxford Book of American Poetry* ('50), *Seven Centuries of Verse* ('57), *How Does a Poem Mean?* ('59), *American Poetry* ('60), *Poet's Choice* ('62), *Modern Poets* ('63), *American Lyric Poems* ('64), *Modern Religious Poems* ('64), *American Poetry* ('65), *Poems and Poets* ('65), *Poems on Poetry* ('65), *This Land of Mine* ('65), *The Norton Anthology of Modern Poetry* ('73), and *Modern Poems: An Introduction* ('73, '76).

HONORS: In addition to the various awards mentioned above, Mr. MacLeish's numerous honors also include the following: Shelley Memorial Award for poetry ('32), Golden Rose Trophy of New England Poetry Club ('34), Levinson Prize ('41), Bollingen Prize ('52), Nat. Book Award in poetry ('53), Sara Josepha Hale Award ('58), Chicago Poetry Day Poet ('58), Antoinette Perry Award in Drama ('58), member of the Am. Acad. of Arts & Letters (Pres., '53-'56), Commander, El Sol del Peru; Legion d'Honneur (Officier), France; The Presidential Medal of Freedom ('77); and these honorary degrees conferred upon him from numerous American and Canadian universities and colleges: Tufts ('32), Colby College ('38), Wesleyan ('38), Yale ('39), Dartmouth ('40), Johns Hopkins U. ('41), Williams C. ('42), U. of

Calif., Berkeley ('43), U. of Ill., Urbana ('46), U. of Wash. ('48), Queen's U., Kingston, Ontario ('48), Columbia ('54), Harvard ('55), Carleton C. ('56), and Princeton ('67). *Pembroke* Magazine has honored Archibald MacLeish in their Bicentennial Issue #7 ('76) with tributes from poets and scholars and essayists in '76 concerning his countless contributions, as have numerous nationwide television programs during the two-hundredth anniversary of the nation.

OBSERVATIONS: In '76, Louis Untermeyer characterized Archibald MacLeish's contribution to poetry in this way for *Pembroke #7:* "Biographers may argue about MacLeish's place as a public figure, but there is little doubt concerning his vitality—and viability—as a poet. As poet, he is concededly a superb craftsman, but he uses craft for more than a display of technique. A virtuoso in a great variety of musical effects—pure rhyme, slant-rhyme, assonance, dissonance—the repercussions emphasize the intention as well as the intensity of his communication....Critics may rationalize their reactions to the variety of MacLeish's contribution. But no matter how widely readers may differ in taste and temperament, they cannot help but recognize the imaginative power of this poetry and respond to it with the caught breath and the quickened pulse." About his poetry, MacLeish observed in '76 in an interview with Stanley Koehler: "I think it is perhaps possible that I have written my way through to a position in which I am—quoting you [Koehler] 'left free.' Left free, that is, to believe. Free to be a happy man although more and more aware of death—I'm close enough to it now so that I can *feel* its presence—but I'm not afraid of it. It doesn't obsess me. And I dare to *say* I'm happy knowing that (snapping fingers) the next moment those iron footsteps on the stair that Cavafy talks about may get me. I know that; but I dare to say so because I really don't care whether they get me or not. What I feel is that I've had my say. It may not be much of a say. I know what it'll dwindle away to: a few poems left somewhere."

CAROLYN (ANNE) MAISEL

BIRTH: 9/20/'42, in Hattiesburg, Miss., grew up in Groves, Texas, a small town outside Port Arthur.

Carolyn Maisel
(June 1975)

EDUCATION: From '60 to '62, and again in the fall of '63, she attended the U. of Tex., Austin. In '62-'63, she attended Lamar U. in Beaumont, Tex. During those years, she majored in government, with a view toward the law. She married Robert Maisel in '64 and they lived in Saudi Arabia and Spain, while traveling in Germany,

Lebanon and France. In Madrid, she attended the American summer course at the U. of Madrid. Her only child, Valerie, was born shortly after they returned to the U.S. in late '65, and they moved to Iowa City, Iowa. Robert Maisel died in '68, shortly after Carolyn resumed course-work at the U. of Iowa. She had done some writing during the intervening years. Fortunately, she came in contact with the Iowa Writers' Workshop, and this decided her upon a professional writing career. She studied with George Starbuck, Marvin Bell, Barry Goldensohn, Donald Justice and others. The staff, in particular, helped her through several difficult years. Although her style does not reflect any particular influence, she notes that she remains indebted to the Workshop for its creative and supportive environment. She received a B.A. in English and Creative Writing ('69), and an M.F.A. from the Iowa Workshop ('71).

CAREER: During her years in Graduate School, she taught a number of literature courses at the U. of Iowa and at Coe College in Cedar Rapids, Iowa. In '69, she met John Benvenuto, a painter and photographer, and they have been together since, moving to Albuquerque, N.M. in '72. She has worked at various jobs since leaving school, including the N.M. Poetry-in-the-Schools Program. She has also taught Science Fiction in the U. of N.M. Community College, and poetry writing in the UNM Free University (Amistad). She has done recent study in Russian literature, including a trip to the USSR and satellites in the summer of '74. With another woman, she has established a Poetry-Arts workshop for delinquent youth at the State Training School in Albuquerque.

EDITORIAL POSTS: Maisel is also the Associate Editor of *Best Friends*, a women's poetry magazine which has been the recipient of several CCLM grants.

PUBLICATIONS: She is the author of *Witnessing*, a book published in '77 by L'Epervier Press. Additionally her poems have been published in *The New Yorker, North American Review, Choice, Hellcoal Annual, Cafe Solo, The Texas Quarterly* and elsewhere. She has also been anthologized in *I Had Been Hungry All the Years: An Anthology of Women's Poetry* (Solo Press), *The New Breed* (Prickly Pear Press), *I Hear My Sisters Saying* (Crowell), *Intro II* (Bantam), *Voices from the Rio Grande, The Indian Rio Grande,* and *Southwest.* A photographer also, she has had two one-woman shows in Iowa City—the first in '68 at the Civic Center and another in '69 at the Unicorn Gallery.

OBSERVATIONS: About Maisel's poetry, Glenna Luschei and Del Marie Rogers have written: "The work of Carolyn Maisel [has] a high level of language-tension, [which she] is able to reach out and sustain: it is as if [she]...tries to push language as far as it will go, to wring the neck of language in order to reveal reality."

HOWARD McCORD

BIRTH: 11/3/'32, in El Paso, Tex., the son of Frank Edward and Sylvia Joy (Coe) McCord grew up there and in southern New Mexico. At eighteen, in '51, he joined the U.S. Navy, in which he remained until '53.

EDUCATION: After his discharge, he drove the Santa Clara Co., Calif. bookmobile for a year, and then returned to El Paso and attended the U. of Texas at El Paso (B.A., '57); M.A. ('60), U. of Utah on a Woodrow Wilson Fellowship, '57-'58).

CAREER: In the fall of '60, he began his teaching career at Wash. St. U., Pullman, where as an Asst. Prof. of English & Humanities, he offered creative writing classes, as well as courses in mythology, Asian civilizations and esthetics. In '73, he moved to Ohio and became affiliated with the Bowling Green State U.;

that same year he used a Research Associateship from the same institution to travel in the highland deserts of Iceland and backpack in Lapland, gathering material for his *The Arctic Desert* ('75). Deserts, mountains, and wilderness areas figure strongly in his work, and earlier, he has also traveled extensively in India and Nepal ('65) on a Fulbright grant, a time when he also studied at the U. of Mysore. He has likewise visited Thailand, Japan, Greece, Great Britain, Canada, and Mexico, and additionally he enjoys exploring his native Southwest. In the summer of '75, he taught at the Navajo Community College in Tsaile, Az., and in '71, when the U. of N.M. named him D.H. Lawrence Fellow, he and his family lived that summer at the Lawrence Ranch, north of Taos. In '76, he served as Visiting Prof. at Calif. State U., Northridge. Since '77, he has been Director of the Creative Writing (M.F.A) Program and Professor of English at Bowling Green State University, Ohio. McCord has read his poetry at The Poetry Center in New York City, on radio, and television, and at more than one hundred universities in twenty states. He is married to the former Jennifer Revis, a poet; they are the parents of four children, the youngest of which was born in Feb. '78. McCord's two sons, Colman and Robert, are by his first marriage.

EDITORIAL POSTS: As an editor of poetry magazines, Howard McCord has been closely affiliated with various periodicals, in particular with *Measure*, which he founded with Donald H. Ross at Wash. St. U. in '71 and produces today in Bowling Green. He is also the founder and editor of Tribal Press ('64). In these capacities, McCord has long been interested in the problems of small press publication in the U.S.A., and is currently the Secretary of the Executive Committee of the Co-ordinating Council of Literary Magazines, which he has served since '71.

Howard McCord
(June 1975)

PUBLICATIONS: His books and pamphlets of poetry include these titles: *Precise Fragments* ('63), *Twelve Bones* ('64), *The Spanish Dark and Other Poems* ('65), *Fables and Transfigurations* ('67), *The Fire Visions* ('68), *Longjaunes His Periplus* ('68), *Ovens: Poems Against the War & Tyranny* ('71), *Maps: Poems Toward an Iconography of the West* ('71), *The Diary of a Young Girl* ('72), *Mirrors* ('73), *Friend* ('74), *Selected Poems: 1955-'71* ('75), *The Old Beast* ('75), *Perfecting an Unspeakable Act* ('75), *Hardtack and Chilled Whisky: Poems and Narratives, 1972-1977* ('78), and *Peach Mountain Smoke Out*, a long poem-pamphlet ('78). Numerous periodicals have featured McCord's poetry: *Penny Dreadful, Measure,*

Kayak, Trace, New York Times, Arena, Bitter-Root, Inland, Miscellaneous Man, New Helios, Old Palace, and *Espacio.* A few of the anthologies featuring it are Paul Carroll's *The Young American Poets* ('68), Walter Lowenfels' *Drum Book: The Poems of Seven Poets* ('67), *Poets of Today* ('64), and the annual *Great Ideas Today* (Encyclopedia Britannica, '64). Additionally, with Walter Lowenfels, he is the author of *The Life of Fraenkel's Death* ('70), which is a study of Michael Fraenkel and Haniel Long. His novella, *The Artic Desert,* appeared in '75, and he is the author of four short stories published in such magazines as *Arena, Western Humanities Review,* and *The Goodly Co.* More than a dozen of his articles appear in selected magazines, *Lillabulero,* among others. Others of his writings include the pamphlets, *Gnomonology: A Handbook of Systems* ('71), and *Some Notes to Gary Snyder's "Myths & Texts"* ('71).

HONORS: In addition to the awards previously mentioned, McCord has been a Danforth Assoc. ('68), an E.O. Holland Summer Fac. Fellow at Wash. St. U. ('67), and has been awarded the Washington St. Governor's Writers' Day Award ('68) as well as an N.E.A. Fellowship ('76). In '76, he was named Chairman of the Division of Poetry, Modern Languages Assoc., and in '77, he was appointed to the Literature Advisory Panels of both the N.E.A. and the Ohio Arts Council.

OBSERVATIONS: Early in his writing career, McCord explained of his work: "I have flowered into the geography of the land: it is the major source of my identity, the myths I inhabit."

SANDRA McPHERSON

BIRTH: 8/2/'43, in San Jose, Calif., grew up in the same region, the daughter of Walter James and Frances (Gibson) McPherson. Her father was a college physical education professor.

EDUCATION: Westmont C. ('61-'63), San Jose St. (B.A., '65), graduate study at the U. of Wash., Seattle ('65-'66).

CAREER: In '66, she worked for a time as a technical writer for Honeywell, Inc. in Seattle, and then married on 7/22/'66, Henry D. Carlile, a university English professor and poet (*The Rough-Hewn Table,* '71). They have a daughter Phoebe.

Sandra McPherson
(March 1973)

Sandra has presented many readings at universities and schools across the nation. During the years '74-'76, she taught creative writing courses as a faculty member at the U. of Iowa Writers' Workshop.

PUBLICATIONS: Elegies for the Hot Season (*'70), Radiation* ('73), and *The Year of Our Birth* ('78). Poems of hers have appeared in various anthologies, a partial listing being: *Borestone Mountain Poetry Awards* ('68 & '75), *Rising Tides* ('73), and *American Poetry Anthology* ('75). Among the periodicals carrying her poetry are these: *The Nation, Poetry, New Yorker, New Republic, Poetry Northwest, Field, The Iowa Review, Ironwood, Antaeus, & American Review.*

EDITORIAL POSTS: Besides writing poetry, she has edited issues of *Poetry Northwest* and *The Iowa Review.*

HONORS: Her *Elegies for the Hot Season* was one of the first three books of verse chosen for the Nat. Council on the Arts program to aid university presses in '70; Helen Bullis Prize of *Poetry Northwest* ('68); Bess Hokin Prize from *Poetry* ('72), the recipient ('72) of a grant from the Ingram-Merrill Foundation, N.E.A. grant ('74), Blumenthal-Leviton-Blonder Prize from *Poetry* ('75), and Guggenheim Fellowship ('76).

OBSERVATIONS: Jonathan Galassi has noted of Ms. McPherson's first book: "...This talented young poet employs a verdant opalescent vocabulary which moves in all directions at once, in an extravagence of language, which may be at times a little too extravagent, but which is normally faultlessly rhythmic....She writes about moving and gardening and pregnancy and the death of friends with a splendid immediacy and a sense of irony that becomes more and more engaging the further one reads."

WILLIAM MEREDITH

BIRTH: 1/9/'19, in N.Y.C., the son of William Morris Meredith, grew up with his sister and attended secondary schools in Conn. & Mass., one of which was the Lenox School, in the latter state, from which he received his high school diploma.

EDUCATION: B.A., *magna cum laude*, Princeton ('40) and also further study at Princeton ('47-'48).

CAREER: His first job was as copy-boy and reporter for the *New York Times* ('40-'41). In '41, he joined the U.S. Army, spending one year in it, and then became a Naval Aviator ('42-'46); during the Korean campaign, he returned to the Navy for another two years ('52-'54). He began his teaching career at Princeton, where he was successively a Woodrow Wilson Fellow ('46-'47), a Resident Fellow in Creative Writing, serving as assistant to the critic and poet R.P. Blackmur ('47-'48), and an Inst. of English ('49-'50). In '50-'51, he spent a year as Asst. Prof. of English at the U. of Hawaii, Honolulu. Since '55, except for leaves-of-absence or invitations as visiting poet-in-residence to other universities, i.e. at Princeton ('65-'66), and Carnegie-Mellon U. ('72), he has taught at Conn. College, where since '65, he has been Prof. of English. Likewise from '58-'77, he has also been frequently on the staff of the Breadloaf Writers' Conference.

EDITORIAL POSTS: From '55-'56, Meredith was opera critic for the *Hudson Review*. Additionally since '64, he has been a Chancellor of the Academy of Am. Poets, and since '68, a member of the Amer. Acad. and Inst. of Arts and Letters. Today he makes his home in a re-modeled barn overlooking the Thames in Uncasville, Conn. As a popular judge for many prestigious poetry awards, he served from '76-'77, and is presently Chairman of the N.E.A. Literary Advisory Panel. Earlier, from '63-'65, he was a member of the Conn. Com. of the Arts, and from '64-'68, was additionally Dir. of Humanities, for the Upward Bound Program.

PUBLICATIONS: Love Letter from an Impossible Land ('44), *Ships and Other Figures* ('48), *The Open Sea and Other Poems* ('58), *The Wreck of the Thresher and*

William Meredith
(March 1970)

Other Poems ('64), *Earth Walk: New and Selected Poems* ('70), and *Hazard: The Painter* ('75). Since '44, he has contributed frequently to *Hudson Review, New Yorker, Poetry,* and other periodicals. Some of the numerous anthologies carrying his work are these: *New Poets of England and America* ('57), *Silver Treasury of Light Verse* ('57), *Modern Verse in English* ('58), *Understanding Poetry* ('60), *Poet's Choice* ('62), *Poems on Poetry* ('65), *Contemporary Poetry in America* ('73), and *The Norton Anthology of Modern Poetry* ('73). Additionally William Meredith is an editor and translator of the works of other poets: his annotated edition of *Shelley* was issued by Dell in '62; his translation of Guillaume Apollinaire's *Alcools: Poems 1898-1933* ('64); and two other editions of his anthologies, *University and College Poetry Prizes, 1960-66,* and *Eighteenth Century Minor Poets,* with Mackie L. Jarrell, have appeared respectively in '66 and '68. Further, Meredith is also the author of the libretto for an opera entitled *The Bottle Imp* ('58), whose music was composed by Peter Whiton, and produced in Wilton, Conn. in '58.

PUBLICATIONS: Beginning with winning the Yale Series' Younger Poets' Award in '43, for his first book, *Love Letter From an Impossible Land,* which was introduced by Archibald MacLeish, Meredith has won numerous other awards and fellowships: the Harriet Monroe Memorial Award ('44), Oscar Blumenthal Prize ('53), the *Hudson Review* Fellowship in Poetry ('56), Nat. Inst. of Arts & Letters' grant ('58), the Russell Loines Prize of the Nat. Inst. of Arts and Letters ('66), the Van Wyck Brooks award ('71), an N.E.A. grant ('72-'73), a Guggenheim Fellowship ('75), and earlier in his career, two Rockefeller grants, one in poetry ('68-'69), and the other in criticism ('48-'49). In '60-'61, he also received a grant from the Ford Foundation for the purpose of studying opera, as a result of his *The Bottle Imp,* the libretto noted above, which is based on a story by Robert Louis Stevenson. In '62, he was one of thirty-one poets asked by John F. Kennedy to read at the Nat. Poetry Festival in Washington, D.C.

OBSERVATIONS: William Meredith has noted: "The voice and strategy of poetry change in a very short span of time and the only ones that can be used by students are the ones of their own time." About his work, Robert Lowell has said that Meredith is "an expert writer, who knows how to make his meters and sentences accomplish hard labors." According to Lowell, his "lines have a lovely voice" and "his intelligent poems, unlike most poems, have a character behind them, one that is solitary, gray, dignified."

CAROL (S.) MERRILL

BIRTH: 10/9/'46, in Tulsa, Okla., grew up and attended schools there.

EDUCATION: In '71, she received her B.A. from the U. of Tulsa, and then moved to Albuquerque to study at the U. of N.M., where she pursued an M.A. in English.

EDITORIAL POSTS: Besides serving as one of the editors of the U. of N.M's literary magazine, *New America*, she, in '75, launched a magazine-project called *Southwest Women's Poetry Exchange*, now in its eighth issue, in which an exchange of one to six of a poet's favorite works are circulated among a growing group of poets who wish to read each other's work. Membership in the organization is not limited simply to women; men may and do contribute too. "Poets need not be

Carol Merrill
(June 1975)

from the Southwest either," Carol says. They may be "traveling through or living halfway around the world." Carol plans for a newsletter to grow out of this exchange. Meanwhile she works very actively with Albuquerque groups of poets organizing readings and workshops, and in '78, presented her first major reading in her native Tulsa for the Living Arts Group.

CAREER: Besides writing poetry and being a student, Ms. Merrill has also worked as a waitress, cook, secretary, and cattlehand.

PUBLICATIONS: With Susan Kilgore and Julie Ryner, she is the author of *Early Light* (Albuquerque, '76). Her poems appear in such periodicals as *Nimrod, Oil of Dog, New America, Best Friends,* and elsewhere. She also has work anthologized in *The Indian Rio Grande* ('77), ed. by Frumkin & Noyes, and in *Southwest: A Contemporary Anthology* ('77), ed. by Kopp, Kopp, & Stafford. Additionally her essay, "Impressionism in Kate Chopin's *"The Awakening"* appears in the Dec. '77 issue of *New America*.

HONORS: In '76, she shared with Joy Harjo the Prize for Poetry at the U. of N.M. offered by the Academy of American Poets.

OBSERVATIONS: Although Carol Merrill has actually been writing poetry since '66, she has decided not to publish much of her beginner's work because she feels her "voice is still changing." However for the past ten years, she has kept a journal "full of dreams, wishes, secrets, and details," which she relies upon now more and more heavily as she begins to produce and publish more of her poems.

(JOHN) CHRISTOPHER MIDDLETON

BIRTH: 6/10/'26, son of Hubert Stanley and Dorothy (Miller) Middleton, in

Truro, Cornwall, England, where his father was cathedral organist.

EDUCATION: Education at Felsted School (Essex, but evacuated to Herefordshire during wartime), and subsequently Merton College, Oxford (B.A., '51; D. Phil., '54).

CAREER: Middleton served in the Royal Air Force, '44-'48, in Germany '45-'46 and '47-'48. After studies at Oxford he taught at the University of Zürich, '52-'55, and in '55 obtained a teaching position at King's College, University of London (until '65). First he came to the University of Texas at Austin as Vist. Assoc. Prof. ('61-'62). Since '66, when he returned to Austin, he has held his present post as Prof. of Germanic Languages there (plus Comp. Lit. since '71). He has traveled widely in Europe, especially in France, and has three children, by his marriage to Mary Freer ('53; divorced '69).

PUBLICATIONS: Two very early books (London, Fortune Press, '44, '45), now repudiated. *Torse 3, Poems 1949-61* ('62); *Nonsequences/Selfpoems* (London/N.Y., '65); *Our Flowers & Nice Bones* (London/N.Y., '69); *The Lonely Suppers of W.V. Balloon* (Carcanet Press, Manchester, and Godine, Boston, '75); and *Pataxanadu and Other Prose* (Carcanet '77). *The Lonely Suppers of W.V. Balloon* includes the 3 pamphlets, *The Fossil Fish* (Burning Deck, '70), *Briefcase History* (Burning Deck, '72), and *Fractions for Another Telemachus* (Sceptre Press, '74). German editions: *Der Taschenelefant* (Berlin, '69, graphics by C. Meckel), *Wie Wir Grossmutter Zum Markt Bringen* (Düsseldorf '70), *Curbaram/Kurzprosa* (Berlin, '77). His work appears in numerous anthologies, the best known being *Penguin Modern Poets, 4* ('63), and in most European languages, including Serbo-Croatian (Knjízevnost, 10,

Christopher Middleton
(August 1976)

Belgrad, '72). Well-known as a translator, especially from German, Middleton has published: Robert Walser, *The Walk and Other Stories* (London, '57); with others, *Primal Vision*, by Gottfried Benn ('60), *Poems and Verse Plays*, by Hugo von Hofmannsthal ('61); and with Michael Hamburger, *Modern German Poetry, 1910-60* ('62), *Selected Poems*, by Günter Grass ('66), and *Selected Poems*, by Paul Celan ('72); also (single-handed) *Selected Letters of Friedrich Nietzsche* ('69), Robert Walser, *Jakob Von Gunten* ('70); *The Quest for Christa T*, by Christa Wolf ('70); *Selected Poems of Friedrich Hölderlin and Eduard Mörike* ('72); Elias Canetti, *Kafka's Other Trial* ('74). He edited the Penguin *German Writing Today* ('67), and Georg Trakl, *Selected Poems* ('68), the latter with his own translations, as well as ones by Michael Hamburger, David Luke, and Robert Grenier. Middleton once also wrote a comic opera libretto, *The Metropolitans*, based on a Menander fragment, for the German composer Hans Vogt (Alkor Ed., '64), performed at Mannheim ('64).

HONORS: Sir Geoffrey Faber Memorial Prize, '64; grants from the National Translation Center, '66, '67,' 69; Guggenheim Poetry Fellow '74-'75; German Academic Exchange Artists' Program for Berlin '75 and '78. On Christopher Middleton, see David Miller, 'Developable Surfaces: The Poetries of C.M. and John Riley,' *Lugano Review*, 6, '75-'76, and Middleton's own statements in *Chicago Review*, 28, 4, Spring '77 ('The Pursuit of the Kingfisher'), and in *Poetry Nation Review*, 4, 3, '77 ('For Márton, Erwin, and Miklos'). *Spindrift*, 3 (March '78, from Paul Smith, University of Kent, England) is a special issue on Christopher Middleton.

JOHN (HERBERT) NEWLOVE

BIRTH: 6/13/'38, in Regina, Saskatchewan, Canada, the son of Thomas Harold and Mary Constant (Monteith) Newlove, was brought up in rural Saskatchewan towns, where his father was a lawyer.

EDUCATION: Attended schools in Saskatchewan, and also the university of the same province briefly.

CAREER: While he wrote his first book of poems, Newlove worked in various parts of Canada at odd jobs. In Saskatchewan, he taught school, was a reporter and a disc jockey. In Edmonton, he was a ditch-digger; in Montreal, a day laborer, and

John Newlove
(March 1965)

in Vancouver, a candy-maker and warehouseman. In August of '66, he married Susan Phillips, who is the mother of his two step-children, Jeremy Charles Gilbert and Tamsin Elizabeth Gilbert. At present, John Newlove and his family live in Toronto, where he is Writer-In-Residence at the Univ. of Toronto.

EDITORIAL POSTS: In Toronto, earlier, he also worked for several years as a Senior Ed. for McClelland & Stewart, Publishers.

PUBLICATIONS: Grave Sirs ('62), *Elephants Mothers and Others* ('63), *Moving in Alone* ('65 & new edition '77), *Notebook Pages* ('66), *What They Say* ('67), *Black Night Window* ('68), *The Cave* ('70), *Lies* ('72), *The Fat Man: Selected Poems: 1962-1972* ('77), and, with John Metcalf, *Dreams Surround Us* ('77). Newlove's poems have appeared in numerous Canadian periodicals and have also known inclusion in some U.S.A. magazines: *Delta, Poetry Northwest, Mountain, Blue Ointment, Evidence, Envoi, Island, Canadian Forum, Fiddlehead, Tish,* and

The Tamarask Review. A few of the various anthologies, which have carried his work are *Poetry '64* and *New American and Canadian Poetry* ('71). He has read his poems on the Canadian Broadcasting Company's recording entitled *Canadian Poets.* As an editor of poetry, he has published *Canadian Poetry: The Modern Era* ('77).

HONORS: For his poetry, John Newlove has been awarded a Koerner Foundation Award ('64), three Canadian Council Grants ('65, '67, & '77), and a Governor-General's Award ('73). About his writing, Robert Gillis notes: "Newlove is a lyric poet; emotion colours his experiences and the emotion for the most part is real and deep." Gillis points out that Newlove's work encompasses 'black irony, black comedy, black pathos and a black near despair." However Newlove carries "the sense of what's past and passing and the existential death, his own and others" through his poems, and "on the whole" remains "remarkably free from bitterness....Love is a primary value to him."

JOHN FREDERICK NIMS

BIRTH: 11/20/'13, in Muskegon, Mich., lived in that city until he entered high school in Chicago.

EDUCATION: De Paul & Notre Dame; B.A. from latter, '37; M.A., Notre Dame ('39), and Ph.D. in Comp. Lit. from U. of Chicago ('45), where he specialized in history and theory of tragedy in Greek, Latin, French and English literature. Especially did he emphasize the study of English drama of the sixteenth and seventeenth centuries in his work in this connection.

CAREER: Nims has traveled widely in Europe, particularly in Greece, France and Poland, and has lived for four years in Italy and Spain. Since '65, except for periods away as Visiting Prof. at various institutions, Nims has taught at the U. of Ill., Chicago campus. Currently he and his wife, the former Bonnie Larkin, whom he married in '47, live in Chicago. They are the parents of four children. Nims began his teaching career at Notre Dame, when from '39-'45, and again from '46-'58, he was a member of the faculty there, with the year '45-'46 spent at the U. of Toronto. For two years, '58-'60, he was Vist. Prof. at the U. of Madrid, and for two others ('52-'53) a Fulbright Lect. at Bocconi U. in Milan and at the U. of Florence, Italy ('53-'54). He has taught at the U. of Ill., Urbana ('61-'65), and has twice been a Vist. Prof. at Harvard ('64, and '68-'69), and a Vist. Prof., both at the U. of Fla. ('73-'75) and at Williams (Fall, '75). From '65-'69, he was a teacher of poetry on the Bread Loaf School of English, and previously he had also been on the staff of the Bread Loaf Writers' Conference in '58 and about a dozen years thereafter, as well as several other writers' conferences: Utah, Colorado, etc.

EDITORIAL POSTS: In addition to all these visiting professorial posts, Nims has also served as Assoc. Ed. of *Poetry* magazine from '45-'48, as Guest Ed. of the same periodical for the year '60-'61, and as Editor, beginning in January, '77.

PUBLICATIONS: Five Young American Poets, Third Series, with others ('44); *The Iron Pastoral* ('47), *A Fountain in Kentucky* ('50), *Knowledge of the Evening* ('60), & *Of Flesh and Bone* ('67). His poetry, as well as his critical articles, have appeared frequently in such periodicals as *Saturday Review, Harper's, New York Times Book Review, New World Writing, Poetry, Hudson Review, Kenyon Review, Atlantic, Sewanee Review, Partisan Review,* and elsewhere. Among the numerous anthologies carrying his poetry are these: *The Penguin Book of Modern Verse, Mid-Century American Poets* ('50), *Modern Verse in English* ('58), *How Does a Poem Mean?* ('59), *Poetry For Pleasure* ('60), *Poet's Choice* ('62), & *Contemporary*

John Frederick Nims
(April 1964)

Poetry in America ('73). As a translator, Nims is widely known for his distinguished translations of poetry from eight languages. His rendering of Euripides' *Andromache* appeared in '58 and has since been published in three different editions, including one released by the Modern Library. It was followed by his text and verse translation of *The Poems of St. John of the Cross* ('59; rev. '68). In addition, he published a collection of his translations entitled *Sappho to Valéry* ('71), and has edited Arthur Golding's sixteenth-century translation of Ovid's *Metamorphoses* ('65). Likewise he has edited with others, *The Poem Itself,* has contributed an essay on Sylvia Plath to *The Art of Sylvia Plath,* and more recently has produced his *Western Wind: An Introduction to Poetry* ('74).

HONORS: Guarantor's Prize ('43); Harriet Monroe Memorial Poetry Prize ('42); the Levinson Prize ('44); N.E.A. grant ('67-'68), Nat. Inst. of Arts & Letters Poetry Award ('68), & Brandeis U. Citation for Poetry ('75).

OBSERVATIONS: John Ciardi has said regarding Nims' poetry, "Nims is one of the current poets I take seriously, gratefully. His poetry has intellect, grace, and feeling. He is one of the really good ones, as I believe time will prove."

SUSAN NORTH

BIRTH: 2/19/'40, in Tucson, Ariz., continues to live in her birthplace with her son David, born in '65, and with the innumerable animals surrounding them.

EDUCATION: She attended Verde Valley School, but terminated a further pursuit of diplomas upon graduation from high school. As Susan has observed, she "resists institutions, incarceration and coercion with considerable experience."

CAREER: She is absorbed by her life in the desert outside of Tucson, where she "feeds coyotes, grows rye for the ducks, tomatoes for the raccoons, zucchini for the crickets. She raises dogs, rides her horse, talks to her son, writes when she needs to write, guards her solitude, reads, listens, looks."

PUBLICATIONS: Susan North's first collection of poetry, *All That Is Left,* was published by Desert First Works in '76. Additionally she has also published poems in various magazines including *Blue Moon News, Kayak, Ironwood, Mazagine, Cedar Rock, Pocket Pal, Greenfield Review, The Spirit That Moves Us, Hyperion,* & *Nitty-Gritty.*

OBSERVATIONS: Ms. North writes: "When someone asks me what I am trying to do in my work, I feel like riding at a gallop up the dry river bed, or taking a long shower, or climbing on the roof to watch the stars. The question is not one I can

Susan North
(May 1976)

answer with any degrèe of coherence. I want what everybody starts out wanting and the lucky ones don't lose: to live *my* life, as wholly and completely as I can, to live out the particular experience that is mine, whatever darkness, whatever light it entails. And the poems, of course, are crucial, are central, are *me* in a way that nothing else is. I am trying to stay alive, alive to the enormous wonder and mystery of the world in all of its minute manifestations, alive to the complexity of human relationships, aware of the intricate fabric of my own existence. The poems are one of the ways I do this; they are absolutely necessary for my survival. If any of my work has relevance for someone else, I am glad—(there are so many barriers, such high walls, so much essential isolation that any points of contact and understanding are blessings); if not, there is no less deliberation on my part to write as honestly and carefully as I am able. Which is what I have tried to do. That is the question and its incoherent answer." Jeff Carter has characterized the poetry in Susan North's first collection in this way: "Ms. North consistently taps (her theme's) power by always being in control of her material. She moves gracefully between the abstract...and the concrete...almost every poem in *All That Is Left* gives what really good poetry must give: a heightened, often painful, sense of being alive."

STEVEN (LESLIE) ORLEN
BIRTH: 1/13/'42, in Holyoke, Mass., grew up in the same area.
EDUCATION: B.A. (U. of Mass., '64); M.F.A., U. of Iowa ('67).
CAREER: For a time, while he was a student, Orlen worked as a tobacco picker, ambulance driver, proof-reader for the *Wall Street Journal,* bartender, waiter, and orderly in a mental hospital. He has also traveled in Europe and lived briefly in Paris and Amsterdam. Since '67, he has been on the faculty of the Department of English at the U. of Ariz., where he was first an Inst. and is presently an Asst. Prof. With his wife, Gail Marcus Orlen, who is a painter, he lives today in Tucson.
PUBLICATIONS: Sleeping on Doors (Penumbra Press, Lisbon, Iowa, '75), *Separate Creatures* (Ironwood Press, 77), & *Permission to Speak* (Wesleyan U. Press, '78). In addition to these collections of poetry, Orlen has published his poems in such magazines as *Poetry, The South Shore Review, Poetry Northwest, Blue Moon News, Ironwood, Field, Choice, American Review #14, Ohio Review, Iowa Review, & Mazagine.*
HONORS: His first poetry prize came in '67 when he won the Hallmark Poetry Contest. He is also the recipient of the George Dillon Memorial Prize from *Poetry;*

in '75, a grant from N.E.A.; a '76 winner in the Associated Writer's Contest, and in '77, a finalist for the Ellison Small Press Award.

Steve Orlen
(February 1976)

OBSERVATIONS: Steve Orlen has noted: "Good poems are a matter of work, compulsiveness, objectivity and love....Good poetry is not 'vague' emotions and making statements. It's solid words close together."

SIMON (JOSEPH) ORTIZ

BIRTH: 5/27/'41, at the Indian Hospital in Albuquerque, N.M., was raised for the most part of nineteen years on the Acoma Pueblo Indian Reservation in the village of McCartys, N.M. Acoma has been the home of all his Keresean ancestors and his mother's and father's birthplace as well. Simon grew up in the Pueblo Indian way of life of his village, and with, as he explains, "our language, customs, values, and the relationships shared among my kinfolk and members of our people." Except for several short periods of time, when his family lived in Ariz. and Calif. because his father worked for the Santa Fe railroad, Ortiz observes: "My life continued that way and I grew with it. That life has been the basis of all that I have done and continue with."

EDUCATION: His formal education consisted of McCartys Day School, St. Catherine's Indian School in Santa Fe, Albuquerque Indian School, and later Grants High School from which he graduated in '60, an athlete—a football player, and an honor student. In '61, he began college at Fort Lewis College in Durango, Colo., but dropped out the winter of '63. After serving in the U.S. Army, he continued his college education at the U. of N.M. for the period '66 through '68. During '68-'69, he was a Fellow in the International Writing Program at the U. of Iowa.

CAREER: In the winter of '63, he joined the U.S. Army and served in it for three years. He studied missile detecting in Air Defense School in El Paso, but wound up a pay clerk in the Finance Section. For the past ten years, Simon Ortiz has been a writer, but has earned his livng additionally at various jobs. In '69-'70, he worked at Rough Rock Dem. School in Rough Rock, Az., editing *Rough Rock News,* which explained the purpose of that Navajo Indian school and the Navajo community it served. Later, in '71-'73, he worked in public relations, again editing a newspaper, *Americans Before Columbus,* for the Nat. Indian Youth Council in Albuquerque. Since '74, Mr. Ortiz has also taught creative writing at various Universities and Institutes. During the Spring semester of '74, he taught at San Diego St. U., and in

81

the Fall of the same year at the Inst. of Am. Indian Arts in Santa Fe. During the summers of '74-'76, he taught at the Navajo Community College, and in '75 was the director of the Acoma Adult Community Education Program which offered various college and community level courses. He worked during the years '73-'76, with the Poets-In-The-Schools-Program in Ariz., Santa Fe, and in the St. Paul-Minn. area. Likewise in the past several years, he has also given lectures and poetry readings at numerous places throughout the U.S.A., including the following: U. of Calif. at San Diego, Pomona C., U. of Ariz., U. of N.M., U. of Neb., U. of Notre Dame, Colo. St. U., Ohio U., Kent St., New York St. U. at Buffalo, & Pima College. Most of his time presently, however, aside from various teaching and reading engagements, is taken up by his writing both his poetry and prose for literary magazines as well as in preparing books for publication. He lives in San Francisco while he teaches Native American Studies at the College of Marin in Kentfield, California. As often as possible, he visits with his parents in their Acoma village near San Fidel, N.M., and likewise with his daughter, Rainy Dawn, the child of a previous marriage to poet Joy Harjo. His son, Raho Nez, child of his first marriage to a talented Navajo Indian artist and educator, lives presently in Tucson, but returns often to the Navajo Reservation. In fact, Simon Ortiz usually observes that his main reason for writing is not only for himself, but also, for his parents, children, and his community of kinfolk. He has composed "horse songs" for his children.

Simon J. Ortiz
(May 1976)

PUBLICATIONS: In '76, Harper and Row published Ortiz's first major collection of poetry, *Going for the Rain*. His second, *A Good Journey*, appeared from Turtle Island Press ('77). However, he had published widely during the "seventies" and late "sixties" in numerous periodicals and anthologies, and his first chapbook of poetry, *Naked in the Wind*, had appeared as early as '70 by Quetzal-Vihio Press. Besides writing poetry, Ortiz also writes fiction. Blue Moon Press published a short story collection entitled *Howbah Indians* ('78), and Ortiz notes currently that his "major-on-going work continues to be a novel." Additionally he has published a children's book, *The People Shall Continue* ('77, Children's Book Press), and an essay booklet, *Song, Poetry and Language—Expression and Perception* ('77), released by the Navajo Community College. Among the many magazines carrying his poetry and fiction are these: *Pembroke, New Mexico Quarterly, Alcheringa, The Western Gate, Fervent Valley, Kuksu, South Dakota Review, Dakota Territory, New Mexico Magazine, Blue Moon News, The Greenfield Review, & Sun Tracks*.

Others of his works, both poetry and fiction, have been included in such major Indian anthologies of the late "sixties" and early "seventies" as the following: *Carriers of the Dream Wheel* ('75), ed. by Duane Niatum, *The Man to Send Rain Clouds*, ed. by Kenneth Rosen ('74), *New Voices from Wah'-Kon-Tah* ('74), ed. by Robert K. Dodge; *The Way: An Anthology of American Indian Literature* ('72), ed. by Shirley Hill Witt and Stan Steiner; *An American Indian Anthology* ('71), ed. by Benet Tvedten, O.S.B.; & *The American Indian Speaks* ('69), ed. by John R. Milton. Other anthologies carrying his work include *Southwest, The Indian Rio Grande, Yardbird Reader, Chronicles of American Indian Protest, North American Indian Reader, America: A Prophecy,* & *Poets West.*

HONORS: NEA grant in '70.

OBSERVATIONS: Simon Ortiz has observed about his poetry: "I write about Indians mainly because I am an Indian and do not feel apart from my people. In fact...it would not be possible for me to write as an individual but only as part of a people....I write in English although I have also done translations from my native language. But the essential languages come from Acoma, the culture, community, and the relations I have tried to share properly. There are any number of changes which occur in a person's life, and I write from that perspective also." Kenneth Rosen has noted about Simon Ortiz's writing, the following summary: "...[He] describes Indians' confrontation with white culture today: a 'crazy' reservation brave who goes to prison rather than join the white man's army; an old chief looking for his grand-daughter, who has gone to San Francisco to become a secretary; an Indian ex-marine who kills a state cop." Of himself as a writer, Ortiz adds: "With humility and the strength from it, one must talk and write about courage. Even when times get bad and hard, you must have courage. Inspiration and hope, that's what Indian people and all oppressed people need in their struggle to keep their humanity. To have courage—that's why I write."

RAYMOND (RICHARD) PATTERSON

BIRTH: 12/14/'29, in New York City, grew up on Long Island, where he attended Public Schools. He is the son of John T. and Mildred (Clemens) Patterson.

EDUCATION: B.A. (Lincoln U., '51), & M.A. (N.Y.U., '56); he did some further summer study at Wagner C., Columbia, & Hunter, too.

CAREER: He served with the U.S. Army from '51-'53. Since his college days, except for two years ('56-'58), when he worked as a children's supervisor for a delinquent boys home called Youth House in New York, he has earned his living as an English teacher. His first post at Benedict C. in '58-'59, took him to Columbia, S.C. Following his year in the South, he returned to the N.Y.C. area for nine years ('59-'68) of teaching reading, as well as English, in a junior high school of the New York Public School system. In '68, he joined the faculty of the City C. of the City U. of N.Y. as a Lect. in English, a post he still holds. He has also participated in the New York St. Council on the Arts poetry reading project, giving readings throughout the state. In '69, he was also spring poet-in-residence for the Minneapolis, Minn. Public Schools. A director of the Black Poets' Reading, Inc. program in N.Y., he has also served as co-chairman with William Stafford in arranging the poetry readings for the NCTE meeting in Las Vegas, Nevada. He lives today with his wife, the former Boydie A. Cooke, whom he married in Nov., '57, and daughter outside N.Y.C. in Merrick.

PUBLICATIONS: Twenty Six Ways of Looking at a Black Man and Other Poems ('69). Among other periodicals, these, have carried his poetry: *Chicago Tribune*

Magazine, The Minnesota Review, Negro Digest, Scholastic Scope, The Transatlantic Review, Phylon, Présence Africain, Practical English, Scholastic Voices, & *Sumac.* Numerous anthologies have carried Raymond Patterson's poems: Adoff, *Black Out Loud;* Adoff, *City in All Directions;* Adoff, *I Am the Darker Brother;* Adoff, *Poetry of Black America;* Baylor & Stokes, *Fine Frenzy;* Brenman, *Sixes and Sevens;* Brooks, *A Broadside Treasury;* Chapman, *New Black Voices;* Coombs, *We Speak as Liberators;* Eisenberg, *Not Quite Twenty;* Hughes, *New Negro Poets: USA;* Hughes, *La Poesie Negro-Américaine;* Hughes & Bontemps, *The Poetry of the Negro: 1746-1970;* Jordan, *Soulscript;* Lowenfels, *The Writing on the Wall;* Major, *The New Black Poetry;* Michel, *Headway;* Pool, *Beyond the Blues;* Randall & Burroughs, *For Malcolm*; Robinson, *Nommo;* Weisman & Wright, *Black Poetry for all Americans;* & Hunter, *The Norton Introduction to Literature: Poetry.* His poems can be heard aloud on a recording entitled, *Tough Poems for Tough People* (Caedman Records). In addition to writing poetry, he has also produced prose. His first work, *Get Caught: A Photographic Essay,* with Lawrence Sykes, appeared in '64. From '60-'62, he wrote a syndicated weekly column on Negro history for three newspapers—*New York Citizen-Call, New Jersey Herald News,* and *Buffalo Empire Star.*

HONORS: Borestone Mountain poetry award ('50), an N.E.A. grant ('70), a Library of Congress poetry reading ('71), and a CAPS Fellowship ('77).

Raymond R. Patterson
(November 1971)

OBSERVATIONS: Patterson has set these goals for his poetry: "To explore, to discover life, as it is lived, to understand and be understood are some of the reasons for my poems. Music, too, is important. Sometimes I want the words to disappear. Sometimes the words are a trace of melanin in the skin." About Raymond Patterson's poetry, Saundra Towns has noted: "Concerned more with the psychological than the physical, Patterson is the poet-chronicler capturing in verse the revolution in Black Thought that created the 1960's...."

BILL (WILLIAM DENNIS) PEARLMAN
BIRTH: 8/19/'43, in Los Angeles, lived in Manhattan Beach, Calif. most of his early years.

EDUCATION: An athlete and a high school standout in football and baseball, Bill attended college at U.C.L.A., where in '65, he was an U.S.V.B.A. All American volley ball star. Meanwhile, in '63-'64, he traveled to Mexico and Europe for the first time. While at U.C.L.A., he met the poet, Jack Hirschman, author of *Cantillations*

(Capra Books, '74), who, as Pearlman observes, influenced him to start "writing after the Dallas Massacre." At that time Pearlman switched his interest from athletics to poetry and was graduated from U.C.L.A. in '67 with a major in English and Theatre. During his last two years in college, he played many roles in Brecht plays. In '67, Pearlman went to N.M. with his friends Steve Katona and Berry Hickman to found a commune, and in August of that year married Meredith Rice. With his first wife, Pearlman left N.M. and started traveling around the country, finally ending up in Mallorca in the summer of '69, "disillusioned with distance" and a marriage which was to end in divorce upon their return to the States. After "wandering around all over the continent again," Pearlman spent a brief period of time as a teaching assistant at the U. of N.M., where he was associated with Robert Creeley, who at that time was directing the Creative Writing program there.

Bill Pearlman
(June 1975)

CAREER: After living in San Francisco in '71 and in N.M. in '72 in communes of poets living there and giving many readings in these places, Pearlman went to New York City "to try a hand at the *whirrld* of swift connections." In New York, his *Galactic Scouting Reports,* a night club act, was "almost a hit," and briefly he had a radio show for WBAI. During this time, Pearlman also made four tapes concerning track with his "rangy voices playing around." In '72, he also went on a reading tour of New England with Fielding Dawson. In '73, Pearlman fled to Hawaii to "recontact" there "old surfing friends," but his reunion there was short-lived, for soon he felt the urge to move on, again, this time to Oregon, where he was to have the happy experience of meeting his present wife, the former Lynn Slingerland, whom he married on 6/9/'73, on a Pacific beach. The following year, on 7/19/'74, the Pearlmans delighted in the birth of their daughter, Wave Adrienne, and for a time lived in Baton Rough, La., where during the years of '74-'76, Lynn taught math while Bill wrote as much poetry and prose as possible and at the same time managed a coffee house, which sponsored poetry readings. Now returned to his native California, Pearlman resides today in San Francisco, a city he called home in the early "seventies."

PUBLICATIONS: In addition to his novel *Inzorbital* (Duende Press, '74), Pearlman has published two books of poetry, *Surfing Off the Ark* (Grasshopper Press, '70), & *Elegy for Prefontaine and Other Track Poems* (Living Batch Press, '77). However Pearlman describes *Inzorbital,* his first novel, as actually "a poemic-prose work," "a light shaded dark rendezvous with 'sixties' & futuristic new left network possibilities." Additionally his work is anthologized in *The Indian Rio Grande* ('77).

OBSERVATIONS: Pearlman says of his writing; "My poetry comes out of the spirited high rise California wilderness with the athletic wonderlands and the filmic switches all banging heads at a home plate." As a poet, he "keeps hoping the shambled dreams of the late 'sixties' will be preserved in a head spouting incantations to the electric mob & coming to terms with its own permutations on the spinning globe...."

CHARLES POTTS

BIRTH: 8/28/'43, in Idaho Falls, Idaho, grew up in the rural town of Mackey, Idaho, and attended nearby schools while his father trapped coyotes for the government, a career, which, as Charlie explains, "ended in bankruptcy."

EDUCATION: After a B.A. in English in '65 from Idaho St. U., Potts began to travel extensively; however by '68, he spent most of his time in Berkeley, where during the demonstrations of that year he was known as "Laffing Water."

CAREER: It was in Seattle, that Potts, who is both a poet and publisher-editor, founded his well-known *Litmus* publications, which he continues to produce today with his wife Judy in his adopted Salt Lake, a city he has called home for several years now after much travel in many places in North America. Their daughter Emily Karen was born 6/12/'77. His magazine ('67-'72) *Litmus,* terminated with #13, and carried poets from a wide range in selection, but emphasized writers from the Black Mountain school and Art Nove poets. Upon receiving numbers 1 & 2 of *Litmus* in '67, Edward Dorn labeled the publication as "the most active thing I've seen coming out of the country since the New York people stopped being active five years ago." Other such poets as Philip Whalen responded to succeeding issues (i.e. #9) in this way: "The entire issue astoundingly alive and charming."

EDITORIAL POST: Presently Potts continues his *Litmus, Inc.* publications as a small press for books, with 18 titles now to his credit, including works by Charles Bukowski, Kell Robertson, Andy Clausen, Peter Koch, David Hiatt, Edward Smith, and two by himself. Of Potts' continued efforts and successes in presenting challenging poetry, even during troubled times for publishers in the '70's, Rich Mangelsdorff in *Margins* has praised Potts' efforts in this way: "It is...hoped that he'll [Potts] continue to embarass the publishing industry....He has co-edited the *Margins* issue on *The Maximus Poems, V. III* by Charles Olson.

PUBLICATIONS: Blues From Thurston County (Grande Ronde, '66), *Burning Snake* (Presna de Lagar-Wine Press, '67), *Little Lord Shiva* (Noh Directions—Aldebaran Review, '69), *The Litmus Papers* (Gunrunner, '69), *Blue Up the Nile* (Quixote, '72), *Waiting in Blood* ('73), *The Trancemigracion of Menzu* (Empty Elevator Shaft, '73), *The Golden Calf* ('75), *Charle Kiot* (Folk Frog Press, '76), *The Opium Must Go Thru* (Litmus, '76), *& Rocky Mountain Man: Selected Poems* (The Smith, '78). In addition to writing poetry, Potts also writes prose. His *Valga Krusa, Psychological Autobiography* appeared in 1977 from his own Litmus Press; among his offerings in fiction is a short story in Gary Elder's *In the Far Side of the Storm* (San Marcos Press, '75). Some of the anthologies carrying Potts' poems include these: *The Smith/17: Eleven Young Poets* ('75), *Hellcoal Annual 3* ('73), *Trubador Anthology* ('72), *The Anthology of Poems Read at the First Annual Cosmep Conference* ('69), *& Do You Want To Be In Our Zoo Too* ('66). Over 100 periodicals, including his own *Litmus,* have carried the poetry of Charles Potts: *Wild Dog, Blitz, Grande Ronde Review, Iota, West Coast Review, Avalanch, Aldebaran Review,*

Meatball, Drunken Boat, New American Canadian Poetry, Nola Express, The Smith, Small Press Review, Wormwood Review, Atom Mind, Street Paper, Kaliedescope, Berkeley Barb, The, Strawberry Field, Northeast Rising Sun, Rocky Mountain Creative Arts Journal, The Paper, Northern Review, People's News Service, Maguey, San Francisco Review of Books, Margins, Fervent Valley, The Independent, Nu, Bricoleur, Cotyledon, Open Arms, Duende, & Camel's Coming. Potts also composes music, and in the past, even formed a Buddhist marching band called *Hot Air,* which received considerable publicity several years ago for its extended campus tours. His critical articles, essays and reviews of various poets works have appeared in such periodicals as these: *The Independent* ('69), *Kaleidescope* ('69), *West Coast Review* ('71), *San Francisco Book Review* ('72), *Litmus* ('71 & '72), & *Camel's Coming* ('72). Charles Potts once claimed ironically that he was "the greatest/mediocre poet/of anytime" with "an answer for

Charles Potts
(June 1975)

everything/even faintly resembling/authority and control/must be destroyed/ immediately." In reviewing Potts' third book of poetry, *Little Lord Shiva,* Paul Buhle has written for *Guardian* that Potts' poetry "contains (a) combination of Berkeley life-style anarchism, Poundian poetic tradition and threads of Eastern mysticism...." Buhle continues to note that "Potts is the classic non-proletarian (but utterly American) revolutionist...and writes occasionally fine poetry....His most powerful stuff is not in the acid-politics poems....Rather, he reaches his height in "The Total Eclipse of Ezra Pound," including Canto 13 'revised by one unlucky/idaho kid for the other'."

LEROY (V.) QUINTANA
BIRTH: 6/10/'44, in Albuquerque, N.M., has as his first memories, instead, his grandfather's ranch near Questa, a mountainous village in northern New Mexico. Later, with his grandparents, Leroy also lived for a time in another New Mexican town high in the mountains, this time in Raton, on the Colo. border. Afterwards his family moved to El Paso, where Leroy attended school for one year, and finally to Albuquerque, settling there in the city with which he most identifies.
EDUCATION: Quintana notes that he "played pool after graduation and worked as a roofer, then started college" at the U. of N.M., but after two years, "dropped out to join the Army" and attend Airborne School. A year in Viet Nam with a reconnaissance unit followed before he was able to return home to Albuquerque again and finish in '71, finally the B.A. in English, which the Army stint had

interrupted after his '64 beginning. In '72, for one quarter, Quintana did post-graduate work at the U. of Denver. Soon he transferred to N.M. St. U. in Las Cruces, where from '72-'74, he studied for his M.A. in English, receiving it in the latter year and writing for his thesis a collection of poems.

CAREER: Leroy Quintana's teaching career began in Albuquerque in '70, while he was still completing his B.A. First he taught for a year at the Casa Linda Private School, and then from '71-'72, he served as an Inst. & Caseworker, again, in Albuquerque, for the "Alcoholism Treatment Program" in the division of "General Addictions Treatment Effort." In the year '74, he also turned to a career of teaching poetry-writing full-time, when he served for the spring term as an Instr. in Santa Fe in the Poetry in the Public Schools Program. In the year, '75-'76, he taught on the faculty of English at the N.M. St. U. at Las Cruces. Presently he and his family live in El Paso where Leroy Quintana is an instructor at the Community C. of that city and is actively associated with various leading Chicano writers of today's scene. His wife Yolanda, whom he married in '70, and their two daughters, Sandra, born in Albuquerque, and Elisa, born in Las Cruces, share with him today his life as an El Paso writer. While Leroy Quintana's main career has been as a teacher, he has also had a variety of odd jobs which have contributed enormously to his poetry writing along the way. As he puts it: "In addition to the soft jobs, I have driven trucks, pulled weeds, cut grass, painted (houses), taught retarded children, taught driver's education to high school students (much more difficult than teaching the retarded), sorted packages during the midnight shift for United Parcel Service, tried to hide out in the basement of the Albuquerque Library while employed as a page boy, worked in construction for a while...and have even accepted a few dollars for publishing poetry(!), but not as much as from, say, painting (houses)."

EDITORIAL POSTS: While at U.N.M. in Albuquerque, Quintana was poetry editor in '70 of the literary magazine, *The Thunderbird.* Latter at N.M.St. U., Las Cruces, while he was a graduate student, he was also fiction editor (for the years '73-'74) of the literary magazine, "Puerto del Sol," and from '75-'76, again served

Leroy Quintana
(May 1976)

as its faculty advisor. In '77, he also served as judge for the U.T.-El Paso-Creative Writing Awards.

PUBLICATIONS: Quintana's first book of poetry *Hijo del Pueblo,* appeared in '76 by Puerto del Sol Publications of N.M.St U., Las Cruces. His poems have been featured with frequency during the '70's in a wide variety of magazines, including:

The Greenfield Review, Colorado State Review, Mango, San Marcos Review, The Pawn Review, The Wormwood Review, Huerfano, Ataraxia, Chicano Voices, Fervent Valley, Texas Portfolio, Mazagine, Cafe Solo, Southwest Heritage, Quoin, The Laureate, New Mexico Magazine, La Luz, Patters, Box 749, Sam Houston Literary Review, Poetry Texas, Dodeca, Contact II, Sailing the Road Clear, Puerto del Sol, Dance of the Muse, Hyacinths and Biscuits, Major Poets, The Thunderbird, Inscape, Arcade, Quintessence, Rocky Mountain Review, Revista Chicano— Riquena, Green Horse for Poetry, National Poetry Press, Voices International, New Worlds Unlimited, & *Stone Country.* Such anthologies as these also carry Quintana's works: *Shore Anthology of Poetry* and *Passing Through: Anthology of Southwest Writers, Travois: Anthology of Texas Writing, Southwest,* & *The Indian Rio Grande.* In addition to writing poetry, Leroy Quintana has also served as a Contrib. Ed. to the Baleen Press in Phoenix in '74, again in '76, and has edited for these publishers the anthology *Metáforos Verdes* ('77). In the future he hopes to write a novel. About his poetry, he has observed: "I think that poetry is made from life, i.e., from the common everyday occurrences (and people) and that it should be written so that those who make poetry happen can understand and appreciate it. This view subject to change without further notice....Majored in English in college and currently trying to unlearn what I needed in order to pass exams and am asking myself at this very moment *WHO* killed Lit. and Why? I know it wasn't The Butler....Also worked as a busboy and waiter. Next time you see me ask me to tell you about the night a man came into the restaurant and claimed a certain part of his anatomy was tattooed and was willing to prove it but his wife would not allow it. I also died in Viet Nam and at too many places too numerous to mention along the road to where I now sit, a night in March, a place called El Paso, at a typewriter, 8:50 p.m., '76. Those deaths were caused by love, hate, jealousy, envy, karma, destiny, hope, despair *y porque soy Chicano.* My children are the finest poems I've created."

A(TTIPAT) K(RISHNASWAMI) RAMANUJAN

BIRTH: 3/16/'29, in Mysore, India, the son of Seshammal and A. A. Krishnaswami Ayyangar, grew up in Southern India, the son of a professor.

EDUCATION: B.A. with honors ('49) & M.A. ('50), both in English from the U. of Mysore; Ph.D. in Linguistics, U. of Indiana ('63).

CAREER: Ramanujan began his career as a Lect. in English at various colleges in S. India ('50-'58), and at the U. of Baroda. In '58-'59, he also gained a post-graduate diploma in Linguistics from Deccan College, and coming to the U.S. in '59, on both Fulbright and Smith-Mundt Traveling Fellowships for the year, he pursued his doctorate in Linguistics. He began his U.S. teaching career in '62 at the U. of Chicago, where since '68, he has been a Prof. of Dravidian Studies and Linguistics. Since '72, he has been a member of the Committee on Social Thoughts also. Meanwhile, during his Chicago appointment, he has also held Visit. Professorships at other institutions. During the summer of '65 and in '72, he was Visiting Professor of Indian Studies at the U. of Wisconsin. In '67 and in '73, he was Visit. Prof. at the U. of Calif., Berkeley, and in '71, at the U. of Michigan. A. K. Ramanujan makes his home in Chicago with his wife, nee Molly Daniels, and their two children, Krittika, a daughter, and Krishna, a son.

PUBLICATIONS: Ramanujan's first volume of poetry in English, *The Striders* (Oxford U. Press), appeared in '66, and was a Poetry Society Recommendation. Additionally he has published these collections of poetry: *No Lotus in the Navel* (in the Kannada language; Dharwar, Manohar Granthmala, '69), *Relations* (Oxford U. Press, London, '72), *Selected Poems* (Oxford U. Press, '76), & *And Other Poems* (in Kannada, '77). He has also published several books of translations of Tamil and Kannada verse. His translations include *Fifteen Tamil Poems* ('65), *The Interior Landscape: Love Poems from a Classical Tamil Anthology* ('67, '70, & '75), *Some Kannada Poems* ('67), *Speaking of Siva: Religious Lyrics from the Medieval Kannada* ('71; '73), and *Samskara* ('76). His works also appear in numerous anthologies: *Best Poems of '61, The Borestone Mountain Poetry Awards* ('62), *Young Commonwealth Poets, 1965* ('65), *Ten Years of Quest* ('66), *Commonwealth Poems of Today* ('67), *New Voices of the Commonwealth* ('68), *Modern Indian Poetry in English* ('69), and *Ten Indian Poets in English* ('76). He has also contributed to many periodicals of poetry in India: *Quest, Illustrated Weekly of India*, and *Poetry India*; to *London Magazine* in England; and in the U.S. to *Atlantic, Poetry*, and *Poetry Northwest*. In addition to his writings in English, Ramanujan has also published several radio plays, poems and stories in Kannada, which is a Dravidian language of South India. His book, *Proverbs*, was published in India in '55 by Karnatiak University; and he has collaborated on a reader for foreign

A.K. Ramanujan
(February 1971)

learners entitled *Modern Kannada Fiction* ('67). His wife has also written novels in English entitled *The Yellow Fish* ('66), which Ramanujan has rendered into Kannada; her *Salt Doll* was published by Vikas, Deli ('77).

HONORS: N.E.A. Fellowship ('77), Padma Sri Award ('76), a nomination for the National Book Award ('74), Tamil Writers' Assoc. Award ('69), Amer. Inst. of Indian Studies Fac. Research Fellowship ('63-'64), and Fellowship of the Indian School of Letters ('63).

OBSERVATIONS: About Ramanujan's first book of poetry, the Indian critic S. Nagarajan noted in '66: "Ramanujan's rhythms are generally very close to the relaxed rhythms of speech; his images are carefully chosen to fit the content in all their details; the ordinary diction is used in a surprising, original and acceptable way; the poems are well balanced and usually contain in themselves the principle of their growth and development. At the moment Ramanujan's poems may not have much to say, but there is a habit of thought in them that, combined with his already strong craftsmanship, promises to make him perhaps the most considerable Indian poet in English."

JOHN CROWE RANSOM

BIRTH: 4/30/1888, in Pulaski, Tenn.

DEATH: 7/3/'74. He was the son of a minister, and was educated in his native state of Tenn.

EDUCATION: Vanderbuilt U. (B.A., '09) & Christ Church, Oxford, as a Rhodes Scholar from '10-'13 (second B.A., '13).

CAREER: During W.W. I, he was stationed for two years ('17-'19) as a 1st Lt. of Field Artillery. After the war, he returned to Vanderbilt where he had earlier begun his teaching career in '14. While at Vanderbilt, he helped found in '22, *The Fugitive,* a poetry magazine, which he edited until '25. At the time of his teaching career, he was also active with Donald Davidson and Allen Tate in a literary movement known as Agrarianism, which attacked the materialism of machine-made culture. Ransom was long a teacher of poetry-writing and inspired such famous students as Allen Tate, Cleanth Brooks, Eric Bentley, Robert Lowell, Randell Jarrell, James Wright, Robert Penn Warren & Andrew Lytle. Except for a stretch in the Army in W.W. I, he taught at Vanderbilt until '37 when he went to Kenyon College, where he served as Carnegie Prof. of Poetry until his retirement from the latter institution in '58. At Vanderbilt, he had risen from the rank of instructor to Full Prof. At Kenyon until his retirement, he was named Prof. Emeritus. However, in the course of his teaching career, he also lectured and taught at other universities, including Colo. St. C., U. of N.M., U. of Fla., Kent St. U., U. of Tex., Chattanooga U., & Harvard.

EDITORIAL POSTS: In addition to *The Fugitive,* mentioned above, Ransom helped to found in '37, with the assistance of Gordon Chalmers, then Pres. of Kenyon, *The Kenyon Review,* and his name is by many automatically associated even today with this now-famous literary quarterly. For it was under Ransom's editorship from '37-'59 that *The Kenyon Review* became world-famous. At Kenyon, he also attracted writers of note from all over the English-speaking world. For his efforts, Kenyon expressed its gratitude by naming its Administration Building Ransom Hall, for the school realized that it owed much of its fine reputation to this poet. Mr. Ransom, who married Robb Reavill in '20, continued to make his home in Gambier, Ohio near the Kenyon campus until his death. He and his wife had three children.

John Crowe Ransom
(March 1967)
deceased

PUBLICATIONS: A careful and precise craftsman, John Crowe Ransom was the first to admit that the total of his verse was "not very large." His *Selected Poems* ('45; rev. ed. '63 & '69) were his last offerings, with his five earlier ones as follows: *Poems About God* ('19), *Chills and Fever* ('42), *Grace After Meat* ('24), *Two Gentlemen in Bonds* ('27), & *Poems and Essays* ('55). He has published poems in numerous poetry periodicals, as well as, of course, in *The Kenyon Review.* His work has also been very widely anthologized: *Armagedden,* with *A Fragment* by William Alexander Percy; *Avalon* by Donald Davidson ('23), *Chief Modern Poets*

('43), *Twentieth Century American Poetry* ('44), *New Poetry* ('47), *Modern American Poetry* ('50), *Oxford Book of American Poetry* ('50), *Modern Poets* ('63), *Poetry in English* ('63), *American Poetry* ('65), *Faber Book of Modern Verse* ('65), *Poems and Poets* ('65), *An Introduction to Poetry* ('67), *Norton Anthology of Modern Poetry* ('73), & *Modern Poems: An Introduction to Poetry* ('73; '76). Ransom can be heard reading his *Poems* for Decca Records in '66. His works of criticism are perhaps as well-known as is his poetry. He has published many critical essays, as well as three full-length books upon such subject matter: *God Without Thunder* ('30), *The World's Body* ('38), & *The New Criticism* ('41), from which the latter term, incidentally, gained currency. His other works and textbooks upon literary themes include *Poetics* ('42), *A College Primer of Writing* ('43), *American Poetry at Mid-Century*, with Delmore Schwartz & John Hall Wheelock ('58), *Exercises on the Occasion of the Dedication of the New Phi Beta Kappa Hall* ('58), & *Beating the Bushes: Selected Essays 1941-1970* ('72). As an editor, Ransom has also published *Topics for Freshman Writing: Twenty Topics for Writing, with Appropriate Material for Study* ('35), *The Kenyon Critics* ('51), & *The Selected Poetry of Thomas Hardy* ('61).

HONORS: In addition to being a Rhodes Scholar to Oxford, Ransom's prizes were many. They included a Guggenheim Fellowship in creative writing ('31), appointment as honorary consultant in Am. Letters to the Library of Congress, Yale's Bollingen award in poetry ('51), the Russell Loines Mem. Fund Prize from the Nat. Academy of Arts & Letters ('51), Chicago Poetry Day Award ('57), Brandeis U. Creative Arts Award ('58-'59), a Fellowship Prize of the Academy of Am. Poets ('62), the Nat. Book Award ('64), N.E.A. Award ('66), membership in the Am. Acad. of Arts & Letters ('67), membership in the Nat. Acad. of Arts & Sciences ('67), Emerson-Thoreau Medal ('68), & Nat. Inst. of Arts & Letters Gold Medal ('73).

OBSERVATIONS: About writing poetry, Ransom once observed in an essay entitled "The Concrete Universal: Observations on the Understanding of Poetry": "Suppose we say that the poem is an organism....Then it has a physiology. We will figure its organs, and to me it seems satisfactory if we say there are three: the head, the heart, the feet. The peculiarity of the joint production is that it still consists of the several products of the organs working individually...the head in an intellectual language, the heart in an affective language, the feet in a rhythmical language." Babette Deutsch has characterized Ransom's poetry in this way: "...one is struck by the delicacy that governs Ransom's diction, happily marrying Latinate words with curt prose, by his careful twisting of syntax for the sake of emphasis, by the way in which he pleasures us with slight variations in his handling of metre. The tone, as usual, is gently ironic. The irony carries the weight of the meaning, which is not light. These felicities are the hallmarks of Ransom's poems."

GEORGE REAVEY

BIRTH: 5/1/1907, in Northern Ireland.

DEATH: 8/11/'76, in N.Y.C., Reavey was the son of a Russian mother and an Irish father who was a mill manager and flax expert; he traveled as a boy all over Europe in connection with his father's work. Finally when his family settled in England, he was educated at various English and Irish schools.

EDUCATION: Royal Belfast Academical Inst. in Ireland and the Chelsea School in London; M.A. from Gonville Caius College, Cambridge; and post-graduate research at the Sorbonne, U. of London, Columbia, and Stanford.

CAREER: Reavey began his literary career in Paris and London, 1930-'39.

EDITORIAL POSTS: He started the Europa Press which published Irish poets, including Samuel Beckett (*Echo's Bones*) & Denis Devlin (*Intrussions*). Also, with Marc Slonin, Reavey started a European Literary Bureau and was instrumental in placing French writers with U.S.A. publishers. During W.W. II, he served from '40'-41 as Sec. and Registrar of the British Institute, Madrid. He was from '42-'45, Second Sec. & Deputy Press Attaché at the British Embassy in Moscow. Later he taught at Manchester U. in England, at N.Y.U., and at the Poetry Workshop of City C. in N.Y. He also gave lectures at Oxford and the U. of Toronto. He was divorced from his first wife, the painter I. Rice Pereia, whom he married 9/9/'50, and with whom he lived in England for a time. Later he moved to N.Y.C., where he lived for the majority of his writing career, with his second wife Jean Reavey, who is a playwright. He devoted most of his time to translating Russian poets' works into English, an occupation which he actually began while still a student at Cambridge and for which he became extremely well-known during the "sixties" and "seventies."

George Reavey
(April 1967)
deceased

PUBLICATIONS: While he was studying at Cambridge, Reavey's first poems appeared in the review *Experiment*. Later, in Paris, he published three related books of poetry: *Faust's Metamorphoses* ('32), *Nostradam* ('35), & *Signes D'Adieu* ('35). In '39, he published his *Quixotic Perquisitions* in London, and in '55, his first American volume, *The Colours of Memory,* appeared from Grove Press. His poems have been published in magazines and reviews in Paris, London, and the U.S.A., among them: *Poetry, The Cambridge Review, The London Bulletin, Transition, The Listener, This Quarter, The New Review, The Tablet,* and *Mademoiselle.* He is also included in such anthologies as *The Pocket Book of Modern Verse* ('53, '55), *The Silver Treasury of Light Verse* ('57, '67), & *A Garland For Dylan Thomas* ('64). He has also read his poetry on B.B.C.'s Third Program, on C.B.S. TV in '57, and on many N.Y.C. radio stations since '56. Nevertheless Reavey is certainly best known for his translations of famous Russian writers and poets, and it is in this capacity that he has made his major contribution not only to the "sixties" and "seventies," but probably to his entire career. During his student days at Cambridge, he began translating the poetry of Boris Pasternak, and published his first translation of four poems of Pasternak's, along with an essay, in *Experiment* No. 7 (Oct., '30). He also began his correspondence and friendship with the Russian poet and novelist at this time; later he and Pasternak met and got to know one another well in Moscow. In '59, Reavey's translation and edition of *The Poetry of Boris Pasternak* appeared. Since that time, he has translated and edited the following works: *The Bedbug and Selected Poems of Vladimir Mayakovsky* ('60; '75); *A Leaf of Spring* by Yesenin-Velpin ('62), *New Life: A Day on a Collective Farm* by Fyodor Abramov ('63), *Fathers and Sons* by Ivan Turgenev, and *A Sky Blue Life, Short Stories* by Maxim Gorky (New Am. Lib., n.d.), *The Poetry of Yevgeny Yevtushenko* ('65, '69), *Petersbourg* and *The Silver Dove* by Andrey Biely (n.d.), *Dead Souls* by Nicolai V. Gogol ('71), and an anthology of which he is likewise the editor, *New Russian Poets* (in English and Russian, '74). As an editor of Russian literature and a critic, as well, he is also the author of several well-known anthologies, including *Soviet Literature: Survey and Anthology*, with M. Slonin ('34; '72), *Soviet Literature Today* ('47; '75), *The New Russian Poets* ('66), and the Russian section in Bantam's '65 *Anthology of European Poetry, 1920-1964*. Additionally as a translator of French poetry, he has also produced *Thorns of Thunder: Selected Poems* by Paul Eulard ('36). Reavey's translations of both Russian and French poems have likewise appeared in numerous periodicals, including these: *Chelsea, Partisan Review, This Quarter, Contemporary Poetry & Prose, Trans-Atlantic Review, Drama Review, Poetry, Poetry Quarterly,* & *Wind and The Rain.*

OBSERVATIONS: Concerning his own work, Reavey wrote: "My poems assume a hero, a stage of history, a battleground, an area of meditation, a stage of enquiry, and a language that is dynamic and symbolic...." About Reavey's work as a translator, Boris Pasternak once wrote him: "Your translations of my work are the best I know of."

PETER (WILLIAM) REDGROVE

BIRTH: 1/2/'32, is a native of Kingston, Surrey, England, whose father worked in advertising.

EDUCATION: Taunton School, Somerset, England, and at Queen's C., Cambridge, England, where he was Open Scholar and State Scholar in Natural Sciences.

CAREER: At eighteen when he was inducted briefly into the National Service Army and was confronted by screaming sergeants, he was hospitalized, labeled an "incipient schizophrenic, and condemned," as British journalist Hugh Hebert says, "to the barbarities of insulin shocks," a treatment that Redgrove called "50 little deaths," but observed later was "perhaps something like the drug trip sought by later youth." Back at Cambridge, Redgrove found peace again and began to write his first poetry. After Cambridge, he worked for a time as a research chemist, and from 1954-'61, as a scientific journalist and editor. He began his teaching career when he won a Fulbright Award and came to the U.S.A. in '61-'62 as Visit. Poet at S.U.N.Y., Buffalo. From '62-'65, he was Gregory Fellow in Poetry at Leeds U., Yorkshire. After this he freelanced for a year before accepting in '66, his present position as Resident Author and Senior Lecturer in Complementary Studies at the Falmouth School of Arts, Cornwall. Since that time, except for leaves and travels, he has taught writing seminars at the Falmouth School modelled on certain of the writing courses he taught first in the U.S.A. at S.U.N.Y., Buffalo, as well as on the procedures of "The Group"—of which he was a founder-member at Cambridge and to whose anthology (O.U.P. 1963) he contributed. In '74-'75, he returned again to the U.S.A., when he served as O'Conner Professor of Literature at Colgate University. He has three children by his first marriage to sculptor

Barbara Redgrove. Presently he makes his home in a Cornwall cottage in Falmouth with poet-novelist Penelope Shuttle with whom he has so productively collaborated since '72, both in poetry and prose.

EDITORIAL POSTS: As an undergraduate, Redgrove started writing poetry and launched the magazine, DELTA. In this capacity, he became closely associated with "The Group," which he helped found in '55 with Philip Hobsbaum, and which contained other such prominent members as George MacBeth and Edward Lucie-Smith. Likewise he was also a friend and contemporary of Ted Hughes' at Cambridge.

PUBLICATIONS: The Collector and Other Poems (London, '60), *The Nature of Cold Weather and Other Poems* (London, '61), *At the White Monument and Other Poems* (London, '63), *The Force and Other Poems* (London, '66), *Work in Progress* (London, '69), *Dr. Faust's Sea-Spiral Spirit and Other Poems* (London & Boston, '72), *Three Pieces for Voices* (London, '72), *Sons of My Skin: Selected Poems 1954-'74* (edited with an introduction by Marie Peel) (London & Boston, '75), *From Every Chink of the Ark: New Poems American and English* (London & Boston, '77), and forthcoming in '79, *The Weddings at Nether Powers,* from Routledge, London & Boston. In addition to these volumes of poetry, Redgrove has also published certain pamphlets and broadsheets with such presses as these: Manuscript Series; Omphalos, Sceptre, Second Aeon, Sycamore, Turret Books, & Words. With Penelope Shuttle, he has also written one volume of poetry, *The Hermaphrodite Album* ('73), and a novel, *The Terrors of Dr. Treviles* ('74). Recognized for his novels as well as his poetry, Redgrove has also produced as a novelist: *In the Country of the Skin* (London, '73; winner of the Guardian Fiction Prize), *The Glass Cottage* (London, '76), and forthcoming, both from Routledge, *The Sleep of the Great Hypnotist* and *The God of Glass.* Currently his manuscript for *The Beekeepers* is in preparation. Redgrove's collections of verse have also appeared in such books as *Penguin Modern Poets II*, with D.M. Thomas and D.M. Black ('68), and his poetry and prose have been widely anthologzied, both in England and America, appearing in volumes too numerous for listing here, but including such collections as these: *The P.E.N.'s* annual anthology *New Poems* ('57, '58, '61, '62, '63, '65, '71-'72, '72-'73, '75-'76, '76-'77, & '77-'78); *The Oxford Book of Twentieth Century Verse; The New Poetry* (Penguin); *British Poetry Since 1945* (Penguin); *New Poets of England and America; Poems of Today; Considering Poetry; Moments of Truth; Penguin Book of "Sick" Verse; Best Poems of '64, '66, & '70* (Borestone Poetry Awards); *The New Modern Poetry; 100 Postwar Poems, British and American: Poetry in the Making; Introducing Poetry; The Voice of Poetry: Poems for Shakespeare 1972 and 1974; Penguin Dictionary of Modern Quotations; Modern Poetry; Poetry of the Sixties; Poetry from Cambridge; Poems of Today; English Poems of the 20th Century; Seasons of Man; Arts Council Poetry Anthologies 1975 and 1976; Introducing Poetry; Seven Themes in Modern Verse; 20th Century Love Poetry; New British Poems; Best SF 1976; Poetry in the '70's; Modernism in Literature; & English Poems of the 20th Century.* In both the U.S.A. and England, his work appears frequently in leading periodicals; particularly in *Poetry* in this country, and in England, he has been a contributor of long standing to the following: *The Time Literary Supplement; The Spectator; The New Statesman; The Observer; The Listener; Encounter; The London Magazine; The Critical Quarterly; Time and Tide; The Poetry Review; Outposts; & Delta.* He has also edited four collections of poetry: *Poets' Playground* ('63), *Universities Poetry 7* ('65), *New Poems 1967: A P.E.N. Anthology*, with Harold Pinter and John

Fuller ('67), and *Lamb and Thundercloud* ('75). Further Redgrove has given widespread readings and lectures during his visits to America in '61, '62, '71, '74, & '75, and at numerous institutions in Great Britain. He can be heard reading on two discs: *British Poets of Our Time* (Argo '75), & *The Poet Speaks* (Argo '61), and has made recordings additionally of his poetry for the Library of Congress, for Harvard University, the British Council and the Leeds University Poetry Room, for Tokyo University and for Argo Gramophone Records. Certain of his works have

Peter Redgrove
(November 1971)

been translated into French, Russian, German, Dutch, Hungarian, Turkish, Polish, Japanese & Italian. Collections of his notebooks and worksheets are lodged in the Lockwood Memorial Library (S.U.N.Y., Buffalo), in the libraries of the University of Texas and University of Indiana, and in the Brotherton Library, Leeds. Redgrove has broadcast frequently for the B.B.C. since '56 and has contributed much writing to their programmes during that time, including several full-length plays. He has also appeared on and written for television. As a dramatist, he has published *In the Country of the Skin* ('73; Best British Radio Drama Script Nomination '74) & *Miss Carstairs Dressed for Blooding, and Other Plays* ('76). His interests are wide, ranging from science and science fiction (he has contributed to several major *SF* anthologies, including more than once to Judith Merril's *The Year's Best S.F.*), through martial arts (he holds brown belts in both the B.J.A. and Otani School of Judo), Verse-Speaking (he was a George Rylands Prizewinner of the Cambridge English Readers) to psychology, psychoanalysis and anthropology. In connection with the latter interest, he studied for over two years, 1968-'69, with the psychologist and anthropologist John Layard. In the fields of psychology and sociology, he has recently published, with Penelope Shuttle, *The Wise Wound: Everywoman and Eve's Curse* (London, Gollancz, '78; forthcoming New York, Marek), a work which concerns the fertility cycle. In preparation are two other manuscripts—*A Feminist Jung* and *The Mirror of the Goddess*. He enjoys traveling, and in addition to his various visits to America, has traveled extensively in Spain.

HONORS: Besides his first Fulbright Fellowship which brought him to the U.S. in '61, he has also won five major Arts Council Awards for his writing (in '69, '70, '73, '75, & '77), and as noted earlier, the '73 Guardian Fiction Prize for his first novel, *In the Country of the Skin*. Two of his books of poetry have been Poetry Book

Society Choices (*The Nature of Cold Weather and Other Poems; & The Force and Other Poems*), and a third (*From Every Chink of the Ark*) has been a Recommendation of the Poetry Book Society. Additionally he has served on numerous prestigious committees, advisory panels, and as a judge for various writers' competitions. In this capacity he has served on the Literature Panel of the Arts Council of Great Britain, on its Poetry Panel, on its New Activities Committee and on its Manuscript Committee. He has been a member also of the Literature Advisory Panel of the South Western Arts Association, on the Universities' Poetry Managing Committee, on the Poets' Advisory Panel of the Poetry Society, on the Advisory Editorial Board of "Modern Poetry in Translation" and on the Leeds University Poetry Committee. He has been a judge for the Cheltenham Festival Poetry Prizes in '68 and '69, a Stroud International Festival Poetry Competition judge in '72, and chairman of the latter's Poetry Workshop in '73.

OBSERVATIONS: Redgrove has observed of his poetry: "I've often satirised in my work the priest and the psychiatrist, because they have usurped the poet's function which is healing....The things that poetry deals with engage people's lives, it is not embellishment, it is a thing that happens to people. If it is true poetry, it accustoms us to the life of dreams, and dreams are life talking back at itself....I think it's socially very important for people to know about their inner selves....The goal is for inner and outer to become the same thing. Writing a poem has always been for me a doorway into a state of being, where I have been more myself, my best being and others have become more themselves." Reviewing his work for N.Y. *Times Book Review* (Jan. '75), M.L. Rosenthal notes: "If you want to read a British poet who leaps with manic glory into sets of perceptions unreducible through art, Peter Redgrove is a pretty close approximation....He always has invited the whole absurdity and awkwardness of being human in the midst of physical nature, and of the torment of desires and dreams and intimations of perhaps supernatural transcendence beyond our ability to deal with, into the wild and yet bravely controlled movement of his poems. All the world's sharp angles and unmanageable realities, the sexual and psychic and cosmic intractabilities, are Redgrove's materials."

MARINA RIVERA

BIRTH: 2/9/'42, in Superior, Ariz., a mining town, later moved to Phoenix.
EDUCATION: She attended Phoenix public schools through high school, and

Marina Rivera
(June 1976)

then lived in Flagstaff where she attended Northern Ariz. St. U. for four years before completing her B.S. in '64 in English and French (*summa cum laude*). In '66, she earned her M.A. in Public Speaking from the U. of Ariz. While at the latter university, she participated actively in the programs and readings of the Poetry Center and served for a year as a student member to the Board of Directors. It was at this time that she met her husband, then a university graduate student in the English department, who also served with her as a student Board member. They were married on 12/7/'66, and make their home today in Tucson.

CAREER: Marina Rivera has been a high school teacher during most of her career. She has taught school in all of the following places: Phoenix, Flagstaff, Hayward, & Santa Ana, Calif. and in Alpine, Tex. For two years, she was also a U. of Ariz. Teaching Asst. Most of her experience has been in the areas of English, speech, creative writing, and advanced studies classes. For a number of years now, she has taught at Tucson High School, and is presently an English Teacher for the Special Projects High School for Advanced Studies of District #1 located at the Tucson High Plant.

PUBLICATIONS: Marina Rivera has been writing poetry since her high school days, and publishing in little magazines since '72, when she first began to send out her poems for consideration. She is the author of two chapbooks of poetry: *Mestiza* (Grilled Flowers, '77) & *Sobra* (Casa Editorial, '77). Her poems and essays have been published also in such anthologies as *I Had Been Hungry All the Years*, ed. by Glenna Luschei and Del Marie Rogers (Solo Press, '75), *Southwest: A Contemporary Anthology* (Red Earth Press, '77), & *The Ethnic American Woman*, ed. by Edith Blicksilver ('79). Individual poems of hers have appeared in the following publications: *Charas, Cafeteria, Casaba, Puerto Del Sol, Quetzal, View Magazine,* & *Quartet.* As a translator of poetry from English into Spanish, she has translated the poetry of Norman Dubie, Steve Orlen, Richard Shelton, Pamela Stewart, and Peter Wild into Spanish for the anthology issue of *Grilled Flowers* entitled *Special Issue on Five Arizona Poets* in '76.

OBSERVATIONS: Concerning the Mexican-American world that frequently is a theme of her poetry, Marina Rivera says: "It's a rich culture with a lot to offer—mainly a re-evaltuation of commitment to outside things, outside the family. The Mexican family is very cohesive and loyal; I think we need more of that in Anglo society." About her poetry, Glenna Luschei and Del Marie Rogers have noted: "...minority-group women writing under quite different cultural stresses have been able to write outside political poems; an example is the work of [this] Chicana poet....It goes without saying that being a member of a minority group does not automatically make a writer able to write political poetry (as apart from propaganda) but minority concerns have combined with other factors in the work of a few women to generate political poems."

WILLIAM A. ROECKER

BIRTH: 1/17/'42, in Madison, Wis., the son of A.W. Roecker, moved to Eugene, Ore. when he was eight.

EDUCATION: B.S. degree in Speech and Broadcasting ('66), & M.F.A. in Creative Writing ('67), both from the U. of Ore.

CAREER: Roecker has worked as a logger, mill employee, truck driver, powder monkey, radio-tv announcer, newsman, and after his schooling, as a college teacher. Beginning his career in '67 as a part-time instructor at the U. of Ore., he also taught English part-time at Lane Community C. in Eugene. In '68, he moved to

Ariz., where he was first Instr., then Asst. Prof., at the U. of Ariz. In '75-'76, he joined the faculty of Pima C., Tucson, where he taught creative writing parttime, and also earned his living as a free-lance journalist. Presently divorced from his first wife Peggy, he spends much of his time traveling and with his avocation of hangglider-piloting. Currently he lives in Encinitas, California, where he writes stories and articles about flying hang gliders, which he publishes in *Hang Gliding* magazine or *Glider Rider* newspaper. One story has been anthologized in Jeppesen Sandersen's *Aviation Yearbook*.

PUBLICATIONS: Bill Roecker's first book of poems, *Willamette,* a chapbook, appeared in '70 from Baleen Press. His second collection, *You Know Me* (Sumac Press, '72) was followed by another chapbook, *Closer to the Country* (Maguey Press, '76). His book in progress in '78 is *Nighthawk*. Numerous magazines have carried his poetry: *The Nation, Prairie Schooner, McCall's, North American Review, Western Humanities Review, Quixote, Consumption, Red Cedar Review, South, Arx, Trace, Druid Free Press, Tongue, Confrontation, Human Voice Quarterly, Iota, Descant, Wisconsin Review, The Dragonfly, Colorado State Review, Northwest Review, Inscape, The Butterfield Express, Redstart, Transpacific, South Florida Poetry Journal, Northeast, Chicago Tribune Sunday Magazine, Sumac, Mediterranean Review, Sun Tracks, Bullfrog Information Service, Ironwood, Measure, Puerto Del Sol, Pure Light, Lotus, The Last Cookie, Guesses, The Monmouth Review, Snowmen and Scarecrows, Hearse, & Mazagine.*

William Roecker
(February 1971)

His poems have also been printed in such anthologies as these: *Poetry of the Desert Southwest* (Baleen Press, '73); *Sequoia* (Littlefield Press, San Francisco, '73), *Yearbook of Modern Poetry* (Young Publ., '71), & *Recycle This Poem* (Dragonfly Press, '71). His short stories have appeared in *Next, Northwest Review, Wisconsin Review, Confrontation, & North American Review*. He has also had two stories published in anthologies: *Intro #1* (Bantam Books, '68) & *The Erotic Anthology* (Signet Books, '72). In addition to writing fiction, he has also edited an anthology of modern and contemporary American stories entitled *Stories That Count*, which was published with his introduction by Holt, Rinehart and Winston ('71). He has written reviews for *Dragonfly*, and has worked for the Ariz. Poetry-In-The-Schools program, giving numerous readings in the Southwest and elsewhere.

HONORS: As a student at the U. of Ore., Roecker won the Ernest Haycox Short Story Award and the Richard L. Neuberger Fiction Award in '66 & '67 respectively.

His poems brought him the Arx Foundation Award in '70, the same year when he was one of the four young poets in the finals for the Yale Younger Poets' series and a finalist likewise in the U.S. Award of the Pittsburgh Series. In '71, he was again runner-up in both the Yale Younger Poets' Series and the U.S. Award, Pittsburgh. In '73, he was awarded an N.E.A. grant. While at the U. of Ariz., Roecker served as a Board member for two years ('70-'72) for the Poetry Center.

EDITORIAL POSTS: In '67, he was asst. ed. for *Northwest Review*, a magazine for which he has written book reviews.

OBSERVATIONS: Roecker notes: "I often think of myself as a romantic moralist, though I will fish with bait."

ORLANDO ROMERO

BIRTH: 9/24/'45, the son of Jose Abel and Ruth Romero, still makes his home in his birthplace of Santa Fe, N.M. However, Orlando grew up in nearby Nambe, a village that has actually been the home of his family and ancestors since the 1600's, for he descends from some of New Mexico's earliest Spanish colonists. As a child, he learned the art of carving images of saints for which his people are famous, and is today a talented *"santero"* with sculptor on permanent display at the Folk Art Museum in Santa Fe. Besides this art, he also learned from his grandfather how to grow herbs for healing. His reminiscences include hallucinative mushrooms as a youngster; also the big adobe home that has been the Romero family's for generations. He still enjoys visiting it with his wife Rebecca and their two chlidren, Carlota, seven years old, and Orlando Cervantes, now six. His writings often concern this home and the teachings of his grandfather, Enrique Romero, and his ancestors, who travel back through three generations in New Mexico. His work always takes up the fact, too, of how northern New Mexicans are bound by myths and culture and explains the process of planting, the joy of religious festivals and the calm of learning how to carve religious statues out of wood.

EDUCATION: Romero received his B.A. in English from the C. of Santa Fe ('75) and his M.L.S. degree from the U. of Ariz. ('76).

CAREER: While he was attending college, he had a variety of jobs in order to support his family, for he and Rebecca were married in '68. From '70-'72, he worked in the Santa Fe Public Library's Bookmobile program. In '73-'74, he served as curatorial asst. for the Hispanic Cultural Com. of the N.M. Lab. of Anthropology. In '75, he worked as a librarian for the No. Region of the N.M. State Library in Espanola, N.M. In the summer of '75, he and Rebecca and the two children moved to Tucson to spend a year while Orlando studied for his M.L.S. degree, which he completed at the U. of Ariz. in August, '76. During his course of study, Romero was one of the fifteen students enrolled in the Grad. Library Inst. for Spanish-speaking Americans at the U. of Ariz., a program funded for one year by the Dept. of Health, Ed., & Welfare. Dr. Arnulfo D. Trejo, himself, an important Chicano prose writer and critic, directed the institute, which handpicked the fifteen students from more than sixty applicants. Of Romero's work, Trejo observed: "It's so important to have writers capturing the heritage of the Spanish-speaking. So much has been done by the outsider; now we have our own writers." After his graduation, Romero returned to a job as a librarian of the Southwestern Special Collection of N.M. St. Lib. in Santa Fe where he is currently employed and where he spends as much time as possible with his writing. A poet as well as a novelist, Romero has published more fiction at present than poetry; however he intends to devote more time to his poetry in the future. He has published in *Puerto Del Sol* and *El Grito Del Sol* publications, and his sculpture has also been featured in *Puerto Del Sol* magazine in

'74. As a novelist, he is the author of the autobiographical *Nambe—Year One,* which was released by Tonatiuh Internationl Inc. publishers of Chicano literature in Berkeley and San Antonio, in June, '76, with illustrations by Dennis Martinez of Albuquerque. A short story is anthologized in *Southwest* ('77). Currently he is at work on a collection of short stories entitled *Fool's Gold*, which he describes as "stories of love, desertion, and regeneration."

Orlando Romero
(May 1976)

OBSERVATIONS: Romero notes: "My work is inspired not only by the indigenous people of the Southwest but by the relationships affecting all human beings....I deal with folklore—mythical and mystical. I think I'm doing something for southwestern literature that's never been done before." About his writing, John Hadsel has called his *Nambe—Year One* "a sensitive confessional," and added in his review that "Romero is obviously talented."

WILLIAM PITT ROOT
BIRTH: 12/28/'41, in Austin, Minn., the son of William Pitt and Bonita (Hilbert) Root. A show-business-director-turned-farmer, his father died while William was a child; in fact, loss of his father figures as a central theme for his first collection, *The Storm and Other Poems.*

EDUCATION: U. of Wash. (B.A., '64); U.N.C.—Greensboro (M.A., '67); in '68'-69, he was a Stegner Creative Writing Fellow at Stanford.

CAREER: Root began his teaching career in '67, as an Instr. at the Slippery Rock St. C. (Pa.); Asst. Prof. of English, Mich. St. U., '67-'68; Lectr.-in-Writing, Mid-Peninsula Free U., '70; Visiting Writer-in-Res. at Amherst C., '71; Wichita St. U., '76; U. of Southwest Louisiana, '76; U. of Montana, '77. He has worked for the Poetry-in-the-Schools programs in Wyo., Ariz., Idaho, Vermont, Mont., Mississippi, and Oregon during "the seventies," spent '74-'75 as Poet-in-Residence at the Galveston, Tex. Art Center, and in '77 served on the Centrum Summer Poetry Symposium at Port Townsend, Washington. Before he began teaching, he worked various odd jobs in warehouses, shipyards, factories, and bars. He married the former Judy Bechtold in '65; they have a daughter, Jennifer Lorca, and were divorced in '70.

PUBLICATIONS: The Storm and Other Poems ('69), *Striking the Dark Air for Music* ('73), *Coot and Other Characters* ('77), and *A Journey South* ('77). His poems have been included in various anthologies: *New Yorker Book of Poems, New*

Voices in American Poetry ('74), *Best Poems of 1974* ('74), *Since Feeling is First* ('71), *Red Clay Reader* ('66, '68), *Greensboro Reader* ('68), and *Intro 2.* ('69). They have also appeared in various magazines: *The Atlantic Monthly, Beloit Poetry Journal, Hudson Review, The Nation, Northwest Review, Harpers, Sewannee Review, Greensboro Review, New Yorker, New Orleans Review, The Floating Island,* etc. Root also writes fiction and critical prose.

HONORS: Academy of Am. Poet's Prize ('66), Mich. St. U. Summer Research Grant ('68), Rockefeller Foundation Fellowship ('69-'70), Guggenheim grant ('70), and an N.E.A. grant ('73).

William Pitt Root
(December 1972)

OBSERVATIONS: Root relates: "The ideal poem would be such that its surface attracts readers while its submarine currents seize, dazzle, baptize and otherwise astonish their souls before letting them worry back onto shore, reborn." *The Virginia Quarterly* reviewed his *The Storm and Other Poems* in this way: "Recent anthologies of the work of young poets resemble in many ways a one-ring circus with poet as small-time acrobat, clown and popcorn peddler. It is our gain that William Pitt Root has refused to join the circus and has chosen rather to demand of his art an honesty and boldness that mark his poems as the work of a serious writer....One has the strong feeling that here is a poet who has been near something important, near enough to have been so haunted that poetry was the inevitable result." Sandra Hutchins of the Texas Commission on the Arts and Humanities has reviewed his second, *Striking the Dark Air for Music,* as "a record of the poet's struggle to dance himself back to life, to change fiercely, to awaken from a sleep of static dreams....poems of death, of constriction and estrangement,...songs of rebirth into participation in the commonalty of the physical and sensory release.

Perhaps a poet who finds language to be at odds with the senses and intuitive knowledge and a source of confusion and mistrust among men must sing his poems, for the song is more directly allied to the body than prose, or other, more cerebral forms of poetry and (is) traditionally more universal. This poet thus sings...."

JEROME ROTHENBERG

BIRTH: 12/11/'31, in New York City, the son of Morris and Esther (Lichtenstein) Rothenberg, grew up there.

EDUCATION: Educated in the city's public schools, he received his B.A. from the City C. of N.Y. ('52) and his M.A. from the U. of Mich. ('53).

CAREER: On 12/25/'52, Rothenberg married his wife, the former Diane Brodatz. They have travelled in Europe, Mexico, & Cuba. For a time ('53-'55), Jerome Rothenberg served with the U.S. Army in Germany. He has taught at various institutions, particularly English at the Mannes C. of Music in N.Y.C., where he was Inst. from '61-'70. Since that time he has served as Regents Prof. ('71), U. of Calif., San Diego; Vist. Lectr. in Anthropology, New Schl. for Social Research, N.Y.C. ('71-'72), Visiting Research Professor at the Center for 20th Century Studies of the U. of Wis., Milwaukee ('75-'76), and is currently Acting Professor with the Visual Arts Department, U. of Calif., San Diego. When not serving as a Visit. Prof. on leaves, he and his wife and their son, Matthew, make their home in Salamanca, N.Y.

EDITORIAL POSTS: During his career, Jerome Rothenberg has founded, edited and directed various distinguished poetry magazines and small presses: *Poems from the Floating World* ('59-'64); with David Antin, *Some/Thing* ('65-'69); and Hawk's Well Press ('58-'65). He also served as ethnopoetics editor of *Stony Brook* ('68-'71). He was co-editor and founder with Dennis Tedlock of *Alcheringa: A First Magazine of Ethnopoetics* ('71-'76), and is the present founder and editor of *New Wilderness Letter.*

PUBLICATIONS: White Black Sun ('60), *The Seven Hells of the Jigoku Zoshi* ('62), *Sightings I-IX* (with *Lunes* by Robert Kelly) ('64), *The Gorky Poems* ('66), *Between 1960-63* ('67), *Conversations* ('68), *Poems 1964-67* ('68), *Offering Flowers,* with Ian Tyson ('68), *Sightings I-IX & Red Easy A Color* (with Ian Tyson) ('68), *Poland/1931* ('69), *The Directions,* with Tom Phillips ('69), *Poems for the Game of Silence 1960-1970* ('71); *A Book of Testimony* ('71), *Net of Moon, Net of Sun* ('71), *Esther K. Comes to America* ('73), *Seneca Journal I: A Poem of Beavers* ('73), *The Cards* ('74), *The Pirke and the Pearl* ('74), *Poland/1931* ('74), *The Notebooks* ('76), & *A Seneca Journal* ('78). His poems have been included in various periodicals including: *El Corno Emplumado, Kulchur, Poor Old Tired Horse, Caterpillar, Trobar, Tree, Poetry Review* (London, & *Montemora.* They have also been anthologized in these works: *A Controversy of Poets* ('65), *New Modern Poetry* ('67), *Where is Vietnam?* ('67), *Notations* ('69), *Caterpillar Anthology* ('71), *Open Poetry* ('72), *East Side Scene* ('72), *New Directions Annual* ('73), *America: A Prophecy* ('74), *Active Anthology* ('75), & *New Naked Poetry* ('76). Likewise he has arranged with David Antin, Jackson Mac Low, and Rochelle Owens, a recording of a series of primitive and archaic poetry, "Origins and Meanings," and "From a Shaman's Notebook" (Broadside Records, '69); also two later cassettes, "Horse Songs & Other Soundings" (S-Press, '75), and "6 Horse Songs For 4 Voices" (New Wilderness Audiographics, '77). Rothenberg is also well-known for his work as a translator and has rendered these books into English: *New Young German Poets* ('59); *The Flight of Quetzalcoatl,* from a Spanish prose version by Angel Maria Garibay of the original Aztec ('67); with Michael Hamburger and the author, *Poems for People Who Don't Read Poems* by Hans Magnus Enzensberger ('68; the British edition is entitled *Poems*); *The Deputy* by Rolf Hochhuth (Broadway Playing version, '74; *The Book of Hours and Constellations* by Engen Gomringer ('68); & *The 17 Horse Songs of Frank Mitchell,* NO. X-XIII from Navajo ('69). An editor, as well as a translator and poet, Rothenberg has also edited the following books: *Ritual: A Book of Primitive Rites and Events* ('66); *Technicians of the Sacred: A Range of Poetries from Africa, America, Asia, and Oceania* ('68); *Shaking The Pumpkin: Traditional Poetry of the Indian North Americas* ('72); with George Quasha, *America A Prophecy: A New Reading of American Poetry from*

Pre-Columbian Times to the Present ('73); *Revolution of the Word: A New Gathering of American Avant-garde Poetry* ('74); with Michei Benamou, *Ethnopoetics: A First Informational Symposium* ('76); & *A Big Jewish Book: Poems & Other Visions of the Jews from Tribal Times to the Present* ('78).

HONORS: Longview Foundation Award for poetry ('61); Wenner-Gren Foundation grant for Anthropological Research for experiments in translation of American Indian poetry ('68); Guggenheim grant ('74); and N.E.A. grant ('76); co-editor of magazine *Alcheringa,* which received a grant from the Co-ordinating Council of Literary Magazines ('71). His collected poems, *Poems for the Game of*

Jerome Rothenberg
(February 1971)

Silence, has been translated into Swedish by Jan Ostergren ('76), and into French by Jean Pierre Faye, Didier Permerle, & Jacques Roubaud ('78).

OBSERVATIONS: Rothenberg has noted: "In general, I think of myself as making poems that other poets haven't provided for me and for the existence of which I feel a deep need. I look for new forms and possibilities, but also for ways of presenting in our language the oldest possibilities of poetry going back to the 'primitive' and 'archaic' cultures that have been opening up to us over the last 100 years. I believe that everything is now possible in poetry, and that our earlier ('western') attempts at closed definitions present a failure of perception we no longer have to endure." Kenneth Rexroth has commented upon Rothenberg's poetry in this way: "Jerome Rothenberg is one of the truly contemporary American poets who has returned U.S. poetry to the mainstream of international modern literature. At the same time, he is a true autochthon. Only here and now could have produced him—a swinging orgy of Martin Buber, Marcel Duchamp, Gertrude Stein and Sitting Bull. No one writing poetry today has dug deeper into the roots of poetry."

RICARDO SÁNCHEZ

BIRTH: 3/29/'41, grew up in east El Paso, Tex., in an old *barrio,* near the Coliseum, known as "El Barrio Del Diablo," the son of Pedro Lucero and Adelina Gallegos Sánchez, both from New Mexico. Ricardo was the first in his family's history, since the 1600's, to be born outside of Southern Colorado or Northern New Mexico. One of a large family of children, he grew up with his brothers Pete and Sefy as *pachucos,* or as *batos* of the X-9 gang, which was sworn to protect the *barrio* and which rivaled other *bato* groups, for instance ones such as those of the *segundo barrio*, south El Paso, to which the poet Abelardo "Lalo" Delgado belonged in those days. Much of Ricardo Sánchez's poetry and prose reflect his experiences in those years before the Chicano movement began—days when he and Abelardo, who was later to serve as *compadre* (godfather) for Ricardo's daughter Libertad-Yvonne, were teen-age rivals from two different *barrios*. In fact, it might be said that Sánchez's poetry and prose are encyclopedias of how the Chicano movement really began; for with Abelardo Delgado, Ricardo Sánchez, looms as one of the most powerful poets of the Chicano movement. Today he lives in Salt Lake City with his wife Teresa, their son Rik-Ser, their daughter Libertad-Yvonne (named to celebrate Ricardo's release from prison), and a baby son Jacinto-Temilotzín, who was welcomed into this family in '76, after the sadness this family experienced in '75 when they lost their infant son Pedro-Cuauhtémoc after a difficult and costly hospitalization. The latter had occurred just after Ricardo Sánchez gained his doctorate in American Studies, and before he became a Visiting Professor of Chicano Studies at the University of Utah, where for the year '77-'78, he teaches.

EDUCATION: Thomas Jefferson High School, El Paso, dropped out before graduation; Alvin Junior College, Tex.; Ph.D., Union Graduate School (Antioch College, Ohio, '75). With understandable pride, Sánchez notes: "I am the first to go from a G.E.D. (High School Equivalency Test), to a doctorate...no bachelor's, nor master's degrees."

CAREER: After attending Thomas Jefferson High School in El Paso, from which, as he writes, he was a "push-out," rather than a "drop-out," Ricardo Sánchez, filled with despair over the injustices to the Chicano in the world he saw around him,

Ricardo Sánchez
(June 1975)

entered the U.S. Army on his eighteenth birthday. After two years in the Army—years in which his anger over such injustices only grew, Sánchez left the Army, feeling as he says, a "flame of need for...liberation—and i vented my furious desperation with gun and madness...and sunny california gave me from one to 25 years in prison." At the Correctional Training Facility, North, Soledad, Calif., he began to write poetry. His well-known, "Soledad," a poem of deep despair over his imprisonment, was written on 11/29/'61, three years after he had been arrested and seven months before his release; it is a product of these lonely years. At twenty-two, he won his first release from prison, returned to his native El Paso, and married his wife, Teresa, daughter of Manuel and Estela Silva of the same city.

Two days before the birth of their first child, their son Rik-Ser, Ricardo Sánchez, jobless and "in anxiety and desperation," committed robbery and was indicted for another four years of prison life—this time at Ramsey Prison Farm #1, near Alvin, Tex. While a prisoner, he took some couses at Alvin Junior College as he worked "first in the fields...later in the education department, ever striving," for the parole he finally was awarded in March, '69, when the son he was to see for the first time was then four years old. This time, Sánchez returned to his El Paso family, even "more dedicated and devoted," as he writes, "to transform the gelatinous globulin of society" than ever. Thus, at twenty-nine years of age, nine of which had been spent in prisons, he began to write and write vigorously for and about the Chicano cause. After his '69 Texas prison release, he was also awarded a Ford Fellowship in Journalism (the Frederick Douglass Fellowship Program in Richmond, Virginia, a one-year-stipend program, which he completed in six months.) His initial work was with the southside El Paso VISTA, the M.M.P., and the *Machos*. Then when he and his wife were expecting Libertad-Yvonne, their first daughter, Sánchez accepted a job as a staff writer, research assistant, for the School of Education, U. of Mass, Amherst, and moved his family to New England. His daughter was born in Northampton while Sánchez worked there for a semester and a half. Meanwhile as Sánchez came to be known more and more for his poetry and Chicano causes, he decided to leave the "vacuousness of new england," where a part of him, he felt, "was dying," and to return to the center of his and his family's being, the Southwest. Thus he and his family moved next to Denver where Sánchez worked for a year for the Colorado Migrant Council as director of the Itinerant Migrant Health Project. In this capacity, he was associated daily with his good friend—the poet, Abelardo Delgado, making fiery speeches with him for the Chicano cause, and living always at this time, as Sánchez notes, "in the jungle of Lalo's (Delgado's) pad."

EDITORIAL POSTS: In '71, he moved back to his birthplace, El Paso, where he founded Míctla Publications with the help of some other friends in poetry. Sánchez's first book of poetry and prose, *Canto y Grito Mi Liberacíon,* was the first book to be published by Míctla Publications; his press first released it in a cloth edition in '71. After the publication of *Canto y Grito Mi Liberacíon*, Sánchez went on to other activism, traveling often across the country giving talks from Virginia to Washington, D.C., N.Y. to Chicago, Denver, Oregon, Michigan, and the Midwest for the Chicano cause. Meanwhile he pursued his poetry and prose writings, was awarded his Ph.D., and became a popular speaker on college campuses and at Writers' Conferences throughout the country, presenting lectures, as he notes, "from Harvard, Yale, etc. to Stanford...along with the U.N.A.M. in Mexico City." Likewise he worked with the Texas Poetry-In-The-Schools program, and with inmates in the poetry-writing programs in Texas prisons and elsewhere. Additionally he founded the annual National Canto Al Pueblo festival of Raza Arts, which held its '78 meeting in Corpus Christi, Texas. In recent years, Sánchez has served as visiting professor of Chicano Studies at various universities; in '78 at the University of Utah.

PUBLICATIONS: After Sánchez's first book appeared, *Canto y Grito Mi Liberacíon*, from Mictla in '71, it was re-issued in '73, by Doubleday which published it in their Anchor Book series in a bilingual edition entitling it the same and adding the sub-title in English, *The Liberation of a Chicano Mind*. Meanwhile Ricardo Sánchez's poetry has also appeared in the important Chicano collection, *Los Cuatro*, which he edited in '70 in Denver for Barrio Publications—an anthology, which also introduced some of Abelardo Delgado's early poetry. The latter publication, as well as the former, also included Ricardo Sánchez's prose, as did *Obras* (Quetzal-Vihio Press, Pembroke, N.C., '71), for Sánchez is a serious writer of fiction, as well as of poetry. His third book, *Hechízospells,* is a 359-page collection of prose and poems published by U.C.L.A.'s Chicano Publication Unit, '76. His fourth *Milhaus Blues & Gritos Norteños*, published by the U. of Wisc./Milwaukee appeared in '77. Additionally his work has been included in numerous periodicals and anthologies, including *Voices of Aztlan: Chicano Literature of Today*, edited by Dorothy E. Harth and Lewis M. Baldwin (New American Library, N.Y., '74).

OBSERVATIONS: Sánchez has commented upon his writings and his people in this way: "Chicanos are a spectral people—a rainbow-like people, whose veins carry all the diverse bloods of humankind, but who were circumstantially forced into vagabondage—now on the final lap home." About his poetry, Philip D. Ortego, well-known Chicano literary critic, has observed: "No contemporary poet reminds me more of William Blake than Ricardo Sánchez. I do not mean in form or style, for Ricardo is a Chicano poet through and through. No. I mean in purpose. Like Blake in his time, Ricardo Sánchez is trying to tell us something. I only hope more of us stop and listen."

JOSEPHINE SAUNDERS

BIRTH: Born in Philadelphia, Pa., grew up there, later moving to its suburbs.

EDUCATION & CAREER: She attended the Agnes Irwin School for Girls in Philadelphia. Josephine studied painting with, among others, Yasuo Kuniyoshi, but was forced to abandon such study because of ill health. Later, again for reasons of health, she and her husband, Frederick Saunders, moved to Arizona. During the early "sixties," they lived in Tumacacori, Ariz. In the late "sixties," they bought a home in Tucson, and now live in the latter city. Josephine Saunders has been writing poetry most of her life.

Josephine Saunders
(March 1972)

PUBLICATIONS: Her work has been widely published in numerous periodicals. Her poems have appeared in *Poetry, Choice, The New Yorker, The Nation, Lillabulero, & Kayak*, and are also anthologized in *The Indian Rio Grande* ('77), edited by Frumkin and Noyes. Currently she is at work on a collection entitled, *"I Am Not, and Never Was, A Bird or a Stone."*

OBSERVATIONS: Concerning her poetry, Jo Saunders relates: "A great deal of my work is autobiographical, and most of it deals with a very strange thing that happened to me, and which, so far as I can find out, has never happened to anyone else. I seem to write two types of poems, one rather prosaic (these are usually the most autobiographical), the other not. But sometimes the two amalgamate.''

HARRIS SCHIFF

BIRTH: Born ''during World War II'' considers himself a poet of the Bronx, for he has spent much of his life in N.Y.C. However, as he notes, ''I was a War Baby, whom destiny flung across the Americas and scarcely gave breath to find home in what at times seems an exile of sorts and not so self-imposed.'' In the mid-''seventies,'' he divided his time living between Cuba, N.M.; Oakland, Calif.; and San Diego; and still devotes much time to traveling.

CAREER: Schiff began practicing his craft in San Francisco in '63-'65. He declares now that he ''will always miss his friends from that era.'' Later, at St. Mark's Church in the Bowerie, he participated, studied, and gave various N.Y.C. readings between '69 and '72 with numerous poets who had gathered there.

EDITORIAL POSTS: For a while, he also edited *The Harris Review.* After '72, he left N.Y. for a time and began to travel extensively, spending sometime in Latin America. Concerning his teachers, he expresses a deep debt to Jack Spicer whom

Harris Schiff
(May 1975)

he says was ''a true friend'' and who gave him helpful encouragement and showed early interest in his work. Currently Schiff lives in New York City, where he writes poetry and gives readings in bars, churches, bookstores, on television and radio. He is still a very active participant at the readings at St. Mark's Church in the Bowerie.

PUBLICATIONS: Harris Schiff's *Easy Street* (No Books Company) appeared in '72. Additionally he has also published several chapbooks, including *Empty Boat* and *Secret Clouds* (Angel Hair Books,' 70), as well as *In the Heart of the Empire* (Angel Hair Books, '78). Such anthologies as these by Anne Waldman also carry his poetry: *The World Anthology* (Bobbs-Merrill, '69), and *Another World* (Bobbs Merrill, '71). Dating from '63, his poems have also appeared in a wide variety of periodicals, including these: *The World, Chicago, Paris Review, Big Sky, The Harris Review, Roots Forming, Sanskaras, Reindeer, Telephone, Adventures in Poetry,* & *Open Space.* He is also recorded reading his poetry on Giorno Poetry Systems Dial-A-Poem. Additionally Schiff writes prose and is the author of a microcosmic novel, *I Should Run for Cover But I'm Right Here* (Angel Hair Books, '77).

RICHARD (WILLIAM) SHELTON

BIRTH: 6/24/'33, in Boise, Idaho, spent his youth in the same region. He is the son of Hazel (Ashlock) Shelton, who still lives in Boise and of the late Leonard P. Shelton.

EDUCATION: Boise High School, Harding C., Ark. ('51-'53) & Abilene Christian College, Tex. (B.A., '58); M.A., U. of Ariz. ('61); post-graduate studies, U. of Ariz. ('62-'67).

CAREER: In '56, Richard Shelton was drafted into the U.S. Army and at the end of the same year, he married Lois Bruce, a talented mezzo-soprano and then a member of the faculty of the Music Department of Abilene Christian College in Texas. Richard was stationed at Fort Huachuca, Arizona, and thus introduced to desert life. In the fall of '58, the Sheltons moved to Bisbee, where for two years Richard taught in the junior high school of the neighboring city of Lowell, and commuted to Tucson to study at the U. of Ariz. When he received his M.A., the

Richard Shelton
(June 1973)

Sheltons built a home in the foothills of the Tucson Mountains, and Richard became an instructor in the English Department at the U. of Ariz., and Lois a teacher of music in the Tucson Public Schools. Since that time they have lived in the Tucson Mountains with their son Brad Scot Shelton, now a married graduate student at U.C.L.A. in the locale Shelton has often described in his poetry. Since '70, Lois Shelton has served as Director of the U. of Ariz. Poetry Center, an institution with which Richard has always been closely identified. He is currently an Assoc. Prof. in the Creative Writing Program at the U. of Arizona where he teachers courses in literature and writing. He has served, for a number of years and at various intervals, as Board member for the U. of Ariz. Poetry Center and was for one year its Director. He has participated in the Poetry-in-the-Schools programs in Arizona, New Mexico, and South Dakota and has presented numerous readings in over a dozen states. For the past four years, he has directed, under the auspices of the Ariz. Commission on the Arts and Humanities, a writers' workshop at the Arizona State Prison in Florence. Six books of poetry or prose by men in the Florence workshop have now been published, and many members of the workshop have published in magazines throughout the U.S. Some of their work has been collected in the anthology *Do Not Go Gentle* (Blue Moon Press, '77), edited by Michael

Hogan. In '77, the P.E.N.-sponsored writing contest for prisoners made a special citation to the Writers' Workshop at the Arizona State Prison for the quality and quantity of entries in poetry.

PUBLICATIONS: The Tattooed Desert ('71), *Of All the Dirty Words* ('72), *You Can't Have Everything* ('75), & *The Bus to Veracruz* ('78), all from the U. of Pittsburgh Press, *Calendar: A Cycle of Poems* ('72, Baleen Press), & *Among the Stones* (Monument Press, '73). Shelton has also published these chapbooks: *Journal of Return* (Kayak Press, '69), and from Best Cellar Press, *Heroes of Our Time* ('72) & *Chosen Place* ('75). Additionally he is the editor of *The Unfinished Man: The Poetry of Paul David Ashley* (Baleen Press, '78). Shelton's poems have been published in over 200 magazines, among them: *The New Yorker, Kayak, Poetry, Poetry Northwest, North American Review, Field, American Poetry Review, The Ohio Review, The Paris Review, The Antioch Review, The Outsider,* & *The American Scholar.* They have also been included in such anthologies as *The New Yorker Book of Poems* ('69), *Borestone Mt. Poetry Awards* ('72, '73), *Modern Poetry of Western America* ('75), *Fifty Contemporary Poets* ('77), *Southwest: A Contemporary Anthology* ('77), & *The Indian Rio Grande* ('77). Besides writing poetry, Richard Shelton has also edited ('63), V. II of *The Spoken Anthology of American Literature,* a series of recordings produced by Ruth Stephan and the University of Arizona Press. Additionally he has published articles and reviews in such magazines as *The American Poetry Review, The Arizona Teacher, The Speech Teacher,* & *Sumac.*

HONORS: Richard Shelton has been awarded the '70 U.S. Award of the International Poetry Forum (for the book, *The Tattooed Desert*), two annual awards from the Borestone Mountain Poetry Awards, and an N.E.A. Writers' Fellowship ('76).

OBSERVATIONS: Shelton notes: "I consider myself a regionalist and a surrealist. I have lived in the desert for years and hope that my work reflects that fact." Charles Simic has commented about Richard Shelton's poetry, noting: "The style he has evolved is remarkable for its precise observation and sensuous memorable imagery. These poems articulate the song of the solitude and drama of the secret traveler in all of us. In that sense, he comes to us with his first book with a voice as old as poetry itself."

CHARLES SIMIC

BIRTH: 5/9/'38, in Belgrade, Yugoslavia, emigrated to the U.S. with his parents in '49, and became, like them, a naturalized American citizen. He settled with his father, George Simic, an engineer, and his mother Helen (Matijevic) Simic in Illinois and attended Oak Park High School there.

EDUCATION: U. of Chicago ('56-'59) & New York U. ('59-'61; '63-'66); B.A. ('66).

CAREER: After completing his public school education in Ill., Simic served in the U.S. Army for two years, '61-'63. He married Helen Dubin, a dress designer, in '65. The next year ('66), after completing his B.A., he worked as an editorial assistant on the photography magazine, *Aperture,* a position he held until '72. As a student in Manhattan, he had held many different kinds of jobs previously to support himself. After a year writing on a Guggenheim Fellowship ('72-'73), he took up a teaching career at Calif. St. U. at Hayward for the year '73-'74. Since '75, he has been poet-in-residence at the U. of New Hampshire. The father of a daughter Anna, he currently makes his home in Strafford, New Hampshire.

PUBLICATIONS: What the Grass Says ('67), *Somewhere Among Us a Stone Is Taking Notes* ('69), *Dismantling the Silence* ('71), *White* ('72), *Return to a Place Lit By a Glass of Milk* ('74), *Biography and a Lament* ('76), & *Charon's Cosmology* ('77). His poems have also appeared in such anthologies as Paul Carroll's *The Young American Poets*, Mark Strand's *The Contemporary American Poets*, Al Lee's *Major Young American Poets*, Quasha & Rothenberg's *America A Prophesy*, Milton Klonsky's *Shake the Kaleidoscope: A New Anthology of Modern Poetry*, Berg & Mezey's *The New Naked Poetry*, & Daniel Halpern, *The American Poetry Anthology*. Many periodicals carry his poetry, including: *The New Yorker, Poetry, The Nation, Esquire, Chicago Review, Minnesota Review, Field, Iowa Review, Seneca Review, Kayak, Sumac, Stony Brook, Lillabulero, Choice, Hearse, Antaeus, Greensboro Review, Chelsea Review, Crazy Horse, Ironwood, Ohio Review, Edge, Alcheringa, Boundary 2, New Republic, American Poetry Review, Agenda, New Letters, Paris Review,* & *The Antioch Review*. Simic has also published numerous translations of Yugoslav and French poetry, and has co-edited with Mark Strand *Another Republic* ('76), an anthology of seventeen European and South American writers. Others of Simic's translations include these books: *Fire Gardens: Poems* by *Ivan V. Lalic*, with C.W. Truesdale ('70); *The Little Box: Poems of Vasko Popa* ('70); & *Four Modern Yugoslav Poets* ('70).

HONORS: In addition to the Guggenheim Fellowship ('72-'73), he has been awarded other prestigious prizes and fellowships for his poetry: P.E.N. International Award for Translation ('70), N.E.A. Grant ('74-'75), Edgar Allan Poe Award ('75), National Institute of Arts and Letters & American Academy of Arts and Letters Award ('76). Additionally his *Charon's Cosmology* ('77) was nominated for the National Book Award in poetry.

OBSERVATIONS: About his poetry, Simic writes: "As for the finished product, the poem, my need requires it to be of, as Whitman said: '...the thoughts of all men in all ages and lands'...on a subjective level, I write to give being to that vibration which is my life and to survive in a hard time." Michael Benedict describes Simic's work in this way: "It has a kind of rock bottom simplicity—a simplicity that is spiritual enough to qualify, I think, as a unique clarity of the heart. Most of Simic's poems are about looking at small, modest things and seeing the sense in which they are indeed, compounded of the stuff of poetry....These simple subjects are always falling open, to reveal other trapdoors to other worlds."

Charles Simic
(March 1970)

GARY (SHERMAN) SNYDER

BIRTH: 5/8/'30, in San Francisco, grew up in the states of Wash. and Ore. He spent most of his youth on the farm of his parents, Harold A. and Lois (Wilkie) Snyder, north of Seattle, Wash.

EDUCATION: Reed College, Portland, Ore., B.A. in anthropology and literature ('51); graduate work in anthropology, Indiana U. ('51), & grad. study of Oriental Languages, U. of Calif., Berkeley ('53-'56).

CAREER: In '48, Gary Snyder interrupted his schooling and worked for awhile as a seaman out of New York. While attending college, he was also employed as a logger, Forest Service crew member, and at forest look-out posts in Ore., Wash., & Calif. These experiences greatly influenced his first writings. During the "mid-fifties," while still a student at Berkeley, he was closely associated with the San Francisco "beat" poetry movement, and with such poets as Allen Ginsberg, Jack Kerouac, Philip Whalen, Michael McClure, and Philip Lamantia. Jack Kerouac outfitted the fictional hero of his *Dharma Bums* on the life and character of Gary Snyder, a fact that also brought considerable notice to the poet and his work. While in San Francisco, Snyder supported himself with various odd jobs, including work for Kodak, a position as a burglar alarm installer, and an assignment as a wiper on an American Tanker, which made runs to the Persian Gulf and the South Pacific Islands. Since his early days of identification with the "beat" generation, Snyder's own work and personal influence on modern poetry, has continued to grow in its own individual direction. Between '56 and '64, and also during the years, '65-'68, Snyder spent most of his time living in Japan, especially in Kyoto, where he studied Zen, and Zen monastery life and training methods. He also spent four months of '61-'62 in India, where he visited temples and ashrams. In addition to his traveling and studying in Japan, he returned to the U.S. during the year of '64-'65. He devoted that year to teaching poetry-writing at the U. of Calif., Berkeley. During the month of July, '65, he participated in the Berkeley poetry conference, and in addition, gave many readings on various college campuses throughout the academic year. Since '69, he has spent most of his time in the U.S., living in California, and making his living by his writings and readings and participation in various writers' conferences throughout the country. His first two marriages were to Alison Gass ('50-'51) and to Joanne Kyger ('60-'64). He is the father of two children and lives currently with his present wife, Masa Uehara, whom he married in '67 in Japan. He now lives at Kitkitdizze, the home he built for his family and himself in the countryside outside Nevada City, Calif. Since '74, he has also served as a member of the California Arts Council, and in '77 was additionally on the faculty of the annual Poetry Symposium at Port Townsend, Washington.

PUBLICATIONS: Riprap ('59), *Myths and Texts* ('60), *The Firing* ('64), *Hop, Skip, and Jump* ('64), *Nanoa Knows* ('64), *Six Sections of Mountains and Rivers Without End* ('65; '68); *Riprap and Cold Mountain Poems* ('65), *Three Worlds, Three Realms, Six Roads* ('66), *A Range of Poems* ('66), *The Back Country* ('68), *The Blue Sky* ('69), *Four Changes* ('69), *South of the Hills* ('69), *Regarding Wave* ('70; '71), *Anasazi* ('71), *Manzanita* ('72), & *Turtle Island* ('74). As always, he continues work on his long *Mountains and Rivers Without End.* Snyder has contributed many poems too numerous for listing here to periodicals, some of which include these: *Poetry, Caterpillar, Nation, Black Mountain Review, Janus, Evergreen Review, Yugēn, Chicago Review, Jabberwock, San Francisco Review, Big Table, Poems from the Floating World, Origin, Kulchur, Journal for the Protection of All Beings, City Lights Journal, Yale Literary Magazine,* & *Beloit*

Gary Snyder
(February 1971)

Poetry Journal. His work has been widely anthologized in such volumes as these: *Beats* ('60), *Helgon and Hetsporper* ('60), *New American Poetry* ('60), *New American Poets* ('60), *June Amerikanische Lyrik* ('61), *Contemporary American Poetry* ('62), *Poesia Degli Ultimi Americani* ('64), *Poets of Today* ('64), *12 Poets and 1 Painter* ('64), *A Controversy of Poets* ('65), *Poems of the Late T'ang* ('66), *Contemporary Poetry in America* ('73), *The Norton Anthology of Modern Poetry* ('73), & *Modern Poems: An Introduction to Poetry* ('73; '76). In addition to his poetry, he has written one volume of essays entitled *Earth House Hold* ('69). He can be heard reading his poetry, with others, on *Today's Poets 4* (Folkway Records).

HONORS: Bess Hokin Prize ('64); scholarship from the First Zen Inst. of Am. for study in Japan ('56), Bollingen Foundation research grant for Buddhist Studies ('65-'67); Nat. Academy of Arts & Letters grant ('66), Am. Academy of Arts & Sciences Poetry Prize ('66); Levinson Prize ('68); Guggenheim Fellowship ('68-'69), & the '75 Pulitzer Prize.

OBSERVATIONS: Snyder has explained elsewhere: "A a poet I hold the most archaic values on earth. They go back to the Palaeolithic, the fertility of the soil, the magic of animals, the power-vision in solitude, the terrifying initiation and rebirth, the lore and ecstacy of the dance, the common work of the tribe." He continues: "For me every poem is formally unique....Each poem grows from an energy-mind field dance...to let it grow, to let it speak for itself, is a large part of the work of the poet....What is needed is a totally new approach to the very idea of form." Of Snyder's poems, Thomas Parkinson writes: "...action and contemplation become identical states of being, and both states of secular grace. From this fusion wisdom emerges, and it is not useless but timed to the event. The result is a terrible sanity, a literal clairvoyance, an innate decorum."

WILLIAM (EDGAR) STAFFORD

BIRTH: 1/17/'14, in Hutchinson, Kansas, grew up and attended public schools there.

EDUCATION: B.A. ('37) & M.A. ('45) from the U. of Kansas; Ph.D. from the U. of Iowa ('54).

CAREER: During W.W. II, Bill Stafford was a conscientious objector, and was active in pacifist organizations. Since '59, he has been a member of the Ore. Board of the Fellowship of Reconciliation. His teaching career began at Lewis and Clark

C., Portland, Ore., where he was a member of the English faculty from '48-'54. He spent the years of '55-'56 at Manchester C. in Ind., and '56-'57 at San Jose C. He has also been a Visit. Prof. of English at San Jose St. C. in Calif. in '56-'57. In '57, he returned to Lewis and Clark C. where, except for absences in connection with grants and leaves, he has remained. From '70-'71, he served as Cons. in Poetry for the Lib. of Congress, and in '72, was U.S. Inf. Agency Lectr. in Egypt, India, Pakistan, Iran, Nepal, and Bangladesh. The father of four children: Bret, Kim, Kathryn, and Barbara, he lives today with his wife, the former Dorothy Hope Frantz whom he married in '44, in the small town of Lake Oswego, Oregon.

PUBLICATIONS: West of Your City ('60), *Traveling Through the Dark* ('62), *The Rescued Year* ('66), *Eleven Untitled Poems* ('68), *Weather: Poems* ('69), *Allegiances* ('70), *Temporary Facts* ('70), *Someday, Maybe* ('73), *That Other Alone: Poems* ('73), & *Collected Poems* ('78). His poetry has also appeared in four volumes with others: *Five American Poets*, with others, ed.by Thom Gunn and Ted Hughes ('63), *Five Poets of the Pacific Northwest*, with others, ed. by Robin Skelton ('64), *Poems for Tennessee*, with Robert Bly and William Matthews ('71), & *Braided Apart*, with his son Kim Robert Stafford ('77). Stafford's work is widely anthologized in addition, some of the latter including: *New Pocket Anthology of American Verse* ('55), *New Poems by American Poets* ('57), *Contemporary American Poetry* ('62), *Poet's Choice* ('62), *Borestone Mountain Poetry Awards* ('63), *A Western Sampler* ('63), *Distinctive Voices* ('66), *Heartland* ('67), and

William Stafford
(December 1976)

Contemporary Poetry in America ('73). His poems have been published widely and with frequency in such periodicals as *Atlantic Monthly, Harper's, New Yorker, Hudson Review, Saturday Review, Poetry, Kenyon Review, Northwest Review, Critical Quarterly,* and *Poetry Northwest.* He has read his poetry on *Today's Poets 2,* with others, for Folkway Records in '68. Additionally Stafford has edited or co-edited these works: *The Voices of Prose,* with Frederick Candelaria ('66), *The Achievement of Brother Antoninus: A Comprehensive Selection of his Poems with a Critical Introduction* ('67), & *Poems and Perspectives,* with Robert H. Ross ('71). He is also the author of three books of lectures and literary criticism, as well as of his first book, *Down in My Heart* ('47), which told of his experiences as a conscientious objector during W.W.II. The former works are entitled *Friends to This Ground: A Statement for Readers, Teachers, and Writers of Literature* ('67),

Leftovers: A Care Package: Two Lectures ('73), and *Writing the Australian Crawl* (78).

HONORS: Yaddo Foundation Fellowship ('55); Ore. Centennial Prize for poetry and for short story ('59); Union League Civic and Arts Foundation Prize ('59), Nat. Book Award ('62); Shelley Memorial Award ('65); N.E.A. grant ('66); Guggenheim Fellowship ('66); & Melville Cane Award ('74). Likewise in both '71 and '66, he was a co-ordinator of the poetry readings of the national conventions of N.C.T.E. in Las Vegas, Nev., and Houston, Tex., and in '71, was also a member of the Nat. Council of Teachers of English Commission on Lit. He has also two honorary D.Litt. degrees, one from Ripon C., Wis. ('65), and Linfield C., McMinnville, Ore. ('70).

OBSERVATIONS: Stafford has written: "My poetry seems to me direct and communicative, with some oddity and variety. It is usually not formal. It is much like talk, with some enhancement. Often my poetry is discursive and reminiscent, or at least is that way at one level: it delivers a sense of place and event; it has narrative impulses. Forms are not usually much evident, though tendencies and patterns are occasionally flirted with." About his writing, Roderick Nordell has written in the *Christian Science Monitor* that Stafford "recognizes an appearance of moral commitment mixed with a deliberate—even flaunted—non-sophistication; an organized form cavalierly treated; a trace of narrative for company amid too many feelings....And the *things* here—plains, farm, home, winter, lavished all over the page—these command my allegiance in a way that is beyond my power to analyze at the moment."

RUTH (WALGREEN) STEPHAN

BIRTH: 1/21/'10, in Chicago, Ill.

DEATH: 4/9/'74, in North Salem, N.Y. She was the only daughter of Charles R. Walgreen, Sr., and Myrtle (Norton) Walgreen, who were the successful drug-chain founders. With her brother C.R. Walgreen, Jr., she grew up in the city of her birthplace.

EDUCATION: Ruth Stephan attended Northwestern ('27-'29), but left in '29 before completing her B.A. degree in order to marry Justin W. Dart, a fellow student and football star. Between '37-'39, she took graduate courses at the U. of Chicago.

CAREER: In the mid-'30's, Ruth Stephan, then the wife of Justin Dart, Sr., and the mother of two small sons, Justin, Jr. and Peter Dart, began writing poetry. In '37, her first poem "Identity," was accepted by *Harper's* Magazine, and shortly afterwards selected for inclusion in the Moult anthology of the best poems of the year in England and the U.S. Thereafter she dedicated the remainder of her life to a literary career of being poet, novelist, historian, editor, record album and film-producer, and to founding Poetry Centers at the U. of Ariz. and at the U. of Tex. Following her divorce from Justin W. Dart, Sr., in '39, she married her second husband, artist John Stephan, with whom she collaborated in planning and producing a distinguished avant-guard poetry journal *The Tiger's Eye*. By this marriage, she had her third and last son, John J. Stephan. After twenty-two years of marriage, she divorced Stephan in '61, but retained her literary name of Ruth Stephan which she had established during the interval throughout the remainder of her life. When she married John Stephan, she also changed her residence from Chicago to the East Coast, and spent most of the remainder of her life, when not traveling, first in Westport, Conn., then in Greenwich Village, N.Y., and later at her estate Stone Legend in Greenwich, Conn. In '66, she married her third and last husband John C. Franklin, a scientist. During her career, she spent much time traveling and living for periods of time in Peru, Japan, India, England, Italy, and Ceylon; vacationing in Tucson, Austin, and in the Carribean. She is survived by her three sons, Justin and Peter Dart, and John J. Stephan, and by her husband, "Jack" Franklin.

PUBLICATIONS: After the publication of her first poem by *Harper's* Magazine, Ruth Stephan began to publish her poems frequently in such magazines as *Poetry & Forum.* Her first collection of poetry , *Prelude to Poetry*, was published in '46. A second collection, *Various Poems*, appeared in '63. As a translator, she rendered into English and edited two volumes of poetry: *The Singing Mountaineers: Songs and Tales of the Quechua People*, with José María Arguedas ('57) & *Poems for Nothing* ('73), a chapbook of Zen verse. Other poems of hers had appeared in various poetry magazines and anthologies, such as *New Directions Annual #10*, in addition to those earlier noted, and were published not only in the U.S., but in England, Peru, and Italy, as well.

EDITORIAL POSTS: As an editor of poetry, she was especially known for *Tiger's Eye*, the quarterly of poetry and art, which she and her husband John Stephan

Ruth Stephan
(April 1971)
deceased

edited together from '47-'50, first in Westport, Conn., and then in Greenwich Village, N.Y.C. Ruth edited the poetry, and John the art; their contributors included such writers as Marguerite Young, Owen Dodson, Marianne Moore, Horace Gregory, Anaïs Nin, Boris Pasternak, Kenneth Rexroth, Paul Goodman, Van Wyck Brooks, Jorge Luis Borges,and numerous other well-known poets and prose-writers of contemporary literature. Among the contributing artists were Jackson Pollock, Mark Rothko, William de Kooning, Mark Tobey, and numerous others. Beginning in '61 and continuing through '65, she also edited *The Spoken Anthology of American Literature* in two volumes, assisted by Arthur M. Kay on V. I, and by Richard Shelton on V. II, for the U. of Ariz. Press. Earlier she had produced a series of recordings, which was also entitled *The Spoken Anthology of American Literature*, for advanced studies in Italian schools. The records were produced in Italy by the Centro Documentazione Phoniche ('60). Besides her own poems, translations and work as an editor of poetry, both written and spoken, Ruth Stephan also wrote two biographical historical novels based on the life of Sweden's Queen Christina, daughter of Gustavus Adolphus, who lived in the seventeenth century. These novels, *The Flight* ('56) & *My Crown, My Love* ('60) were both published by Alfred A. Knopf and were praised for their fine style and attention to historical detail. Also she wrote one unpublished autobiographical novel entitled "Jegerson's Daughter," which she completed in '69, and which, with the rest of her manuscripts and other papers, forms a part of the Ruth Stephan Collection today at the Yale University Library. In addition to her fiction, and other contributions to poetry previously noted, she also produced a documentary movie entitled *Zen in Ryōkō-In*, ('72), which deals with life in a Zen Buddhist temple—that of Daitokuji, in Kyoto, Japan. In '61, Ruth Stephan had had the rare privilege of living in Ryōkō-In, one of Daitokuji's constituent temples as the guest of Nanrei Kobori, the English-speaking abbot, and his family. Her friendship with this Zen priest and his family blossomed, and she described it, both in an article of hers in *Harper's* Magazine (June '62) and ten years later in the film concerning not only her experiences at the temple, but also its daily routine of activities and its priceless Zen art treasures and philosophy. As a sponsor and patroness to poetry and the arts, she likewise endowed and helped to create and found two poetry centers—one at the U. of Ariz., which was dedicated by Robert Frost in November, '60, and a second, on a smaller scale, in November, '65, at the U. of Tex., Austin. Her work as a friend to the arts had begun in '37 when she was invited to head the committee, as chairman, for the book selection of Chicago's Lib. of International Relations. It was here that she met the young attorney on the Library's board, Adlai Stevenson, who was to remain a lifelong intimate friend of hers. She held the post on the Book Committee for the Library until '43. Later, in '64, she helped organize as a part of the Civil Rights movement, the Freedom Schools throughout the southern part of the U.S.A., supplying poetry books for their libraries. In this connection, she also edited a special issue of *Mankind,* a social journal published in India, which was dedicated to black Americans and their experiences, and which carried a lead article by her good friend Owen Dodson. At the time of her death, Ruth Stephan was involved in producing a second film entitled "Wabi," which concerned the lives of three individuals and their artistic achievements, and which was left uncompleted.

HONORS: In addition to the honors mentioned above, Ruth Stephan's achievements include the Friends of Literature Award, Chicago ('57) for *The Flight,* and an honorary Doctor of Letters degree in '63 from the U. of Ariz., for her "high achievement as a poet, novelist, translator, and editor with international recognition, and as a sponsor and patron of imaginative literature."

OBSERVATIONS: Ruth Stephan's editorial policy for *The Tiger's Eye* can be offered as her criteria for what her own poetry, or else that of some contributor to her magazine should ideally be. Of contributor's work, she asked these questions: "Is it alive? Is it valid as art? How brave is its originality? How does it enter the imagination?" About Ruth Stephan's poetry, Marianne Moore once wrote: "Throughout these various revelations, poems are embedded in the words, attesting indigenous, contagious, deep-rooted poetic imagination." Kenneth Rexroth also characterized her work in this way: "Reading Ruth Stephan's poems is a most lucid experience—they are so perfectly like herself—they are gracious as she is gracious; it would be incredible if they were more beautiful—but they approach that comparison."

ALAN (ARCHER) STEPHENS

BIRTH: 12/19/'25, in Greeley, Colo., grew up on the farm of his parents, Alan Archer and Ellen (Meyers) Stephens, located near the same town. After high school, he served in the U.S.A.F. from '43-'45.

EDUCATION: Stephens worked on his B.A. degree at three universities—the U. of Colo. ('46-'48), Colo. St. C. of Ed., and at the U. of Denver. He received this degree, as well as his M.A. in '50 from the latter institution, and his Ph.D., in '54, from the U. of Missouri. In '58, Stephens was awarded a poetry fellowship at Stanford and studied there for a year, as a pupil of the poets Donald Drummond and Yvor Winters.

Alan Stephens
(December 1964)

CAREER: He began his teaching career in '54 at the Ariz. St. U. in Tempe, where he was an Asst. Prof. of English until '58. Since '59, and presently, he is a Prof. of English at the U. of Calif., Santa Barbara, where he makes his home with his wife, the former Frances Jones, whom he married in '48. They have three sons, Alan, Daniel, & Timothy.

PUBLICATIONS: The Sum ('58), *Between Matter and Principle* ('63), *The Heat Lightning* ('67), *Tree Meditation and Others* ('70), & *White River Poems* ('76). His poems have also appeared in various periodicals, among them: *The Nation, Paris Review, Beloit Poetry Journal, Arizona Quarterly, Genesis West, Poetry, Denver Quarterly, & Southern Review.* He has edited *The Selected Poems of Barnabe Googe* ('61), with an introduction and notes concerning the Elizabethan poet.

EDITORIAL POSTS: For a number of years, Stephens was a member of the editorial board of *Twentieth Century Literature* magazine.

OBSERVATIONS: Alan Stephens has said that his poems are "descriptive meditations rather than meditative descriptions...." About his poetry, E.D. Blodgett notes that Stephens writes "careful poetry" and "enjoys the world as problem, as an object for science in the positivistic sense. Thus, matter is not quite flesh but a front or form; 'matter' is " 'engrained and tough' where destiny and chance evolve in time and imagination."

PAMELA STEWART

BIRTH: 2/3/'46, in Boston, grew up in New England.

EDUCATION: She received her B.A. from Goddard College in '73. She took her M.F.A. in Creative Writing at the U. of Iowa in '74.

CAREER: She is currently Lecturer at the Ariz. St. U. and lives in Tempe with her husband, poet Norman Dubie, and their daughter Hannah.

PUBLICATIONS: Pamela Stewart's first chapbook was entitled *The Hawley Road Marsh Marigolds,* published by Meadow Press (Iowa City, '75). Another pamphlet,

The Figure Eight at Midnight, appeared from Arion's Dolphin ('75). Her first book of poems *The St. Vlas Elegies* was published by L'Epervier Press in '77, and a chapbook, *Half-Tones,* came from Maguey Press ('78). Additionally her work has

Pamela Stewart
(May 1976)

been published in such anthologies as *Stepping Out* ('75), *Best Poems of 1976* (Borestone Mountain Poetry Awards, '76), & *Five Arizona Poets* ('76). Her poetry has appeared in numerous magazines, including *The New Yorker, The American Poetry Review, Poetry, The Goddard Journal, The Black Warrior Review, The Ohio Review, Antaeus, Field, Seneca Review, The Iowa Review, Poetry Now. Grilled Flowers,* and *Agenda* (London).

PRIMUS ST. JOHN
BIRTH: '39, in N.Y.C., was raised in his birthplace.
EDUCATION: U. of Maryland & Lewis and Clark C.
CAREER: In '69, while still a student at the U. of Maryland, he did voluntary work conducting writing workshops with elementary students in Wash., D.C. in a

Primus St. John
(December 1976)

cultural enrichment project sponsored by the Friends of the Arts. He has taught communications at Mary Holmes Junior C., Miss.; black literature at Steilacoon Com. C., Tacoma, Wash., and during the year '71 served as poet-in-residence for the Tacoma, Wash. Public Schools. In connection with this project, which was

119

sponsored by the Wash. St. Arts Com. with funds made available from the state and the N.E.A., he worked in several Tacoma elementary schools, attempting to instill in young students (mostly fourth graders), feelings of joy and appreciation over what for many of them was their first experience writing poetry. He has also worked for the Minn.-Poetry-In-The-Schools program. In '71, he was one of a number of poets who were asked to read their work at the Las Vegas, Nev. meeting of the Nat. Council of Teachers of English. He has also given readings for Black Poets' Reading, Inc., directed by Raymond R. Patterson. During the academic year '72-'73, he taught poetry writing courses at the U. of Utah, Salt Lake City, and since '73, has served as poet-in-residence at Portland St. U. in Oregon.

PUBLICATIONS: In '76, Copper Canyon Press published his *Skins in the Earth.* He is also the ed. of a junior high school poetry anthology entitled *Zero Makes Me Hungry* ('75). His poems have appeared in such college texts as *What Is A Poem* (Scott Foresman) and in such anthologies as *Agenda for Survival,* ed. by Harold W. Helfrich, Jr. ('70), *Poems and Perspectives,* ed. by Robert H. Ross & William Stafford ('71), & *The Poetry of Black America,* ed. by Arnold Adoff ('72). St. John's poems appear in various periodicals, including these: *The Calvert Review, Dryad, The Southern Poetry Review, Concerning Poetry, Poet Lore, Voyages & Poetry Northwest.*

HONORS: In '70, his poetry won for him the Discovery Award; he has also been the recipient of a creative writing fellowship of the N.E.A.

OBSERVATIONS: St. John notes: "Poetry is one of my verbal ways of delighting and despairing in all the possibilities of being human."

RUTH (PERKINS) STONE

BIRTH: 6/8/'15, in Roanoke, Va., the daughter of Roger Perkins, a musician, and Ruth (Ferguson) Perkins, a painter, grew up in Indianapolis, Indiana.

EDUCATION: She attended the U. of Ill. (B.A.) and Harvard.

CAREER: She worked first as an assistant to the literary and dramatic editor of *The Indianapolis Star.* After her marriage to poet and fiction writer Walter Stone, she lived first in Cambridge, Mass., and then in Poughkeepsie, N.Y. During those years her husband taught English at Harvard, Radcliffe and Vassar Colleges. He died in '59.

Ruth Stone
(December 1965)

EDITORIAL POSTS: After his death, Ruth Stone worked for a time as an editor for the Wesleyan U. Press. During her fellowship years at Radcliffe Institute for

Independent Study, she began teaching in the Radcliffe Seminars' Program. She has pursued a parallel teaching career (except for leaves and fellowships) since that time at various institutions: Wellesley College ('65), Brandeis ('65-'66), Wis. ('67-'69), Ill. ('71-'73), Indiana ('73-'74), Center C., Ky. ('75), Hurst Prof. at Brandeis ('76), & Univ. of Virginia ('77-'78). She has also traveled in the Poets-In-The-Schools programs of Ariz., Ky., and other states. The mother of three grown daughters: Marcia (Stone) Croll, Phoebe and Blue Jay A., Ruth Stone makes her home permanently now in Goshen, Vermont when she is not lecturing or away on teaching or reading assignments.

PUBLICATIONS: In an Iridescent Time ('59); *Topography and Other Poems* ('71), & *Cheap: New Poems and Ballads* ('75). Her poems have also appeared in such magazines as *Poetry, The New Yorker, Kenyon Review, Partisan Review, Accent, Green House, California Quarterly,* & *Poets: On.* Her work is included in such anthologies as *The New Pocket Anthology of American Verse, Best Poems of 1965, No More Masks,* & *The Women Poets in English.* A 16 mm. documentary film in color called "The Excuse: The Poetry of Ruth Stone" is distributed by the U. of Calif., Berkeley.

HONORS: Radcliffe C. Fellowship; Shelley Award; & Guggenheim fellowships.

OBSERVATIONS: Ruth Stone has noted concerning her career of teaching poetry: "I enjoy teaching—I feel it is right and proper to be of assistance to the young." About her poetry, Richard Wilbur writes: "Many of the subjects of Ruth Stone's new book (*Cheap*) are hard ones...but she rises to everything with her familiar verve and resource, and without evasion turns it to the stuff of delight."

MARK STRAND

BIRTH: 4/11/'34, in Summerside, Prince Edward Island, Canada, considers himself a poet of the U.S.A.

EDUCATION: Antioch C., B.A. ('57); B.F.A., Yale ('59); U. of Florence, Italy (Fulbright Fellow, '60-'61); U. of Iowa, M.A. ('62). At Yale where Strand won the Cook Prize and Bergin Prize, he studied painting with Joseph Albers. At Antioch, earlier, Nolan Miller, and at the U. of Iowa, Donald Justice, later, were other teachers who deeply influenced Strand while he was a student.

CAREER: Strand's teaching career began in '62, when he was an Instr. at the U. of Iowa, a post he left in '65 to accept an appointment for one year ('65-'66) as a Fulbright Lectr. at the U. of Brazil, Rio de Janeiro, '65-'66. He returned to the States as an Asst. Prof. of English at Mount Holyoke in '67. He then served twice ('68; '70) as a Visit. Prof. at the U. of Wash., and for the year-in-between, '69, as an Adj. Assoc. Prof. at Columbia U., for part of the year, and at Yale, as a Visit. Prof. for the other part. For the years '70-'72, he was Assoc. Prof. at Brooklyn C., N.Y., and since '73, has been Bain-Swiggett Lectr. at Princeton U. Divorced from his first wife Antonia Ratensky in '73 (married in '61). Mark Strand has one daughter. He lives today in New York City with his second wife, and commutes to Princeton. In the summer of '76, he was also was on the faculty of the Breadloaf Writers' Conference.

PUBLICATIONS: Sleeping With One Eye Open ('64), *Reasons for Moving: Poems* ('68), *Darker: Poems* ('70), *The Story of Our Lives* ('73), *The Sergeantville Notebook* ('73), & *Elegy For My Father* ('73). Represented in various anthologies, some of Mark Strand's poems appear in these collections: *Poems For Our Moment* ('68), *Young American Poets* ('68), *Contemporary Poetry in America* ('73), *New Voices in American Poetry* ('73), *The Norton Anthology of Modern Poetry* ('73), &

Modern Poems: An Introduction to Poetry ('73; '76). Published likewise in many periodicals, his poems also appear in such magazines as these: *The Atlantic, The*

Mark Strand
(May 1971)

New Yorker, Partisan Review, The New York Review of Books, Poetry, Antaeus, Georgia Review, Andover Review, Seneca Review, Nation, Ploughshares, & American Poetry Review. Mark Strand has likewise served as editor of two well-known anthologies: *The Contemporary American Poets: American Poetry Since 1940* ('69) & *New Poetry of Mexico* ('73). His notes and observations appear in *The Monument* ('78). Additionally, as both editor and translator, he has produced *The Owl's Insomnia: Selected Poems of Rafael Alberti* ('73), *Souvenir of the Ancient World* ('76), the latter being a selection of poems of Carlos Drummond de Andrade, and has co-edited with Charles Simic, *Another Republic* ('76), an anthology of seventeen European and South American writers. As translator he has also published a pamphlet of 18 Quechua Indian poems from Peru, entitled *18 Poems From the Quechua* ('71). As a playwright, he is the author of an original screenplay entitled *I Knew A Girl.*

HONORS: In addition to the Cook Prize & Bergin Prize from Yale and the Fulbright Scholarship to Italy previously mentioned, Strand's honors include an Ingram Merrill Fellowship ('66), an N.E.A. grant ('67-'68), Rockefeller Award ('68-'69), & a Guggenheim fellowship ('75-'76).

OBSERVATIONS: Laurence Lieberman has written that Strand's poetry is "a kind of elegantly flawless art...that bespeaks a perfect tuning of the instrument."

ROBERT SWARD
BIRTH: 6/23/'33, in Chicago, Ill., the son of Irving M. and Gertrude (Huebsch) Sward, attended public schools in his birthplace.

EDUCATION: B.A. with honors & Phi Beta Kappa, U. of Ill. ('56); M.A., U. of Iowa ('58); study in creative writing at the Breadloaf School of English ('56-'58); & post-graduate study, U. of Bristol, England ('60-'61).

CAREER: After serving in the Navy from '51-'53, during the Korean War, Sward received his formal education at the institutions just noted. His teaching career began at Conn. C., where he was an Instr. in English ('58-'59), and continued after a year in England, at Cornell U., where he was also an Instr. from '62-'64.

HONORS: For several years, Sward studied and traveled both in the U.S. and in Mexico and lived on various grants and fellowships, among them a '64 Guggenheim

Fellowship for creative writing in poetry (spent in Mexico), a '66 D.H. Lawrence Fellowship from the U. of N.M. with a residency at Lawrence's Kiowa Ranch above Taos, and taught from '69-'73 at the U. of Victoria, B.C. Earlier in his career, he had received the Dylan Thomas Poetry Award and had been a poetry fellow at Breadloaf Writers' Conference, '58. In '59-'60, he also held fellowships to Yaddo and MacDowell Colonies.

CAREER: (continued from above): More recently, Robert Sward has resumed his teaching career; this time, in Canada, at the U. of Victoria, B.C., where from '69-'73, he was Poet-in-Residence. Earlier in '67, he had served as poet-in-residence at the Aspen Writers' Workshop and for a term as Writer-in-Residence the same year at the U. of Iowa.

EDITORIAL POSTS: Since '76 he has worked as Senior Editor with a commercial publishing house. Today in Victoria, B.C., where Sward makes his home, he also edits *Soft Press,* a publishing house which has produced 21 poetry books since '70. Earlier he served for a time as a member of the editorial board of *Epoch* magazine. He is married to Irina Schestakowich. He is the father of five children, Barbara, Michael, Alexis, Cheryl, & Hannah by his first marriage to Diane Kaldes, a dancer.

PUBLICATIONS: Advertisements (chapbook of satires, '58); *Uncle Dog & Other Poems* ('62) *Kissing the Dancer* ('64), *Thousand-Year-Old Fiancee* ('65) *Horgbortom Stringbottom, I Am Yours, You Are History* ('70), *Selected Poems* ('78; issued in Canada as *Poems: New & Selected 1957-78* ('78)), & *Honey Bear on Lasqueti Island, B.C.* ('78). Additionally he has published one novel, *The Jurassic Shales* ('75), and has likewise presented many readings of his poetry throughout

Robert Sward
(October 1965)

the United States and Canada. As an editor, he has produced *Cheers for Muktananda* ('76). A wide variety of anthologies have published Sward's poems: *A Controversy of Poets,* edited by Paris Leary and Robert Kelly ('65), *Penguin Animal Book of Poetry,* edited by George MacBeth ('67), *Contemporary American Poets,* edited by Mark Strand ('69), *Inside Outer Space,* ed. by Robert Van Dias ('70), *Some Haystacks Don't Have Any Needles,* edited by Dunning, Lueders and Smith ('70); *Silver Screen (Neue Amerikanische Lyrik),* edited by Rolf Dieter Brinkmann, with English & German translations by Verlag Kiepenheur & Witsch ('70), *New Yorker Book of Poems* ('70), *The Voice That Is Great Within Us,* ed. by Hayden Carruth ('73), *New: American & Canadian Poetry,* No. 20, Special Issue, edited by John Gill ('73), & *Cheers for Muktananda,* edited by Robert Sward ('76,

Soft Press). Numerous magazines have also carried Robert Sward's poetry, including *Poetry, The New Yorker, The Hudson Review, Paris Review, The Nation, Chelsea Review, Carleton Miscellany, Beloit Poetry Journal, Extensions, Denver Quarterly, Transatlantic Review, Tamarack Review, Malahat Review, Kayak, Iowa Review, Chicago Review, Massachusetts Review, Underground, Prism International, Ambit, Poetry Northwest, & El Corno Emplumado.*

OBSERVATIONS: Robert Sward notes of his poetry that its themes and devices are "person, place and thing. Things of this world, things of that world. Measures based upon speech phrases and syllable-count. Collage, free-verse, song, speech, protest. Rock. Acid-Rock. Architecture. Stand-up burlesque comedians. Flashing lights. Lights that are not flashing. Silence. Silence. Space. New Hampshire. Canada. Mt. Monadnock. Love....White houses and yellow houses. The thousand-year-old fiancee." William Meredith has commented upon Sward's poetry, noting that it has "the air of having been made for people rather than for other artists." Meredith has also observed that Sward's lines "come out of original experience, and they exist in the language that the experience discovered."

MAY SWENSON

BIRTH: 5/28/'19, in Logan, Utah, of immigrant Swedish parents, the eldest of several children grew up in her birthplace. Her father, Dan Arthur Swenson, was a teacher.

EDUCATION: Utah St. U., Logan, B.A. ('39).

CAREER: May Swenson's first career was as an editor, and it began while she was still a student at Utah St., where she edited the campus literary magazine and wrote for the college newspaper.

EDITORIAL POSTS: After a year on the *Salt Lake Deseret News,* she came to New York City, where she held various editorial posts, and beginning '49-'66, worked as an editor for New Directions Press. Since '66, she has devoted all her time to her writings, except for intervals of teaching special poetry workshops at various universities, and for readings, lectures, and travels. In '66-'67, she was

May Swenson
(February 1965)

Writer-in-Residence at Purdue. She has since held these posts: Poetry Seminar Instr., U. of N.C., Greensboro ('68-'69) & ('73-'74); Lothbridge U., Alberta ('70); U. of Calif., Riverside ('75); & Utah State U. ('76). During the summer of '76, she taught on the staff of the Breadloaf Writers' Conference in Middlebury, Vermont.

Ordinarily she makes her home, when not traveling, in Sea Cliff, N.Y. in a house overlooking Long Island Sound.

PUBLICATIONS: Another Animal (included in a volume with other collections of poetry by Harry Duncan and Murry Noss, '54); *A Cage of Spines* ('58); *To Mix With Time: New & Selected Poems* ('63); *Poems to Solve* ('66); *Half Sun, Half Sleep* ('67); *Iconographs* ('70); *More Poems to Solve* ('71), and *New & Selected Poems* ('78). She can be heard reading her poetry on a Folkways' recording, *Today's Poets 2*, with others, produced in '68, and on a Caedmon Record ('75). Poems by May Swenson appear in magazines too numerous for complete listing here, but include *New Yorker, Hudson Review, Harper's, Saturday Review, New American Review, Atlantic, Tri-Quarterly, Southern Review, New Republic, The Nation, Paris Review, Western Review, & New World Writing.* Likewise her poems have been widely anthologized; a partial listing follows: *Treasury of Great American Poetry* ('55), *New Poets 2* ('57), *New Poets of England and America* ('57), *Poetry: Theory and Practice* ('62), *Arts in Society; Poetry in Our Time* ('63), *Borestone Mountain Award Annual* ('63), *The Modern Poets* ('63), *Erotic Poetry* ('63), *Twentieth Century American Poetry* ('63), *Of Poetry and Power* ('64), *Voices No. 2, New Modern Poetry* ('67), *Poems of Our Moment* ('68), & *New Yorker Book of Poems* ('69). Besides writing poetry, she has also rendered into English the poetry of Tomas Tranströmer in a volume entitled *Windows and Stones: Selected Poems* ('72). Her own poems have also appeared in translation by others in German and Italian anthologies. Additionally she has written a play, *The Floor*, which was produced at the American Place Theatre in New York in '66 and published in *First Stage* (Lafayette, Indiana, vi, 2, '67). Articles by May Swenson related to criticism and literature include the following: "An Introduction" to Edgar Lee Masters' *Spoon River Anthology* ('62), "A Matter of Diction" in *Festschrift for Marianne Moore's Seventy-seventh Birthday* ('65), and "The Experience of Poetry In A Scientific Age" in *Poets on Poetry* ('66). She has been a judge for several distinguished poetry awards: the National Book Award, the Lamont Award of the Academy of Am. Poets, and the U.S. Award of the Pittsburgh International Poetry Forum.

HONORS: May Swenson's honors, awards, and fellowships include the following: Poetry Introduction Prize from the Y.M.H.A. Poetry Center in New York ('53), Rockefeller Writing grants ('55; '67); Robert Frost Fellowship of the Breadloaf Writers' Conference ('57); Guggenheim Fellow ('59); William Rose Bénet Prize ('59); Longview Foundation Award ('59); Amy Lowell Traveling Fellowship ('60); fellowships at the Yaddo and MacDowell Colonies, as well as the National Inst. of Arts & Letters Award ('60); Ford Fellowship for Drama ('64); Brandeis U. Creative Arts Award ('66); Distinguished Service Gold Medal from Utah State U. ('67); Lucy Martin Donnelly Fellowship from Bryn Mawr College ('68); Shelley Memorial Award ('68); N.E.A. Arts Grant ('75); and membership in the Nat. Inst. of Arts & Letters.

OBSERVATIONS: May Swenson relates: "I devise my own forms. My themes are from the organic, the inorganic, and the psychological world. I sometimes create a typographical or iconographic frame for my poems *after* the text is complete." Elizabeth Bishop has commented upon Ms. Swenson's poetry in this manner: "[She] looks, and sees, and rejoices in what she sees. Her poems are varied, energetic, and full of a directness and optimism that are unusual in these days of formulated despair and/or careful stylishness."

BIRTH: 1/27/'35, in Redruth, Cornwall, England, is a British poet, who spent most of his early life in the same locale of his birthplace.

EDUCATION: Redruth Grammar School and Univ. High School, Melbourne; New College, Oxford, B.A., from which he graduated in English with First Class Honors. In '58, he received his M.A. from Oxford.

CAREER: Since '63, except for leaves and travel, he has held the post of Senior Lecturer in English at Hereford College of Education. In '67, he came to the U.S.A. as Visiting Lecturer in English at Hamline U., St. Paul, Minn., and also returned to

D.M. Thomas
(November 1971)

the U.S.A. in 11/'71 to give a series of poetry readings, including one at the U. of Ariz. Ordinarily he makes his home at a cottage in Hereford, England, near the institution where he teaches.

PUBLICATIONS: Two Voices ('68), *Logan Stone* ('71), *The Shaft* ('73), *Love and Other Death* ('75), & *The Honeymoon Voyage* ('78). A selection of his poetry also appeared with that of Peter Redgrove & D.M. Black in the same year in *Penguin Modern Poets II* ('68). Thomas's poems have also been anthologized in such volumes as: *The New S.F., New Worlds S.F., Inside Outer Space, Tri-Quarterly 21, New Poems: P.E.N. Anthology* ('65, 68), *Frontiers of Going* ('69), *Holding Your Eight Hands* ('69), & *Postwar British Verse* ('70). He has also published poetry in such periodicals as *London Magazine, Encounter, New Worlds, American Scholar, Transatlantic Review, New York Times,* & *London Times Literary Supplement.* As an editor, Thomas has also published two volumes: *The Granite Kingdom: Poems of Cornwall* ('70) and *Selected Poems of John Harris* ('77). As a translator, he has rendered *Anna Akhmatova: Requiem and Poem Without a Hero* ('76).

HONORS: For his poetry, he has received the Richard Hillary Memorial Prize ('60) & British Arts Council Award ('75).

OBSERVATIONS: About his poetry, Thomas comments: "Like all poets, my themes are simply love, death, and human destiny, both individual and collective. I have sometimes used science-fiction themes, as myths, regarding S.F. [Science Fiction] as a powerful mythology of our time. Our present moment is a broad spectrum, taking in the potentialities of the future." He also notes: "I am not aware of precise influences, but of the poets of our century, Akhmatova, Yeats and Frost mean the most to me. I aspire more and more to the strength and clarity of the great

126

twentieth century Russian poets." About Thomas's poetry, Edward Lucie-Smith has observed: "What is new and fresh about Thomas's work is its interest in narrative—an aspect of their work which most contemporary poets neglect. He is an extremely able craftsman, and his poems are very effective when read aloud. The deliberate, considered style, instead of seeming dull and unspontaneous, helps to carry the listener along with the story the poet is teling. One's interest is seized by the content itself, rather than by the manner."

TOMAS TRANSTRÖMER

BIRTH: 4/15/'31, in Stockholm, Sweden, is descended from a long line of ship pilots who worked in and around the Stockholm Archipelago.

EDUCATION: Educated as a psychologist at the U. of Stockholm ('51-'56), he is still today employed in this capacity even though he is now a poet of international fame, and has been awarded Sweden's Aftonbladets Litteraturpris ('58) and Bellmanpriest ('66).

CAREER: Tranströmer's career as a psychologist began at the Psychotechnical Inst. in Stockholm, where he practiced from '57-'59. From '60-'65, he served as Roxtuna in the south of Sweden at an Inst. for Delinquent Youths. Since '66, he has been employed as an occupational psychologist at Pa-rådet, in Västerås, Sweden. There he works in vocational guidance for handicapped people in the province where he also makes his home with his wife and family.

PUBLICATIONS: Tranströmer's career as a poet began in '54 when he published in Swedish the first of his six volumes of poetry, *17 Dikter* (17 Poems). His other volumes include *Hemligheter Pa Vägen* ('58), *Den Halvfärdiga Himlen* ('62), *Klanger Och Spår* (*Sounds and Traces*, '66), *Kvartett* (*These Four*, '67), *Mörkerseende* (*Night Vision*, '70), *Stigar* (*Paths*, '73), & *Baltics* ('75), which has

Tomas Tranströmer
(November 1975)

been translated into English by Samuel Charters for Oyez Press. In addition to the '75 Charters' translation of *Baltics*, there are four other English translations of Tranströmer's work. These include *Night Vision* and *20 Poems by Tomas Tranströmer*, translated by Robert Bly, *Windows and Stones*, translated by May Swenson with Leif Sjöberg, Robin Fulton's translation, *Selected Poems* (Penguin, '74), and *Five Swedish Poets* (Seton Hall, '72).

HONORS: See mention of his honors noted above in connection with the section concerning Tranströmer's education.

OBSERVATIONS: Robert Bly has perhaps given the best description of the Swedish poet both physically and emotionally. Additionally of his poetry, Bly observes: "Tomas Tranströmer seems to me the best poet to appear in Sweden for some years....He is at home on islands. His face is thin and angular, and the swift, spare face reminds me of Hans Christian Anderson's or the young Kierkegaard's. He has a strange genius for the images—images come up almost effortlessly. The images flow upward like water rising in some lonely place, in the swamps, or deep fir woods." About his poetry, Ivar Ivask and Gero von Wilbert have noted in their *From World Literature Since 1945:* "Tranströmer...has been his own man, filled from the start with confidence in his own poetic vision. The volume *17 Dikter* ('54, *17 Poems*) indicated that he was at ease with the world he perceived (not the same, of course, as being at peace with it), that he was able to express his ease in original but by no means enigmatic images and to control them. His oeuvre has been small; his fourth volume, *Klanger Och Spår (Sound and Traces)* appeared only in '66. But...every poem has value."

DIANE WAKOSKI

BIRTH: 8/3/'37, in Whittier, Calif., grew up in her birthplace.

EDUCATION: She received her B.A. in English from the U. of Calif., Berkeley, '60, and that same year moved to N.Y.C., where she began her career in earnest as a poet.

CAREER: For the first three years of her life in New York, she worked in the British Book Centre (a bookstore) as a clerk ('60-'63), and then for the next three years ('63-'66) taught English in Junior High 22 of the N.Y.C. public schools.

EDITORIAL POSTS: It was at this time of her life that Diane Wakoski also edited for a while two small periodicals, first *Dream Sheet* and then *Software.* In '66, when she was awarded the Robert Frost Fellowship for her *Discrepancies and Apparitions,* her poetry came to be so widely recognized that she has since that time devoted all her time to her writings, her readings, or to being poet-in-residence at numerous institutions. In the latter capacity, she has held these posts: Lectr., New School for Social Research, New York ('69); Poet-in-Residence, Calif. Inst. of Technology, Pasadena (Spring '72), U. of Virginia (Autumn '72-'73), Wilamette U., Salem, Ore. (Spring '74). Beginning in '75 and presently, she is Poet-in-Residence with the Michigan St. U., and living in East Lansing. Briefly married to S. Shepard Sherbell in '65, she married her second husband poet Michael Watterlond in '73, on George Washington's birthday. She still considers the West Coast and California as her real home although she has continued to live in N.Y.C. for the major part of her writing career.

PUBLICATIONS: Coins and Coffins ('62), *Discrepancies and Apparitions: Poems* ('66), *The George Washington Poems* ('67), *Greed Parts One and Two* ('68), *The Diamond Merchant* ('68), *Inside the Blood Factory* ('68), *Thanking My Mother for Piano Lessons* ('69), *Greed Parts 3 and 4* ('69), *The Moon Has a Complicated Geography* ('69), *The Magellanic Clouds* ('70), *Greed Parts 5-7* ('70), *The Lament of the Lady Bank Dick* ('70), *Love, You Big Fat Snail* ('70), *Black Dream Ditty for Billy "The Kid" Seen in Dr. Generosity's Bar Recruiting for Hell's Angels and Black Mafia* ('70), *Exorcism* ('71), *On Barbara's Shore* ('71), *The Motorcycle Betrayal Poems* ('71), *The Pumpkin Pie, or Reassurances Are Always False, Though We Love Them. Only Physics Counts* ('72), *The Purple Finch Song* ('72), *Sometimes a Poet Will Hijack the Moon* ('72), *Smudging* ('72), *The Owl and the Snake: A Fable* ('73), *Greed Parts 8, 9, 11* ('73), *Dancing on the Grave of a Son of a Bitch* ('73),

Winter Sequences ('73), *Trilogy: Coins and Coffins, Discrepancies and Apparitions, The George Washington Poems* ('74), *The Fable of the Lion & the Scorpion* ('75), *Virtuoso Literature for Two and Four Hands* ('75), *Waiting for the King of Spain* ('76), & *The Man Who Shook Hands* ('78). Her poems have also appeared as a part of the collection—*Four Young Lady Poets*, with others, edited by Leroi Jones ('62) and additionally she has been published as a playwright in *A Play and Two Poems*, with Robert Kelley and Ron Loewinsohn ('68). Anthologies too numerous for listing here have also included Diane Wakoski's poems. Some are these: *A Controversy of Poets* ('65), *The Young American Poets, Poetry: A Premeditated Art* ('68), *Technicians of the Sacred* ('68), *Contemporary American Poets* ('69), *An American Literary Anthology 2* ('69), *Five Blind Men* ('70), *Contemporary Poetry in America* ('73), *The Norton Anthology of Modern Poetry* ('73), & *Modern Poems: An Introduction to Poetry* ('73, '76). Among the numerous magazines which have carried her poems are *Caterpillar, Chelsea Review, Poetry Now, Crazy Horse, El Corno Emplumado, Galley Sail Review, Lillabulero, Poetry, Set, Tuatra, Works, Sumac, Grain, Noose, Armadillo, Stony Brook Journal, New American Review*, and *Kayak*. In addition to her poetry, Ms Wakoski has also written a book entitled *Form Is an Extension of Content* ('72).

Diane Wakoski
(September 1971)

HONORS: Ms. Wakoski's honors include these: N.E.A. grants, '66, '68, & '73; Breadloaf Writers' Conference Robert Frost fellowship, '66; Cassandra Foundation Award, '70; N.Y. State Council on the Arts grant, '71; & Guggenheim grant, '72. In '77, she served with two other poets on the selection committee for the Bollingen prize.

OBSERVATIONS: Diane Wakoski has written about her poetry in this way: "The exterior events of my life are not very noteworthy and all the interior events are recorded in my poems....In my poems, I try to speak to men and communicate what it's like to be a woman so that they could feel and know." About her poetry, Louis Simpson has commented: "I found Wakoski...absorbing. The poems are full of experience, and feeling, honestly expressed. She is more than merely confessional, however. I was constantly being surprised by new angles of vision." Hayden Carruth says: "...there is no doubt that she has become in a very few years one of the two or three most important poets of her generation in America."

DAVID RAFAEL WANG
BIRTH: 11/20/'31, and raised in Shanghai, China of an aristocratic family, he

was a direct descendant of the T'ang dynasty poet, painter, and physician Wang Wei, who lived from 701-761.

DEATH: 4/8/'77, in New York City, while attending an academic conference. Wang's legal name, which he always used for his work as a University professor and critic, was David Hsin-Fu Wand. In an anthology *Asian-American Heritage* (N.Y.: Washington Square Press-Pocket Books, '74), which he edited under his legal name, he explained the reasons why he had used two different names for his writings: "Basically, I don't want the critic-professor to be compared with the poet. Unlike some professors, I am not an academic poet. I don't even write in the English poetic tradition..." David Rafael Wang came to the U.S.A. in '49, when he was seventeen years old, and became a naturalized citizen of the U.S. in '64.

David Rafael Wang
(June 1975)
deceased

EDUCATION: Dartmouth College (B.A., English, & Class Poet, '55); M.F.A. (Creative Writing), San Francisco State College; M.A. & Ph.D. (Comparative Literature), Univ. of So. Calif. From '57-'61, while he studied in San Francisco and spent his time constantly translating Chinese poetry into English, he came to know well various poets—Gary Snyder, Philip Whalen, Diane Wakoski and Jack Anderson, and noted that his associations with these friends deeply influenced his craft at the time. Later, in '66, he also studied poetry under Robert Creeley and Paul Blackburn at the Aspen Writers' Workshop; their teachings, too, were to leave their mark on his writings. In fact Wang's doctoral dissertation at USC (1972, under his legal name—David Hsin-Fu Wand) concerns Gary Snyder and is entitled *Cathay Revisited: The Chinese Tradition in the Poetry of Ezra Pound and Gary Snyder.* Wang had also known personally Ezra Pound and had visited and corresponded with him often at St. Elizabeth's in 1956-'58. A portion of the section of his unpublished dissertation related to Pound was published as an article in *Paideuma: A Journal of Ezra Pound Scholarship* 3, 1 (Spring 1974), 3—12.

CAREER: A Professor of Comparative Literature at the University of Texas at Dallas ('75-'77) at the time of his sudden, untimely death, Wang had taught previously at various institutions in the U.S.A. From '74-'75, he was Visiting Professor of English & Humanities at the U. of N.M. Earlier he had taught literature and creative writing courses at Occidental College and at the State University of New York, Genesco. He was the son of Mrs. S.T. Ting Wong, author of *Madame Wong's Long-Life Chinese Cookbook,* who now teaches Chinese cooking courses at UCLA. Yuet-Fun, his wife of eleven years, is a native of

Shanghai, who speaks little English. They had one daughter, a baby Angelina, born 5/3/'76.

PUBLICATIONS: The Goblet Moon (Stinehaur Press, '55); *The Intercourse* (Greenfield Review Press, '75), & *Rivers on Fire* (Basilisk Press, '76). When he died, Wang was preparing a new collection of poetry entitled "Grandfather Series," which may be published posthumously. Poems by Wang appeared in 72 or more U.S., Canadian, English, and Australian literary magazines, including such periodicals as these: *Western Humanities Review, The Edge, Venture, Beloit Poetry Journal, Delta, Odyssey, Neon, Folio, Nomad, The Fiddlehead, Yūgen, Sparrow, Combustion, Targets, Approach, Mica, Coastlines, San Francisco Review, Satis, Poet & Critic, The Minnesota Review, The Free Line, Between Worlds, Outcry, Trace, Sumac, Original Works, The Dragonfly, The Seneca Review, New York Quarterly, The American Pen, Cloud Chamber, & Tri-Quarterly.* Such anthologies as these also carried his poetry: *Beatitude Anthology* and *Southwest: A Contemporary Anthology* ('77). Additionally a translator, Wang had not only edited the previously mentioned anthology, *Asian-American Heritage* ('74), he also appeared as a translator in four well-known anthologies. *The Cassia Tree* was a work of Chinese translations, which he did in collaboration with William Carlos Williams between '57 and '61. *New Directions #19*, ed. by J. Laughlin, issued it in '66. In '68, Jerome Rothenberg's *Technicians of the Sacred* (Doubleday) presented some of Wang's translations of Samoan and Hawaiian poetry. His rendering of Chinese and Italian nuptial poetry was included in *High Wedlock Then Be Honoured,* edited by Virginia Tufte for Viking Press ('70). Lastly Wang's translation of the Samoan "Legend of Saveasi'uleo" appeared in *Munching on Existence* (ed. by Robert Gilner and R.A. Raines, '74, Free Press-Macmillan). His prose articles appeared in *Trace, The Chinese World, San Francisco Stars,* and elsewhere. Additionally he was especially interested in presenting readings of classical Chinese and Japanese poetry with English translations and commentaries. Fluent in both Asian languages, he spoke some Italian as well. A black belt in karate, he was further fascinated by correlations between athletic ability and the arts—especially in poetry, and presented various readings at the U. of N.M.and elsewhere which demonstrated the correlations he recognized.

HONORS: Besides being Dartmouth Class Poet ('55), Wang was a finalist in '57 in the Nat. Writing Contest sponsored by the Writing Center of N.Y.U., a contest judged by Louise Bogan, M.L. Rosenthal, and Russell F.W. Smith.

OBSERVATIONS: David Rafael Wang once noted that he considered himself "an heir of the Greco-Sino-Samurai-African tradition," and tried in his poetry "to emulate the qualities of Miles Davis, John Coltrane, Muhammad Ali, and Bruce Lee." In '74, in Albuquerque, he delighted in discussing poetics with Muhammad Ali. Such major American poets as William Carlos Williams and Gary Snyder, both of whom Wang came to know well, frequently praised and encouraged his work. Wang, who first met Williams in '57, had continued as his collaborator in translating Chinese poetry until '62. In a letter dated 12/14/'59, Williams wrote Wang: "Your own poems have given me so much pleasure of late that I have been forced to think of you as an expert in the art, that (which) was printed recently in *Folio* is quite up to the rule, excellent." Gary Snyder had this to say about Wang's craft in a letter he sent him dated 6/29/'59: "Those two poems you sent me make me think of you as a modern Catullus, very neatly done....I like you Wang, because you're as cranky as I am (& a good poet too.)" Several years later, Snyder sent Wang a postcard dated 6/6/'63; further observing: "You are developing a new style, I see, concojones & deep-breathing." An article by Hugh Witemeyer entitled: "The Flame-Style King," concerning David Rafael Wang and his friendship with Ezra Pound (and Pound's fascination with the Chinese meaning of the *Hsin*, part of Wang's legal name) appears in the Fall-Winter '75 issue of *Paideuma: A Journal of Ezra Pound Scholarship, IV,* and reveals that Pound's contacts with the youthful Wang lead to Pound's references in *Thrones* about "Wang's middle name not in Mathews [dictionary]." It shows how Pound associated Wang "with the flame-style kings of the orient."

LARRY WEIRATHER

BIRTH: 4/23/'44, in Savana, Ill., grew up near the Mississippi River of his birthplace and has always been deeply interested in rivers; for, as he notes: "It seems that my life so far has been centered around rivers, which have made a deep impression on me and my writing." After growing up along the Mississippi, when it came time for college, he "moved to Iowa along the Skunk River. From there it was the Platte in Colo. Having fallen in love with the mountains there, I moved to the Yellowstone River in Montana."

EDUCATION: B.A., Iowa Wesleyan C.; M.A. U. of Denver.

CAREER: Larry began his career as a reporter and writer for *Savanna Times—Journal* and *Northwestern Illinois Dispatch,* and continued it as a work

Larry Weirather
(June 1976)

supervisor for the Clinton, Iowa Job Corps, and later as a consultant in technical writing for Wirth Associates, Environmental Planning. He has also served as an Instructor for the Indian Drug Rehabilitation Program. In addition to being Chairman of the Department of English at Rocky Mountain College in Billings, Mon., where he lives today, Weirather has spent most of his time teaching poetry and creative writing courses, as he explains it, "to cowboys and Indians." In '76-'77 while on sabbatical from Rocky Mountain, Larry devoted the entire year to writing poetry, when his interests in "The Big Sky Country" and in fishing, backpacking, cross-country skiing, geology, archeology, golf, tropical fish, photography, mushrooming and stamp collecting did not interfere. Married, he has traveled widely, especially in connection with archeological field trips to Brittany, France, and to Pre-Columbian sites in Mexico. He is also a frequent participant in various creative writing and popular culture workshops throughout the U.S.A.

PUBLICATIONS: Weirather's poetry has appeared in various poetry periodicals, including these: *The Rocky Mountain Review, Foothills, The Monitor, The Rectangle,* & *Lyrical Iowa.* He is currently at work on his first collection of poetry.

Additionally he has published articles and reviews in various journals and newsletters, and has contributed numerous "Environmental Impact statements" for the Corps of Engineers. He has also written a defense of art as a chapter in a textbook entitled *The New Journalism* and has been a slide show lecturer on the megalithic archeological sites of Brittany.

OBSERVATIONS: Weirather comments: "The second movement in my life has been a steady movement west. I have tried in my poetry to explore the peculiar problems in writing a western poetry that is not trite in the face of the staggering natural landscape of the West. I am also interested in experimenting with longer poetic narrative structures."

RICHARD (PURDY) WILBUR

BIRTH: 3/1/'21, in New York City, the son of a portrait painter, Lawrence Wilbur, Richard Wilbur grew up in New Jersey.

EDUCATION: B.A., Amherst ('42); M.A., as a Junior Fellow, Harvard ('47).

CAREER: Richard Wilbur served in W.W. II with the 36th Div. in Italy, Sicily, and western Europe, as a member of the U.S. Army from '43-'45. He began his academic career at Harvard, where he was a member of the Soc. of Fellows from '47-'50, and Asst. Prof. of English, '50-'54. From '55-'57, he taught at Wellesley C. as an Assoc. Prof. of English, and from '57-'77, served as a Prof. of English at Wesleyan U. In '77, he became Writer-In-Residence at Smith College. During the year '54-'55, he also lived in Rome, and in '61, traveled to the Soviet Union on a cultural exchange program.

EDITORIAL POSTS: Since the early "sixties," he has also served as Gen. Ed. for the Laurel Poets' series of Dell Publishing Co., N.Y. He married the former Charlotte Ward in '42. They have four children—a daughter and three sons. Presently the Wilburs live at their mountain home in the Berkshires in Cummington, Mass. They have also lived in New Mexico, Texas, Italy and France.

PUBLICATIONS: The Beautiful Changes and Other Pomes ('47), *Ceremony and Other Poems* ('50), *Things of This World: Poems* ('56; one section reprinted as

Richard Wilbur
(April 1973)

Digging to China, '70); *Poems, 1943-56* ('57); *Advise to a Prophet and Other Poems* ('61; '62); *The Poems of Richard Wilbur* ('63); *The Pelican From a Bestiary of 1120* (privately printed, '63); *Prince Souvanna Phouma: An Exchange Between Richard Wilbur and William Jay Smith* ('63); *Complaint* ('68); *Walking to Sleep: New Poems and Translations* ('71); *Seed Leaves* ('74), & *The Mind-Reader* ('76). He has made two recordings of his poetry, *Poems* (Spoken Arts, '59) & *Richard Wilbur Reading His Own Poems* (Caedmon). Poems by Wilbur have also appeared in such periodicals as *The Atlantic Monthly, New Yorker, Poetry, New York Review of Books, Nation, Hudson Review, The New England Quarterly, The Kenyon Review,* and *Parisan Review,* among other publications. Anthologies too numerous for mention here have included poetry by Wilbur, a selection being: *Faber Book of Modern American Verse* ('56), *Modern Verse in English* ('56), *New Poets of England and America* ('57), *Modern American Poetry and Modern British Poetry* ('58), *Chief Modern Poets of England and America* ('62), *Contemporary American Poetry* ('62), *Twentieth Century Poetry: American & British: 1900-1970* ('70), *Contemporary Poetry in America* ('73), *Norton Anthology of Modern Poetry* ('73), & *Modern Poems: An Introduction to Poetry* ('73, '76). Widely recognized as a translator and playwright, Richard Wilbur has rendered the works of such French authors as Molière, Baudelaire, Valéry, Voltaire, Jammes, & Phillipe de Thaun into English. His verse translations of Molière's *Tartuffe* ('63) was awarded the Yale Library's Bollingen Prize for the best translation of poetry into English in '64 and was produced by the Lincoln Center Repertory company in New York in '65, after having been premiered in Milwaukee, Wis. in '64. An English edition of the play was published by Faber in '64. Earlier, in '65, his verse translation of Molière's *The Misanthrope* was produced off-Broadway, and also in Cambridge, Mass. in '55. *The Misanthrope* adaptation has been published by Harcourt Brace in '55 and by Faber in London in '58. In England, there have also been performances of his translations from Molière. In '56 Wilbur collaborated with Leonard Bernstein and Lillian Hellman and produced most of the lyrics of the comic operetta, *Candide*, based on Voltaire's satire, an operetta, which was produced on Broadway that same year and in London in '59. Random House published the *Candide* adaptation of Wilbur's in '57. Likewise Wilbur's adaptation of Molière's play, *School for Wives*, was produced in N.Y.C. in '71 and published the same year by Harcourt Brace. Besides the works already named, Richard Wilbur has also translated *The Funeral of Bobo* by the Russian poet Joseph Brodsky into English (Ann Arbor, Mich., Ardis Publ., n.d.), Molière's *The Learned Ladies* ('78), and has also contributed prose translations, criticism and fiction to such works as *French Stories and Tales, Mid-Century American Poets, Prize Stories of 1946, & New Yorker Anthology.* His *Responses* are a collection of his prose pieces published in '76. Also well-known for his distinguished work as an editor, Richard Wilbur has published critical editions of various poets: *Emily Dickinson. Three Views*, with Louise Bogan & Archibald MacLeish ('60); *Modern American and Modern British Poetry*, rev. shorter ed., with Louis Untermeyer and Karl Shapiro ('55); *A Bestiary* (anthology; '55); *Complete Poems of Poe* ('59); *Selected Poems* by John Keats (Dell, '59); *Poems of Shakespeare*, editor with Alfred Harbage (London, Penguin, '66; rev. ed., as *The Narrative Poems, and Poems of Doubtful Authenticity*, '74). As literary critic, he has further contributed articles such as "The House of Poe" to *Anniversary Lectures* (Lib. of Congress, '59) & "Round About A Poem of Housman's" in *The Moment of Poetry* ('62). Lastly as an author of juvenile books, he has published *Loudmouse* ('63) and *Opposites*, with his own drawings as illustrations ('73).

HONORS: In addition to the awards noted above, Wilbur's recognition has been far-reaching: Harriet Monroe Memorial Prize, '48; Oscar Blumenthal Prize, '50; Guggenheim Fellowships, '52 & '63; Am. Academy in Rome Fellowship, '54; Pulitzer Prize, '57; Nat. Book Award, '57; Edna St. Vincent Millay Memorial Award, '57; Ford Fellowship for drama, '60; Melville Crane Award, '62; Bollingen

Prize for translation, '63, and for verse, '71; Sarah Josepha Hale Award, '68; Brandeis U. Creative Arts Award, '70; Prix Henri Desfeuilles, '71; Shelley Memorial Award, '73; Mem. of the Amr. Acad. of Arts & Sciences; Chancellor of the Am. Academy of Arts & Letters; & Chancellor, Acad. of Amr. Poets. He has had numerous honorary degrees bestowed upon him, including these: L.H.D.; Lawrence C. (Appleton, Wis., '60); L.H.D., Washington U., St. Louis ('64); and D. Litt.; Amherst ('67).

OBSERVATIONS: Richard Eberhart has called Wilbur "one of the best poets of his generation." John Ciardi has echoed this praise, noting that "with his enormous gifts grown into their mature assurance, Wilbur certainly emerges as our serenest, urbanest and most melodic poet." About his own work, Wilbur has observed: "I write poems as it suits me, enjoy the work of some very dissimilar contemporaries, and deplore theories, especially dead-serious talk about breath-groups."

PETER WILD

BIRTH: 4/25/'40, in Northampton, Mass., the son of Arnold Arthur and Edith (Meshivkovsky) Wild, grew up in the same city and attended high school there.

EDUCATION: But Peter became a confirmed Southwesterner when he started college in '58 at the U. of Ariz. where he received his B.A. ('62) and M.A. ('67). Additionally he holds an M.F.A. from the U. of Calif., Irvine ('69).

CAREER: In '63-'65, Wild interrupted his education at the Tucson campus to join the U.S. Army, where he was a writer/researcher, whose job involved answering correspondence from Congressmen and government officials of all ranks. Much of his time in the Army was spent abroad in Heidelberg, West Germany. After his discharge from the Army and his pursuit of his degrees at the Ariz. and Calif. institutions earlier noted, Wild began his teaching career in '69 as an Asst. Prof. of

Peter Wild
(September 1972)

English at Sul Ross St. U., Alpine, Tex., where he taught until '71. Since '71, he has been associated with the English faculty of the U. of Ariz., where today he is an Assoc. Prof., who teaches courses in poetry writing. He and his wife, the former Sylvia Ortiz, whom he met when they served together as student board members of the U. of Ariz. Poetry Center, and whom he married on 12/17/'66, make their home today in Tucson, where Peter continues to be an active hiker and conservationist when he has time free from writing poetry.

135

PUBLICATIONS: One of the most widely published young poets in America today, Peter is the author of the following chapbooks and collections: *The Good Fox* ('67), *Sonnets* ('67), *The Afternoon in Dismay* ('68), *Mica Mountain Poems* ('68), *Joining Up and Other Poems* ('68), *Mad Night With Sunflowers* ('68), *Love Poems* ('69), *Three Nights in the Chiricahuas* ('69), *Poems* ('69), *Fat Man Poems* ('70), *Terms and Renewals* ('70), *Grace* ('71), *Wild's Magical Book of Cranial Effusions* ('71), *Peligros* ('72), *New and Selected Poems* ('73), *Cochise* ('73), *The Cloning* ('74), *Tumacacori* ('74), *The Island Hunter* ('75), *Chihuahua* ('76), and *Gold Mines* ('78). As an undergraduate poet at the U. of Ariz., Peter Wild participated actively in the then beginning Ruth Stephan Poetry Center, and began to publish his poetry in numerous little magazines at the time, a practice he continued even during the years '63-'65 when his stretch in the Army interrupted his academic studies. Beginning with the "sixties," poems by Wild have been published in over 600 small magazines, and continue in the "seventies" to appear in similar publications despite his recognition. Among others, Wild has published in such periodicals as these: *Poetry, Foxfire, Poetry Northwest, Lillabulero, Tri-Quarterly, Ironwood, Inscape, Antaeus, Kayak, Trace, Beloit Poetry Journal, Northwest Review, Ann Arbor Review, Poetry Now, Apple, Beyond Baroque, Chicago Review, Corduroy, Minnesota Review, & Descant.* He is also represented in numerous anthologies, including these: *Poems Southwest* ('68), *Poetry Extra 1* ('68), *Southern Poetry Review* ('69), *Poets of the Desert Southwest, Modern Poetry of Western America* ('75), *Five Arizona Poets* ('76), *Southwest* ('77), & *The Indian Rio Gande* ('77).

HONORS: Peter Wild has won various prizes for his poetry; First Prize for Poetry, *Writers' Digest* Competition, ('64), a Hart Crane and Alice Crane Williams Memorial Fund Grant, ('69), and *Art River Review* Prize ('72). Additionally he has had the honor of seeing his book *Cochise* ('73) nominated for the Pulitzer Prize. In addition to writing, Mr. Wild writes articles regularly for various national environmental publications and is a very active member of the Sierra Club in Tucson. He also has served as Co-Chairman of the Wilderness Committee of Arizonans for Quality Environment.

OBSERVATIONS: About his poetry, Peter Wild says: "Both figuratively and in reality, I have always felt a necessity to spend a great deal of time in the open, in the outdoors, Hence, the deterioration of the natural environment, over-population, and the erosion of man's cultural diversity are conditions of great concern to me. Furthermore, due to a strong sense of place, as a resident of the American Southwest, a region of the Anglo, Mexican, and American Indian, I often hold conflicting sympathies and allegiances. This is not to imply that I consider myself either a "nature poet" or a regional poet—a poet must write for all men—but in general it may be of help for a reader to remember that the above concerns and circumstances of my life undoubtedly underlie and temper much of my writing." Diane Wakoski has observed concerning Peter Wild's poetry, these tendencies: "Peter Wild is one of my favorite wild poets. He is droll and serious. His relentless surrealist imagery magnetizes the reader into another dimension of his own experiences. It is the poetry of a deadly world, illuminated by a laughing death. I am always excited by his imagination." Ormond Seavey has noted further in *The Little Magazine:* "Peter Wild seems to stand apart. The most basic issues of his poetry, taken as a whole are public issues, the reconciling of Americans with their continent and with their history."

C.(HARLES) K.(ENNETH) WILLIAMS

BIRTH: 11/4/'36, in Newark, N.J., grew up in that area.

EDUCATION: Bucknell U. & U. of Penn., '55-'59 (B.A., '59).

CAREER: Williams has lived for varying periods of time in France, Spain, Mexico and Greece. He makes his home now in Philadelphia and Paris with his wife Catherine Mauger, and he has two children, Jessica and Jed. He has taught at the Poetry Center of the "Y" in Philadelphia, at Beaver College, Drexel University, & Franklin and Marshall College. He has also worked as a part-time group-therapist and as a ghost-writer.

EDITORIAL POSTS: Since '72, Williams has been a Contributing Editor of *American Poetry Review*, and in '76-'77, was the literary editor of *The Philadelphia Arts Exchange*.

PUBLICATIONS: A Day for Anne Frank ('68), *Lies* ('69), *I Am the Bitter Name* ('72), & *With Ignorance* ('77). Additionally, with Gregory Dickerson, he has translated Sophocles' *Women of Trachis* ('78). Williams' poems have been

C.K. Williams
(February 1970)

published in the following periodicals: *The American Poetry Review, Carleton Miscellany, Chicago Review, Colorado State Review, December, Iowa Review, Ironwood, Lillabulero, Mademoiselle, The New American Review, The New Yorker, North American Review, Poetry & Transpacific Review.* Among the various anthologies in which he is represented are *A Book for Open Learning* ('70), *Other Tongues* ('70), & *The Major Young Poets.*

HONORS: Guggenheim Fellowship, '74.

OBSERVATIONS: Williams once said of his poetry: "What I would really like would by simply to sing without meaning anything....But we do suffer, hunger and love and war. And find how much war there is within us...the apparently vicious, apparently irrational....and how much love, how much hunger, and so song becomes charm, aversion, prayer, and we become all the painful, necessary abstractions that are meant to make us mean something. And more love again, so song is never lost, no matter how brutal or truthful. And again the intensity of the joy of life and song, which, when it looks, has been riding oppression and shame toward death and cries out then with its double again. And finally the desperate last hope that poetry does something, does anything, and to keep on with it." Morris Dickstein, reviewing Williams' *With Ignorance* said, "Williams' poems sacrifice eloquence for energy, epigram for affect, song for speech. I find them deeply inspiriting."

KEITH WILSON

BIRTH: 12/26/'27, in Clovis, N.M., attended fifteen different grammar schools and three different high schools as he followed his father, an engineer, about the Southwest. For a time, he also worked on ranches and farms as a cowboy and ditch-digger.

EDUCATION: In '45, he received an appointment to the U.S. Naval Academy, and after his graduation from Annapolis in '50, spent four years at sea, mainly in Korea, where he earned five battle stars. In '54, he resigned his commission as a Lieutenant in the Navy to begin work on his M.A. ('56) at the U. of N.M.

CAREER: His teaching career also began in '56, when he spent a year as an Instr. at the U. of Nevada, Reno. From '58-'60, he was employed as a technical writer with the Sandia Corporation, Albuquerque. Then, in '60, he came to the U. of Ariz., where he was an instructor actively associated with the then newly created Poetry Center in Tucson, until '65. Since '65, he has been teaching at the N.M. St. U. in Las Cruces, where he is now Prof. of English and Poet-In-Residence. In '72 & '76,

Keith Wilson
(November 1969)

he was on the staff of the Writers' Workshop at Utah St. U., and traveled with his family to Romania as a Fulbright Prof. in the year '74-'75. He has also worked for the Poetry-In-The-Schools programs of Ariz., N.M., N.Y., & Mich., and from '61-'65, while at the U. of Ariz. served as a member of the Board of Directors of the Poetry Center and started some of the first poetry-writing courses now offered there. In '58, he married his wife Heloise, the only child of Roy and the poet Besmilir Brigham. The Wilsons have four children and live today in Las Cruces, N.M.

PUBLICATIONS: Keith Wilson is the author of these chapbooks and collections: *Sketches from a New Mexico Hill Town* ('66), *The Old Car and Other Black Poems* ('68), *II Sequences* ('68), *Lion's Gate* ('68), *Graves Registry and Other Poems* ('69), *The Shadow of our Bones* ('69), *Psalms for Various Voices* ('69), *Homestead* ('70), *Rocks* ('70), *The Old Man and Others* ('70), *Midwatch* ('72), *While Dancing Feet Shatter the Earth* ('77), *The Streets of San Miguel* ('77), *Thantog: Songs of a Jaguar Priest* ('77), *Desert Cenote* ('77), *Stone Roses: Poems from Transylvania* ('78), *The Wind of Pentecost* ('78), and in preparation ('78), *The Early Southwestern Poems.* His poems have appeared in numerous poetry periodicals, some of which follow: *Poetry, Poetry Now, Tri-Quarterly Review, Matter, Camels Coming, New Mexico Quarterly, New Mexico Magazine, Outsider, Magdalene Syndrome Gazette, Tolar*

Creek Syndicate, Ninth Circle, Open Letter, Colorado State Review, Confrontations, Descant, El Corno Enplumado, Floating Bear, Puerto Del Sol & From a Window. Wilson's poetry is also included in various anthologies, a partial listing of which follow: *Poems Southwest, 31 New American Poets, The Now Voices, Some Haystacks Don't Even Have any Needle, Inside Outer Space, Enter the Young, America: A Prophecy, The Belly of the Shark, The Indian Rio Grande, Southwest, & Metáforos Verdes.* Wilson also writes fiction and has two novels, *Martingale,* and *In His Father's House* in manuscript, as well as a book of stories and a book of plays.

HONORS: D. H. Lawrence Creative Writing Fellowship at the U. of N.M. ('72), Westhafer Award for Creative Activity (the first granted in research outside of the Sciences) by N.M. St. U. ('72), N.E.A. Writing Fellowship ('74), and Senior Fulbright Hays Fellowship ('74-'75).

OBSERVATIONS: Wilson has noted that he has these "three major areas of concern" in his writing: "(1) New Mexico Southwest, (2) the Sea, (3) Emotional Geography. I often use methods derived, in part or at least, from Charles Olson's *Projective Verse*—he, Robert Duncan, and Robert Creeley have been large influences on me, as have both William Carlos Williams, and—from childhood—Robert Burns." Duane Ackerson has observed that "Keith Wilson's poetry is informed by a strong sense of history; both the sometimes violent history before his time in his own Southwest, and his own personal experience with violence as a naval officer during the Korean War....It is this sense of our own complicity, whether through repetition or reincarnation, in past history, that makes his pre-occupation with his own ancestral past and New Mexico's roots in the past valuable; it is not merely nostalgia, but rather a desire to learn from the past how to avoid bumping into it again in the future...[His] poems are ultimately heartening: Wilson brings a compassion rather than self righteous anger to human follies, a forgiveness that may help us to forgive ourselves."

JAMES (ARLINGTON) WRIGHT
BIRTH: 12/13/'27, in Martin's Ferry, Ohio, grew up there.
EDUCATION: He received his B.A. ('52) from Kenyon College, where he studied

James Wright
(February 1973)

with John Crowe Ransom, and was elected to Phi Beta Kappa. He also spent the year of '52-'53 at the U. of Vienna studying on a Fulbright Scholarship. He was awarded his M.A. ('54) & his Ph.D. ('57) degrees from the U. of Wash., where he did further study of poetry-writing with Theodore Roethke.

CAREER: From '57'-63, Wright began his teaching career at the U. of Minn., Minneapolis as an Asst. Prof. of English; he also taught in the same capacity at Macallester C., St. Paul, Minn. ('63-'65). Since '66, and presently, he is a Prof. of English at Hunter C., the City U. of New York. He and his wife, the former Anne Runk live in Manhattan and have two sons. The Wrights have traveled widely in Japan, Austria, France, and Italy, and have lived for awhile in France ('74). They also spent part of '76 in Hawaii.

PUBLICATIONS: James Wright's first book of poems, *The Green Wall* won the '57 Yale Series of Younger Poets' Competition, and brought his work into prominence from that time forward. His other works include these: *Saint Judas* ('59), *The Branch Will Not Break: Poems* ('63), *Shall We Gather at the River* ('68), *Collected Poems* ('71), *Two Citizens* ('73), *Moments of the Italian Summer* ('76), & *To A Blossoming Pear Tree* ('77). A collections of his poetry entitled *The Lion's Tail and Eyes: Poems Written Out of Laziness and Silence,* also appears with works by Robert Bly and William Duffy included in the same volume ('62). Many anthologies have carried Wright's poetry, among them: *New Poets of England and America* ('57), *Poetry for Pleasure* ('60), *Contemporary American Poetry* ('62), *Erotic Poetry* ('63), *American Poems* ('64), *Faber Book of Modern Verse* ('65), *Poems on Poetry* ('65), *Heartland* ('67), *An Introduction to Poetry* ('67), *Poetry: An Introductory Anthology* ('68), *Poets of Our Moment* ('68), *Contemporary Poetry in America* ('73), *The Norton Anthology of Modern Poetry* ('73), & *Modern Poems: An Introduction to Poetry* ('73; '76). Likewise numerous periodicals have carried his verse, a partial listing being these: *The New Yorker, Harper's, Field, Poetry, Choice, Chelsea, The Ohio Review, Modern Poetry Studies, The Nation, The Paris Review, Antaeus,* and *The American Poetry Review.* The Fall '77 issue of *Ironwood* magazine was dedicated to his work. Well-known for his translations, Wright has often collaborated, particularly with Robert Bly, and others to produce the works of various poets into English, and has also rendered several volumes alone. In this connection, Wright's work includes: *Hypos Waking* by Rene Char, selected and edited by Jackson Matthews with the colaboration of Barbara Howes, W.S. Merwin, William Jay Smith, Richard Wilbur, William Carlos Williams, and James Wright ('56); *Twenty Poems of Georg Trakl,* with Robert Bly ('61); *Twenty Poems of César Vallejo,* with Robert Bly & John Knoepfle ('63); *The Rider on the White Horse* by Theodor Storm ('64); *Twenty Poems of Pablo Neruda* ('67), with Robert Bly; *Poems* by Herman Hesse ('70); & *Wandering: Notes and Sketches* by Herman Hesse, with Franz Wright ('72). Additionally Wright has been recorded reading his poetry on *Today's Poets 3,* with others, which was produced by Folkway Records.

HONORS: In addition to the Yale Series of Younger Poets' Award ('57) and other honors mentioned above, Wright has received such other distinguished recognition for his poetry as the following: *Kenyon Review* Poetry Fellowship ('58-'59), Robert Frost Poetry Prize ('52), Eunice Tietjens Memorial Prize ('55), Martha Kinney Cooper Ohioana Library Award ('60), Guggenheim Fellowship ('65), Rockefeller Grant ('70), Ingram Merrill Foundation Grant ('70), Brandeis U. Creative Arts Award ('71), Fellowship to the American Academy of Poets ('72), The Pulitzer Prize ('72), & Member of the National Institute of Arts and Letters ('74). In '74, Kenyon also conferred the honorary Doctor of Humane Letters degree upon him.

OBSERVATIONS: James Wright says of his poetry: "I have written about the things I am deeply concerned with—crickets outside my window, cold and hungry old men, ghosts in the twilight, horses in a field, a red-haired child in her mother's arms, a feeling of desolation in the fall, some cities I've known. I try and say how I love my country and how I despise the way it is treated. I try and speak of the beauty and again of the ugliness in the lives of the poor and neglected. I have changed the way I've written, when it seemed appropriate, and continue to do so." About his writing, James Dickey has noted: "James Wright is one of the few authentic visionary poets writing today. Unlike many others, James Wright's visions are authentic, profound, and beautiful. Moreover, even among visionaries, he is rare, for he is a visionary not with an unearthly or heavenly vision, but a human vision. He is a seer with an astonishing compassion for human beings. We are lucky to have James Wright among us."

MARGUERITE (VIVIAN) YOUNG

BIRTH: 1909, in Indianapolis, Indiana, is a member of a large family, one of whose patriarchs was Brigham Young. But she traces her writing talent back to her ancestor John Knox, "whose dour, fantastic visions and wild imaginings were passed on to his descendants, among them Lord Byron, Jane Carlyle, Herman Melville, Robert Louis Stevenson, and James Boswell." Ms. Young grew up in the midwest and attended universities there.

EDUCATION: Indiana U.; Butler U. (B.A., '30); M.A., U. of Chicago ('36); post-graduate, U. of Iowa.

CAREER: The poet-novelist Marguerite Young has long been a teacher of creative writing. She began her career at the Indiana U. ('42), and continued it at

Marguerite Young
(February 1966)

the following institutions: U. of Iowa ('55-'57); Columbia U. ('58); New School for Social Research, N.Y. ('58-'67); Farleigh Dickinson ('60-'62); Seton Hall University ('71-'77); & Fordham ('66-'77). Presently she teaches workshops from time to time at various institutions in the New York City area, where she continues to devote as much time as possible to her writing in her Greenwich Village apartment. Among her various current projects are continued work on a biography of James Whitcomb Riley and the nearly completed two-volume history of Utopian politics centered upon Eugene Debs—two works to which she has already devoted much attention and research.

PUBLICATIONS: Marguerite Young began her career as a poet in '37 when she published her first book of poems, *Prismatic Ground.* Another volume of her poetry, *Moderate Fable*, followed in '45. A work in non-fiction, *Angel in the Forest: A Fairy Tale of Two Utopias*, which concerned a Utopian community at New Harmony, Indiana, appeared also in '45, and in a second edition, with a preface by Mark Van Doren, in '66. In '45, she embarked on a fiction project she anticipated would take two years. Eighteen years later, she delivered the 3,449 page typescript of her manuscript of *Miss MacIntosh, My Darling*, to her publishers, Charles Scribner's. A monumental novel, the book, published in the U.S.A. in '65 and in London in '66, has the style of a prose epic. Young has characterized the work as a "poetic novel concerned with dreams and the sub-conscious." When this novel, which took so long in the making, was finally published in '65, John Barkham of *Saturday Review* noted that it is a work, in which, "The English language is put to its finest use." Ms. Young's work has appeared in *Saturday Review, Partisan Review, Accent, The Nation, Poetry, The New Republic, Kenyon Review, Mademoiselle, Harper's Bazaar, New World Writing, Botteghe Oscure, Discovery, Furioso, & The Tiger's Eye*. In '77 and '78 various articles upon Marguerite Young have appeared in *Book Forum, Paris Review, & Ms*. Her poems have also been included in such anthologies as these, among others: *New Directions* ('41), *New Poems*, edited by Howell Sockin, *Modern American Poetry*, edited by Oscar Williams, *Reading Modern Poetry*, edited by Paul Engle and Warren Carrier, & *Modern Poetry*, edited by Kimon Friar and John Malcolm Brinnin. Reviews by Marguerite Young appear in *The New York Times Book Review*, and elsewhere.

HONORS: Amr. Assoc. of Univ. Women grant ('43); Nat. Inst. of Arts & Letters Award ('45); Guggenheim Fellowship ('48); Newberry Library Fellowship ('51); & Rockefeller Fellowship ('54).

OBSERVATIONS: Marguerite Young has explained her methods used in writing *Miss MacIntosh, My Darling* in this way: "Every sentence in my book has to do with one of four categories of a dream world everyone inhabits. Sometimes reality is a dream that crumbles before your eyes, as when someone you deeply love is taken from you, and everything you cherished suddenly vanishes. Sometimes the reality you thought was a dream turns out to be real. You might see an elephant walking down the road. You think you are dreaming, but it turns out that an elephant has escaped from the circus and *is* walking down the road. Sometimes a dream is a dream. Knowing this fact is the difference between being sane and crazy. And the greatest tragedy of all is when reality turns out to be reality and the unbelievable thing must be faced as true." About her writing, William Goyen has praised it in this way: "It (*Miss MacIntosh, My Darling*) is a mammoth epic, a massive fable, a picaresque journey, a Faustian guest and a work of stunning magnitude and beauty. Her only published fiction to date, it is her masterwork. Its style is one of musicalizations, rhapsodies, symbolizations that repetitively roll and resound and double back upon themselves in an oceanic tumult. Its force is cumulative; its method is clarification through amassment, as in the great styles of Joyce or Hermann Broch or Faulkner."

PAUL ZIMMER

BIRTH: 9/18/'34, in Canton, Ohio, grew up in his birthplace.

EDUCATION: Kent St. U. (B.A., '68). However, concerning his education, Paul Zimmer always quickly observes: "I was a dismal student from the first grade right through to my last year of college. In fact, I was dismissed twice from Kent St. U. for failing to meet standards. I blame this as much on 'education' as myself. Kent St. finally awarded me my degree in '68...nine years after I had left the campus."

CAREER: Paul Zimmer began his career as a salesman, and then from '65-'67, served as manager of the Bookstore of the U. of Calif, Los Angeles.

EDITORIAL POST: In '67, he became Asst. Director of the U. of Pittsburgh Press, and editor in charge of the Pitt Poetry series, positions he still holds. He lives with his wife Sue and their two children—Justine and Erik—in Pittsburgh. He has taught and also served as poet-in-residence at Chico State College in Calif. for the Spring '71 semester. He has also worked for the Penn. and Michigan Poetry-In-The-Schools programs and has given numerous readings both on the East and West Coasts and in the Midwest and Southwest.

PUBLICATIONS: A Seed on the Wind: Poems (privately printed, '60); *The Ribs of Death* ('67); *The Republic of Many Voices* ('69), & *The Zimmer Poems* ('76). Among the various anthologies carrying his work are *Poetry: An Introduction and Anthology* ('67), *The Voice That is Great Within Us* ('73), & *American Poets in 1976.* His poems have appeared in numerous periodicals, including *Poetry Now, Poetry Northwest, Yankee, Prairie Schooner, Virginia Quarterly Review, Massachusetts Review, Southern Poetry Review,* & *Field.*

Paul Zimmer
(February 1971)

HONORS: Borestone Mountain Award, '71; & N.E.A. grant, '74.

OBSERVATIONS: Zimmer writes: "I suppose I have a characteristic style, but I hesitate trying to identify it, as I might disturb whatever it is I have going. I spend a good deal of time making my own mythologies and casting my voice into various personae; I seem to write in a more sombre tone when I work this way, and when I work in a personal form I tend to write more humorously. In either case, I am always casting my own voice into the poem. I'm not so concerned that people 'understand' my work, but I want very much for them to experience it. I work into the form that which seems to fit whatever I'm working on." Joseph Parisi has reviewed Zimmer's poetry in this way: "Paul Zimmer is a protean poet whose personae are not so much depicted as created: we witness poet and subjects in process of becoming. A vivid verbal imagination projects the common, lonely, unwanted, neurotic, merely eccentric, and truly mad people of these poems into the elements which surround them and are soon to reclaim them in death, while inanimate objects assume the habits and attributes of human life. Zimmer makes the stock-in-trade of synaesthesia and personification his own by force of an original, often startling point-of-view...." Zimmer's work has been reviewed in

Partisan Review as follows: "[His] poetry is of real fulfillment...[it] beats with an almost subliminal and yet somehow irrepressible gaiety. All is weighted in value and proportion, and the results are precious, hard, almost gemlike in clarity."

Poets listed in *Focus 101* are anthologized in

THE FACE OF POETRY
first published, 1977 by Gallimaufry Press;
second printing, 1979 by Heidelberg Graphics.